מסורה

ArtScroll Series®

Rabbi Nosson Scherman / Rabbi Meir Zlotowitz

General Editors

Contemporary Questions

Discussions of common dilemmas in daily life

Published by

Mesorah Publications, ltd

in **Halachah**
and **Hashkafah**

Rabbi Yosef Viener

FIRST EDITION
First Impression … September 2011

Published and Distributed by
MESORAH PUBLICATIONS, LTD.
4401 Second Avenue / Brooklyn, N.Y 11232

Distributed in Europe by
LEHMANNS
Unit E, Viking Business Park
Rolling Mill Road
Jarow, Tyne & Wear, NE32 3DP
England

Distributed in Australia and New Zealand
by **GOLDS WORLDS OF JUDAICA**
3-13 William Street
Balaclava, Melbourne 3183
Victoria, Australia

Distributed in Israel by
SIFRIATI / A. GITLER — BOOKS
6 Hayarkon Street
Bnei Brak 51127

Distributed in South Africa by
KOLLEL BOOKSHOP
Ivy Common
105 William Road
Norwood 2192, Johannesburg, South Africa

ARTSCROLL SERIES®
CONTEMPORARY QUESTIONS IN HALACHAH AND HASHKAFAH
© *Copyright 2011, by* MESORAH PUBLICATIONS, Ltd.
4401 Second Avenue / Brooklyn, N.Y. 11232 / (718) 921-9000 / www.artscroll.com

Typography by CompuScribe at ArtScroll Studios, Ltd.
Printed in the United States of America by Noble Book Press Corp.
Bound by Sefercraft, Quality Bookbinders, Ltd., Brooklyn N.Y. 11232

Contemporary Questions in Halachah and Hashkafah

This *sefer* is dedicated to the memory of

אבי מורי
ר׳ יוסף מיכל בן חיים יצחק ז״ל

ואמי מורתי
אסתר דבורה בת אריה ליב ע״ה

ויינר

Who worked tirelessly on behalf of *Klal Yisrael*

for *harbatzas Torah* and *hatzalas nefashos*.

אשר צבי ורעיתו פסיה לאה ויינר

לזכות

שרה בילא בת חנה בלימא

שמואל קמנצקי
Rabbi S. Kamenetsky

2018 Upland Way
Philadelphia, PA 19131

Home: 215-473-2798
Study: 215-473-1212

בס"ד יום ל' לחי' תשס"ז

ולואי"ט ידי' הרב' וכו' כש"ת וכו' שי'

כ' ולד הנוי' שלי"ט

וראשי"ל ברכה וברכה ושלום,

רבני דפעיה שליט"א לבי' אות יתוד שבו בע"מ
שלא' דכמאה וכמל ורסופ' ובותאר ובילא' אתל
שלום ורכ' ובם ושלופ' לפבס שחיו' יכו' וכן את
נסכיית ולפבא'.

ברכתו כשמון לבר' ורב' וכבב' לאשי' ולבביני
וכל זה דכבכ ושפס כי לדעל' וכמ"ו

א' ברכת ושבם המורח' ו',

בידדי' מלו' תשס"ז ולפבנ
[signature]

Rabbi Y. Belsky
506 EAST 7th STREET
BROOKLYN, NEW YORK 11218

ישראל הלוי בעלסקי
941-0112

קבלתי המכתב מכתב"ק איש יצחק ר' יוסף וינד שליט"א
רב"ג מאנשוואג וישוורי הלבב בצנעינ"ת פנים אכ"ו אבו"ג מיפי
שמוש גאונוא, ובכא"ו קבלף יהף צורונ בין לוחות ספר פלפ
ותרטום לצינו, ובזוני נצינתי לבהראות ואזרתי על חלק גאול
אכף ומאמותיף בזילף בכמית הלשון סוכף מביר מכוססיא יבה
מביאור מתקיף מתהילת יסוף' הצינין צ' סול מסרכת הלבבירון
התלעשי"ף, והבל קולא סול תצערה ולאו יהלאלו הלקבוק קאול
שלם יהאו נשה יאה ימין ואמסוא מבוון התמימי. שאהל' מסוא
לתאות בר' צאו אם יציף' תרה 'ונסף נ"ו כי ביאוריו גצ'או
מאמאתקח להבי"ף יוסי והלאכבב בתוכבי מאתרי הקלורת לצאת
הברך 'לכו בה והאמאסר סאר ישאו, ורוטוה סונ מאמריו שא
כובכ מאמיר-רב ומורת בישראל תרואב אות צרנרו בלוב
שלא וצאת ונעדיץ על צרך קיור ואתהא הכלורת, סוהי
הלקנו והלוך צצאן, בקבל'ב יבל לצאות בתמצות הכלורה הב
ביאות גולות לבדק הב"ל

יומ ג' לחיב מאכים טוב שנ עסא"ו לב"ק בצרונל נ'.
ישראל הלוי בעלסקי

בס״ד

שלמה אליהו מילר
רה״כ ואב״ד דכולל טאראנטא

הנה ידידי הרב יוסף ווינער שליט״א כבר אתמחי גברא ואתמחי קמיע שכבר
כתב בירורים בעניני הלכה כמה שנים ומצא חן בעיני הקוראים ועכשיו אזר
חיל להוציא לאור הדפוס ממה שכבר כתב, ומכיר אני מכבר מלפני כמה שנים
את האיש ואת שיחו הרב יוסף הנ״ל ואשרי חלקו שהולך תמיד ביישרות
ומבקש האמת בלימודו. ואף שלא עיינתי בכל דבריו, המקצת שראיתי יעידו
על הכל שלא הלך הלך בגדולות ונפלאות, ורק רוצה לקוטב האמת ואשרי חלקו.
והנני מברכו שיצליח להוסיף עוד להוציא לאור עוד ספרים בעניני הלכה כמו
שעושה עכשיו.

וע״ז בעה״ח היום ד׳ תמוז תשע״א לפ״ק פה טאראנטא

Table of Contents

SECTION THREE
WAYS AND MEANS OF TEFILLAH AND TEHILLIM

SECTION FOUR
V'ACHALTA V'SAVATA U'VEIRACHTA —
EATING AND BENTCHING

SECTION FIVE
BERACHOS

SECTION ELEVEN
MAASER, MONEY, AND MORE

SECTION TWELVE
PRACTICAL HASHKAFAH MATTERS

Preface

We are all quite fortunate to be living at a very special time. This is an era in which Torah learning is pursued and idealized, and exacting adherence to *halachah* is gaining momentum with each passing day. The Torah is increasingly accessible and all the precious details of *halachah* are sought after by Jews from all walks of life.

I am greatly inspired by the thirst for knowledge and *yiras Shomayim* I witness daily. These encounters take many forms, the most common being the many inquiries a rav receives concerning the myriad situations and circumstances to be found on the contemporary Jewish scene.

Although most of these questions have been dealt with for generations, the complexity of our ever-changing world, coupled with the erudition of even the average layman, have brought the quality and quantity of *she'ailos* to a level not seen in many years.

It is a great *chessed* from *HaKadosh Baruch Hu* that our communities boast *chashuvah Yidden*, whether they are young or old, full-time learners or professionals, *frum* from birth or *ba'alei teshuvah*, who are sincere *mevakshim* of the highest caliber. These incredible people constantly push themselves to grow in their knowledge of Torah and in their adherence to *mitzvos*. They continuously look for the truth and are successful in finding it — a true fulfillment of the words of Chazal: *yagati u'matzasi ta'amin.*

This *sefer* contains a sampling of halachic issues faced at home, in shul, and in the office. It deals with real-life challenges that arise between parents and children, neighbors and friends, employers and employees, Jews and non-Jews. Struggles involving *emunah*, *bitachon*, and *hishtadlus* are explored. Also focused upon are halachic issues concerning *kashrus*, *tefillah*, *berachos*, Shabbos, Yom Tov, *tzedakah*, *shidduchim*, obligations in Torah learning, and many other timely topics.

The fact that one can obtain clear answers and comprehensive solutions for each unique situation testifies to the eternity and truth of Torah and to the everlasting applicability of *halachah*. The fact that there are so many who are interested in asking these questions and applying the answers is a testimony to the greatness of *Klal Yisrael*.

We must stand in awe and appreciation, for we continue to see the fulfillment of *HaKadosh Baruch Hu's* promise: *Lo yamushu mipicha umipi zaracha ... mai'atah v'ad olam.*

Acknowledgments

The most important gift that Hashem has given us is the ability to learn Torah and the opportunity to apply its teachings. I therefore begin with expressing my *hakaras hatov* to the *Ribono Shel Olam* for allowing me to dwell *beohalo shel Torah ubedaled amos shel halachah*. This gratitude will perhaps be expressed in a small way through the publication of this work on *halachah* and *hashkafah*, which I hope will serve to increase *limud haTorah* and *dikduk behalachah*.

Siyata di'Shemaya is generated to a great degree through the *zechusim* and efforts of others.

My father, Rabbi Asher Zvi Viener, *shlitah*, has taught me through shining example the supremacy of *limud haTorah*. Leaving a promising business carreer to go live and learn in *Eretz Yisrael* is a rare, inspiring story of idealism, focus, and *mesiras nefesh*. Yet, that is exactly what he did with the encouragement and help of my mother, *shetichye*, over a quarter century ago. My parents have shown our family what is truly important in life, and I have no doubt that their sacrifice has been a major source of *siyata di'Shemaya* for whatever we have accomplished.

May Hashem grant them many more years together with *nachas* and good health so that they may continue to set the tone for *aliyah* in Torah and *mitzvos* for many generations to come.

This book has been dedicated in part to the memory of my grandparents — builders of Torah and *askanim* of the highest caliber. Hashem bestowed upon them unusual *chein* and prominence in their Washington DC community among Jews and non-Jews alike, putting them in a unique position to help thousands of *Yidden* during the Holocaust, as well as establishing shuls and yeshivos for the expanding Jewish community.

It is only due to the tireless self-sacrifice and hard work of my wife that I have had the time to learn, teach, and write. Her total being is dedicated solely to my *limud haTorah* and the *chinuch* of our children. May *HaKadosh Baruch Hu* grant her continued wisdom, health, and *siyata di'Shemaya*, so that we be *zoche* together to raise *bonim uvenei bonim oskim baTorah uvemitzvos*.

Her esteem and *meseiras nefesh* for Torah were not created in a vacuum. She grew up in a home where *limud* and *chashivos haTorah* permeated every aspect of their lives, and saturated every fiber of their existence. For this I am forever indebted to my father-in-law Rabbi Yaakov Landesman. A *talmid chachom* and educator of note, he has put his imprint on generations of *talmidim*. My mother-in-law, from a family renowned for its role in transporting Torah and tradition from the old world to these shores, remains the dependable partner and co-architect of their successful home. I and my children have been the direct beneficiaries of the *eishes chayil* they have produced.

My partners in the dissemination of *shiurim* have been R' Dovid Roth and his wife, Barbara. With ambition and vision, these dear friends and loyal *mispallelim* have been responsible for countless hours of *harbatzas Torah*. Continuing their tradition of support in all Torah endeavors, they have graciously co-dedicated this *sefer*. May the *zchus* of their efforts on behalf of *harbatzas Torah* continue to be a benefit for them and their children for many generations to come.

Selected parts of the *Hashkafah* portion of this work has been transcribed from audio CD by Rabbi Yehudah Heimowitz. His expertise is evident in the final product.

I would like to thank HaGoan HaRav Hillel David *shlita* for his precious time, invaluable suggestions, and guidance.

A special *yasher koach* to my dear friend and *chavrusah*, Rabbi Tzvi

Goldberg, a *talmid chochom* and excellent sounding board. I have enjoyed and benefited from the *pilpul chaveirim* that he has provided. His valuable insights have contributed immensely to many of the topics that appear in this book.

Most of the articles in this *sefer* originally appeared in *Hamodia* newspaper. Truly a paper for Torah Jewry, its dedication to the dissemination of *divrei Torah, machshavah,* and *halachah* has enhanced and enriched the homes of *Yidden* across the globe. It has been a privilege to offer a *halachah* column in *Hamodia's* weekly magazine.

My debt of gratitude to the staff at *Hamodia* begins with the request for the column from Mrs. Ruth Lichtenstein,and continues with the encouragement of Mr. Yonason Moller and Mrs. Rochel Roth, as well as the dedicated efforts of Mrs. Esther Henny Ehrlich and Mrs. Simi Lemmer.

Last but certainly not least, the amazing staff at ArtScroll were inviting, helpful, and accommodating. Rabbi Meir Zlotowitz and Rabbi Nosson Scherman asked me years ago to write, yet were patient and encouraging as they waited until I found the time and opportunity to take them up on their gracious offer. Rabbi Avrohom Biderman has enhanced the manuscript with his valuable comments and insights.

Mendy Herzberg shepherded the book to completion.

Eli Kroen's attractive cover design is yet another feather in his cap of achievements, and Devorah Bloch's page design makes the book a pleasure to read.

Mrs. Judi Dick made invaluable comments and suggetions. Mrs. Frimy Eisner brought her considerable editorial and organizational skills to bear as she enhanced the content of the book and compiled the subject index. Mrs. Faigie Weinbaum proofread and made important suggestions.

May Hashem grant us all the ability to work together on many such projects.

Yosef Viener

Monsey, New York
Elul 5771

SECTION ONE

TO WASH OR NOT TO WASH

Hand-Washing Before Davening

Is there an actual obligation to wash before Shacharis, Minchah, and Maariv, or is it merely a stringency that some have adopted?

There is an absolute obligation to wash one's hands before *every tefillah*.[1] Even if one was learning before *davening* and had washed his hands before learning, there is still an obligation to wash prior to *tefillah*, unless he is sure that there was no *hesech hadaas* (loss of awareness and focus) from the obligation to keep the hands clean for *davening*.[2]

It is ironic that in the age of modern plumbing, where every home, shul, and yeshivah has ample running water, the important obligation to wash one's hands before *davening* is often ignored. Many claim that they do not have time to wash before *davening*. Although it is true that one should not miss *davening* with a *minyan* for the sake of finding water for washing,[3] coming to shul only a

---

1. *Gemara Berachos* 15a; *Shulchan Aruch Orach Chaim* 92:4; 233:2.
2. *Rema*, ibid.; see *Perishah* 92:6.
3. *Shulchan Aruch Orach Chaim* 92:4.

minute earlier will make it possible for him to observe this important mitzvah for the sake of *kavod haTefillah* (treating prayers with the appropriate deference).

If one *davens* Maariv shortly after Minchah, there is no obligation to wash again, because we assume that there was no *hesech hadaas* in such a brief time span.[4] It is obvious that if one touched shoes or a covered part of the body during that time, he would be obligated to wash.

---

4. *Mishnah Berurah* 233:16.

Hand-Washing in Various Situations

When I touch my shoes or any covered part of the body, I wash my hands three times. I do this after coming from the bathroom as well. Is this practice absolutely required, or is it merely a chumrah?

Let us explore the various requirements of hand-washing (*netilas yadayim*) based on *halachah*, as well as accepted practice (*minhag Yisrael*).

One who wakes up in the morning must wash to remove the *ruach ra'ah* (an impure spirit that rests on the hands when one sleeps at night)[1] and in preparation for *davening* Shacharis.[2] This washing must involve pouring water three times alternately on each hand.[3]

There is an obligation to wash one's hands after using the bathroom.[4] There is a dispute in the *poskim* concerning the need to

---

1. *Gemara Shabbos* 109b. See *Teshuvos HaRashba* 191 for a third reason.
2. *Rosh Berachos* 9:23.
3. *Mishnah Berurah* 4:17 and 39.
4. *Shulchan Aruch Orach Chaim* 4:18.

wash from a utensil (such as a cup) after coming out of the bath-room.[5] There is also a question regarding the need to wash each hand three times. Common custom is to attempt to fulfill both re-quirements whenever possible.

Some *poskim* rule that the obligation to wash applies even if one entered the bathroom without actually using the facilities.[6] One could argue that the stringent opinions may not apply this rule to contemporary restrooms.[7]

When one touches shoes or any part of the body that is normally covered, he also has an obligation to wash his hands. The *Mishnah Berurah*[8] rules that this obligation of *netilas yadayim* is for cleanli-ness purposes only and is unrelated to any issue of *ruach ra'ah*.[9] There is therefore no requirement to use a utensil or to wash each hand three times.[10]

[In our discussion "Talking After Washing" (page 82), we suggest that if one washed for bread and spoke before reciting the *berachah* of *Al Netilas Yadayim,* he should touch his shoes in order to trigger an obligation to wash again. This suggestion follows the majority of the *poskim,* who do not require washing three times after touching shoes. It is therefore sufficient to wash twice, as one would normally do when he washes for bread.]

---

5. See *Mishnah Berurah* 4:39, who quotes a dispute on the matter but is lenient on the issue. *Shelah* (*shaar ha'osiyos* 9) requires a utensil. *Eliyahu Rabbah*, however, quotes opinions that require washing three times but do not require a utensil. This dispute might apply to the obligation to wash hands after cutting hair and nails as well.
6. *Mishnah Berurah* 4:40 rules this way. However, *Beur Halachah* 613:3, *d"h ve'im rotzeh*, records lenient opinions on the matter.
7. See *Chazon Ish, Orach Chaim* 17:4, *Igros Moshe Even HaEzer* 1:114, *Halichos Shlomo* 20:24 and note 86, *Minchas Yitzchak* (1:60), *Yabiya Omer* (3:2).
8. Loc. cit. 41.
9. If water is not available, one may even wipe his hands with or on any material that cleans.
10. However, some *poskim* understand that the obligation to wash after touching shoes and the like is not simply for cleanliness but to remove the *ruach ra'ah* as well. This might necessitate the use of a utensil as well as washing each hand three times. One should follow his personal custom on this matter..See *Olas Hatamid:* 11 and *Shulchan Aruch HaRav* 128:27.

Washing Hands
After a Haircut

In an attempt to save time and money, I give my small children their haircuts at home on a fairly consistent basis. I always make sure to train them to wash their hands after I cut their hair (our minhag is three times per hand, using a cup). My friend mentioned recently that she believes that I also have an obligation to wash my own hands after giving the haircuts. I would like to verify whether she is correct or not. If so, am I obligated to wash my hands after I cut their nails as well?

You should wash your hands after you finish cutting your children's hair. This is because one often touches the scalp and hair that is not clean during the haircutting process.[1]

1. *Kaf HaChaim* 4:92.

If one snips a small amount of hair during an *upsherin*, there is no need to wash, because hands do not become unclean during the process.[2]

After cutting your children's nails, there is no need for you to wash your hands.[3]

You should continue to train the children to wash their hands after you cut their hair or nails.

---

2. *Halichos Shlomo* 2, footnote 33.
3. *Kaf HaChaim* ibid.

HOW-TO'S: TZITZIS, TEFILLIN, AND MEZUZAH

Wearing Tzitzis During Sports

As the weather turns hot, my son is increasing his outdoor activities during recesses and time off from yeshivah. He is under the impression that it is prohibited to get sweat and dirt on his tzitzis and wants to remove them during the game. Should I suggest that he keep them on?

Although technically there is an obligation to wear *tzitzis* only if one happens to be wearing a four-cornered garment, *Klal Yisrael* has accepted the practice of pursuing the mitzvah at all times by constantly wearing a four-cornered garment with *tzitzis*.[1] Therefore, the correct practice is to always wear a four-cornered garment with *tzitzis*. *Chazal* tell us that wearing a garment with *tzitzis* earns us tremendous reward,[2] as well as providing powerful protection from *aveiros* and acting as an

---

1. See *Shulchan Aruch* 24:1; *Tosafos Yeshanim*, Shabbos 32b, s.v. *be'avon tzitzis*; *Igros Moshe*, *Orach Chaim* 4:4.
2. *Menachos* 43b.

impetus to perform *mitzvos*.[3] We therefore want to always be in a position where we can fulfill this relatively easy-to-perform mitzvah.

Harav Moshe Feinstein (O.C. 3:1) rules that one fulfills the mitzvah of wearing *tzitzis* even with a garment that is not needed for warmth or protection against the elements, and even if it uncomfortable. Therefore, even if one sweats more while playing ball due to the fact that he is wearing *tzitzis*, a *mitzvah min haTorah* is still being fulfilled.

There is no *issur* against getting sweat or dirt on *tzitzis* if it occurs through normal usage (and therefore it is permissible to wear *tzitzis* in the bathroom[4]). Your son's situation is no different from that of a person who wears *tzitzis* while working from nine to five in a hot warehouse. Such a person is simply wearing *tzitzis* while doing his job. It is, of course, *kavod hamitzvah* to wash the *tzitzis* when the need arises.

It is important to encourage your son to wear *tzitzis* while playing ball, thereby fulfilling this special mitzvah at every possible moment. The *Navi*[5] relates the story of King Shaul's pursuit of David ben Yishai (later to become David HaMelech). Shaul thought that David was trying to kill him and felt the halachic necessity to execute him in self-defense. The *Navi* states that when David and his men chanced upon Shaul HaMelech in a cave, David's men wished to finally rid themselves of their pursuer. Due to his attributes of extraordinary *rachamim* and sensitivity, David stopped them, not wanting to kill Hashem's anointed under any circumstances. Instead, David tore Shaul's garment as a sign that he had been there and spared his life. David hoped that the message would teach Shaul that he, David, was not a threat and meant no harm to the throne.

The Midrash[6] comments that David later experienced pangs of regret for having cut off the corner of the garment, as this left Shaul HaMelech temporarily bereft of the mitzvah of *tzitzis*. David suffered much anguish over this, despite the fact that, now that he was wearing a garment with one corner removed, Shaul was not longer actually obligated in the mitzvah. *Chazal* teach us that at the end of his life

---

3. *Shulchan Aruch* 24:1.
4. See *Rambam, hilchos tzitzis* 3:9.
5. *Shmuel* I Ch. 24.
6. *Yalkut Shimoni* 133.

David HaMelech suffered from an illness through which clothing could not warm his body and that this illness was in retribution, *middah kenegged middah*, for David's having ruined Shaul's garment.[7]

Some commentators[8] maintain that this punishment was for the slight disregard on David's part for the value of each and every moment of fulfilling the mitzvah of *tzitzis*.

The Vilna Gaon cried on his deathbed while holding his *tzitzis*. The Gaon explained that he was saddened that he must leave a world where for such a small amount of money and effort one can be *zocheh* to perform the incredible mitzvah of *tzitzis*. One should certainly not forgo every precious opportunity to fulfill it.

---

7. *Berachos* 62b.
8. See *Torah Shebe'al Peh, Shmuel I* 24:5 in *Remez BiMelo*, quoting *Chiddushei Hagaonim*; see also *Iyun Yaakov* to *Berachos* 62b and *Shocher Tov #7.*

Making a Berachah When Donning a Tallis After the Shabbos Seudah

I often go to my in-laws for the Shabbos seudah. Since I come directly from shul, I often wear my tallis to their house and remove it as the meal begins. The seudah lasts about an hour and a half, after which I like to wear my tallis home again. Do I make a new berachah when I put on the tallis for the second time?

The *mechaber* in *Shulchan Aruch*[1] rules that if the *tallis* is taken off even with the intention to wear again immediately, a new *berachah* is recited. The Rema[2] argues, ruling that if one intends to wear the *tallis* again, a new *berachah* is not recited. The *Mishnah Berurah*[3] paskens

---

1. *Orach Chaim* 8:14.
2. Ibid.
3. Ibid. 37.

that no *berachah* is recited as long as there was no *hesech hadaas* (lapse or diversion of attention) and an interruption of more than a short duration.

Although Sephardim usually follow the rulings of the *mechaber*, many Sephardic *poskim* point out that when the case involves the possible reciting of a *berachah* in vain, we apply the rule of *safek berachos lehakel*. This means that when there is halachic doubt whether a *berachah* should be recited, we opt not to do so. Therefore, even those who follow Sephardic custom would not make a *berachah* if the *tallis* is taken off with intention to put it on again after a short break, and this is what was done.[4] The *Beur Halachah*[5] quotes the *Artzos HaChaim* as ruling that if one removes *tzitzis* in order to enter a bathhouse, he must make a new *berachah* upon donning the *tzitzis*, because of the lengthy interruption. The *Beur Halachah* quotes the Bach, who rules that such an interruption is not lengthy enough to require a new *berachah*.

Although a trip to the bathhouses of old probably required more time than taking a simple shower does today, we do see doubt in the *poskim* as to the length of time that is considered an interruption and therefore requires a new *berachah*.

With regard to *tefillin,* the *Shulchan Aruch HaRav* (25:29) rules that an interruption of two or three hours requires a new *berachah*. HaRav Shlomo Zalman Auerbach[6] applies this to a *tallis,* ruling that an interruption of up to three hours does not require a new *berachah* (understanding that the *Shulchan Aruch HaRav* did not set a specific time but only a general guideline of two to three hours). HaRav Auerbach suggested the possibility that even more than three hours would not be considered a *hefsek* and that each scenario would have to be examined independently.[7]

Other *poskim* also feel that such a long interruption would not necessitate the recital of a new *berachah*.[8]

Based on this, if you are sure that you will be putting the *tallis* back

---

4. See *Birkei Yosef, Orach Chaim* 7:3; *Kaf HaChaim* ibid.8:52; *Yechaveh Daas* 3:80.
5. Ibid. *d"h veyesh omrim she'ein mevarchim.*
6. *Halichos Shlomo* 3:7.
7. See footnote 25, ibid.
8. See *Orchos Rabbeinu, Orach Chaim* 1:30, and *Hosafos;* see also *Tzitz Elizer* 13:4.

on after the *seudah* in order to wear it home, no new *berachah* is required. If the meal lasts a long time but is still within the time frame of a few hours, no *berachah* must be recited.

To avoid the gray area of doubtful *berachos* that your interruption will entail, I would suggest that when you make the *berachah* on the *tallis* before *davening*, you have in mind that it should cover the mitzvah of wearing the *tallis* only until such time as you remove it (which for you is right before the meal). This will enable you to make a new *berachah* when you don the *tallis* again before going home, without any hesitation or halachic doubt.[9]

---

9. See end of *Beur Halachah*, ibid., who advises the same practice to avoid the question concerning the bathhouse mentioned above.

Tefillin the "Right" Way

Q *I am a 28-year-old "lefty" who performs all labor and activities with my left hand, with the exception of writing, which I do with my right hand. (This inconsistency was a result of my strong-willed grandmother's insistence that her grandson was going to write the "normal" way!)*

The instructions given to me before my bar mitzvah were to put tefillin on my left arm, as a right-handed person would normally do. I recently began learning the laws of tefillin, and I see the matter is far from simple. Should I be wearing the tefillin on my right hand, as lefties do, since I am really a lefty except for writing? Does anyone wear the tefillin on both arms consecutively?

The good news is that the original ruling you received at your bar mitzvah was not wrong. The better news is that the information you will now receive will assist you so that if you desire to ask the question again, you will understand the issues. (One need not ask any *she'eilah* twice, but in this particular case, there might be room to re-examine the issue, as we shall soon explain.)

The *Gemara*[1] presents various sources to explain why a left-handed person puts *tefillin* on his right arm. Rav Nassan learns from the juxtaposition of two *pesukim* — "וּקְשַׁרְתָּם לְאוֹת עַל יָדֶךָ", *Bind them as a sign upon your arm.....*" and "וּכְתַבְתָּם עַל מְזֻזוֹת בֵּיתֶךָ", *And write them on the doorposts of your house...*"[2] — that the binding of the *tefillin* (וּקְשַׁרְתָּם) is done by the same hand that does the writing (וּכְתַבְתָּם). This means, then, that a person who writes with his left hand will put *tefillin* on his right hand, thereby tying it with his left hand. According to this understanding, left- or right-handedness is determined solely by which hand does the writing (even if a person was forced to use that hand in order to conform with societal "norms").

The second source learns it from the Torah's adding the letter *hei* to the end of the word "*yadcha*" (your hand) in the *pasuk*, "וְהָיָה לְאוֹת עַל יָדְכָה וּלְטוֹטָפֹת בֵּין עֵינֶיךָ,"[3] that the *tefillin* is placed on the weaker hand — the word יָדְכָה aluding to a contraction of the words יַד כֵּהָה, *the weak hand*. Rashi[4] adds that "*yadchah*" as spelled is a feminine form, indicating the weaker hand. According to this explanation, *tefillin* would be worn on the arm that does less of the daily activities (e.g., using a fork or hammer or lifting heavy objects), and writing does not count more than any other activity. Once the dominant hand is identified, the *shel yad* is placed on the other hand.[5]

Interestingly, an ambidextrous person dons his *tefillin* as a right-handed person would.[6] This applies only to one who performs all activities equally with both hands. Many who profess to being ambidextrous

1. *Menachos* 37a.
2. *Devarim* 6: 8-9.
3. *Shemos* 13:16.
4. *Menachos* 37a d"h *miyadchah.*
5. *Beis Yosef*, siman 27, d"h *v'itur.*
6. *Shulchan Aruch Orach Chaim* 27:6; *Mishnah Berurah* 5 .See *Beur Halachah*, ibid. d"h *yesh omrim.*

cannot really write well with both hands and often do not perform other activities with nearly the same strength in both hands.

There is a dispute among the *Rishonim* and early *Acharonim* about whether strength or writing is the deciding factor in determining which hand will be used.

The *Shulchan Aruch*[7] quotes both opinions. The general rule of the *Shulchan Aruch* is that when two opinions are quoted and both are quoted as a *"yesh omrim,"* the *halachah* follows the second opinion. In this instance, the deciding factor is which hand does the writing.[8]

The Rema, who generally represents the *minhag* of Ashkenazim, agrees that the custom is to use the hand that writes as the determining factor. The Gra (Vilna Gaon),[9] however, and others[10] take the opinion that it depends solely on which hand performs most of the daily activities.

The Bach brings a third opinion[11] that states that if either writing *or* the other activities are done by the right hand, then the man is considered a "righty" and wears the *shel yad* on the left hand. It is only when *all* activities and writing are done by the left hand that a person is considered a lefty. There are notable *poskim* who concur with this opinion.[12]

HaRav Moshe Feinstein, *z"tl,*[13] points out that it is difficult to declare that there is a clear *minhag* in regard to this matter. He points out a discrepancy between two works by HaRav Moshe Isserlis, *zt"l:* his glosses to *Shulchan Aruch* (commonly referred to as *Rema)* and his *Darkei Moshe.* In his glosses to *Shulchan Aruch* he states, *"v'hachi nahug* — that is the custom." However, the *Darkei Moshe* states *"v'nireh li linhog* — it appears to me that this should be the practice."

Rav Moshe then raises the possibility that one should be *machmir* and put the *shel yad* on each arm alternately, since it is prohibited to wear *tefillin* on both arms at the same time, before putting on the *shel rosh.* Others suggest that the second *shel yad* should be donned at the end of *davening.* The advantage of doing this at the beginning of *davening* rather than at the end is that the *berachah* recited on the

---

7. Ibid.
8. See *Yabiya Omer* 6:2 and 8:108.
9. Ibid. 17.
10. See *Beur Halachah* ibid.; *Aruch HaShulchan,* ibid. 16.
11. Ibid. *d"h v'itur yad.*
12. See *Beur Halachah,* ibid.; *Igros Moshe Orach Chaim* 4:11.
13. *Igros Moshe,* ibid.

first *shel yad* will be *chal* on whichever hand is the correct one. If one puts on the second *shel yad* at the end of *davening*, no *berachah* can be recited.

In his written *teshuvah*, Rav Moshe rejects this approach because it is a difficult thing to do every single day. We also do not see that the earlier *poskim* suggested such an idea, even though it would cover both halachic opinions.

Interestingly enough, not only do other contemporary *poskim* endorse the suggestion that one should (although certainly not obligated to) try to wear the additional *shel yad*, but Rav Moshe himself has advised others to do so.

The story begins on the Lower East Side over forty years ago ....

Rabbi Mordechai Goldstein, now Rav of the Mishkenos Yaakov community in Ramat Beit Shemesh, *Eretz Yisrael*, and the son of the noted American *posek* HaRav Tuvia Goldstein, *zt"l*, is left-handed. Nevertheless, when he was growing up, he was taught to write with his right hand. Although he wrote exclusively with his right hand, his left hand performed all other activities.

Before his bar mitzvah, the question arose: On which arm should he lay his *tefillin?*

Rav Tuvia took his young son with him to pose this question to the venerated *Posek HaDor,* HaRav Moshe Feinstein, *zt"l*, who resided in the apartment directly above theirs.

Rabbi Goldstein vividly recalls what occurred during that visit. After listening to the *she'eilah,* Rav Moshe began to dissect the issue from every angle. After clarifying all aspects of the *sugya,* he concluded that in this situation, the bar mitzvah boy should lay *tefillin* on his right arm, in accordance with the opinion of the Vilna Gaon, since even though young Mordechai wrote with his right hand, that was not his natural way of writing, and he had had to be trained in order to write that way.

Over thirty years later, Rabbi Goldstein was talking in learning with the *Posek HaDor,* HaRav Yosef Shalom Elyashiv, *shlita.* The topic under discussion was upon which arm an individual should place his *tefillin* if he writes with one hand but does all other *melachos* with the other. After clarifying all aspects of the *sugya,* Rav Elyashiv concluded that the halachah is in accordance with the *minhag ha'olam* brought by the Rema, that the writing hand is considered the primary hand.

"Well," Rabbi Goldstein began, "what about someone like myself, who's been laying *tefillin* on his right arm since his bar mitzvah, as per the Gra?"

"Perhaps it would be best for you to switch and begin to lay *tefillin* on your left hand," Rav Elyashiv replied.

"But Rav Moshe told me to be *noheg* like the Gra," Rabbi Goldstein said.

"Ahhh," said Rav Elyashiv. "If Rav Moshe told you to do it this way, you should certainly continue to be *noheg* like the Gra."[14]

At the conclusion of the conversation, Rabbi Goldstein was already at the door when Rav Elyashiv suddenly called him back in. "Although I said to continue to do as you were told by Rav Moshe, nevertheless, toward the end of *davening* — after *U'va L'Tzion* — it would be worthwhile for you to remove the *shel yad* from your right arm, without removing the *shel rosh,* and put it on your left arm for a few minutes to be *mekayem* the *shitah* of the Rema." (Many who practice this stringency do not have a second *shel yad* and simply adjust the one they have for use on both arms. The *bayis* (box) of the *tefillin* is turned around so that the *yud* is on the inner side.)

Rabbi Goldstein followed HaRav Elyashiv's advice, at the same time wondering if Rav Moshe would have had any objection to this added *chumrah.* It was likely he would never know since Rav Moshe was no longer here to ask ....

After many years of wondering, Rabbi Goldstein received the good tidings that there were people close to Rav Moshe who had been advised to put *tefillin* on both arms, due to the doubt regarding their status. A *yungerman* in Yerushalyaim who writes with his left hand and performs all other activities with his right hand was wondering if Rav Moshe was truly opposed to the idea of putting *tefillin* on the other arm. He called his uncle, Rabbi Avraham Pessin of Monsey, New York, a close *talmid* of Rav Moshe.

---

14. Most *Rishonim* hold as the Gra does; see *Beur Halachah*, ibid.

Rabbi Pessin related, "I myself asked Rav Moshe this question, and he told me that for a scrupulous individual it would be appropriate to put *tefillin* on both arms to fulfill the opinion of the Rema."

HaRav Ephraim Greenblatt, the author of *Teshuvos Rivevos Ephraim*, also reports that although he himself never heard directly from Rav Moshe on the topic, he did hear from a *rebbi* in Mesivtha Tiferes Jerusalem, Rav Moshe's yeshivah, that once, when discussing the *she'eilah* with Rav Moshe, the latter did indeed endorse the idea of a scrupulous individual putting the *shel yad* on the other arm as well.

It seems that the written *teshuvah* discourages the practice for young bar mitzvah *bachurim* and others who are not prepared to take on a stricter practice, but Rav Moshe did advise older, conscientious individuals to do so.

An important question must be raised for those who choose to put the second *shel yad* on the other arm at the end of *davening*. Must one remove — or move to the side — one's *tefillin shel rosh* before taking off the *shel yad* to transfer it to the second arm?

One could argue that he must, because it is prohibited to wear the *shel rosh* without a *shel yad*. This is based on the *halachah*[15] that the head-*tefillin* are donned after the arm-*tefillin* are already in place.

However, many *poskim* rule that once the *shel rosh* is on one's head, one need not remove it or move it off center in order to switch the *shel yad* from arm to arm. (This was an oral *psak* of both Ha-Rav Elyashiv and HaRav Chaim Kanievsky. This may also be the position of the *Beur Halachah*.[16] The *Aruch HaShulchan* disagrees with this conclusion.[17])

In conclusion, there is clearly no obligation to change your present custom, and you definitely have every right to continue following the *psak* you originally received before your bar mitzvah. However, if you want to be extra-scrupulous in your fulfillment of the mitzvah of *tefillin*, many *poskim* recommend placing a *shel yad* on the other arm *l'chumrah*, once you are at a stage in life when you feel you are ready for it.

---

15. *Menachos* 36; see *Shulchan Aruch* 28:2.
16. *Beur Halachah* 25:6 d"h *paga*, although one can possibly differentiate between our case and the case discussed there.
17. *Orach Chaim* 26:5.

The fulfillment of the *mitzvah d'Oraisa* of *tefillin* is predicated on wearing the *shel yad* on the correct arm. It is a very serious question that deserves careful deliberation and assessment of both the practical *metzius* and the correct direction of the halachah. As always, one should always consult his Rav, because what may appear to the questioner to be "insignificant" details may, in fact, influence the halachic decision.

Purchasing the "New" Tefillin Straps

My son is becoming bar mitzvah this year, and I am in the process of purchasing tefillin for him. Tefillin with retzuos that are completely black on both sides and throughout have recently come on the market. Is this a hiddur that I should opt for? I would be more than happy to provide my son with the best tefillin money can buy if there is a halachic advantage in purchasing these types of straps, yet I wonder why this hiddur was not practiced in earlier generations.

It is clear from the *Gemara*[1] that although one is required to dye the outer surface of the *tefillin* straps black, he has the option to leave the

---

1. *Menachos* 35a.

inner part without any dye at all, or to dye it any color of his choice (except red).[2]

The Rambam *paskens* that while there is no requirement to blacken the inner side of the *tefillin retzuos*, there is a halachic advantage in doing so, because it would beautify the mitzvah (*"vena'eh hu la'tefillin sheyihiyu chulan shechoros, haketzitzah veharetzuah kulah"*).[3]

The *Beis Yosef*[4] cites the Rambam but observes that it is not the *minhag* to follow the Rambam and blacken both sides of the *retzuos*. *Darkei Moshe*[5] cites the *Ohr Zarua*, who suggests that one should indeed blacken both sides. *Darkei Moshe*, however, concludes that it is not the common custom to do so. The *Mishnah Berurah*[6] quotes both the *Beis Yosef* and the *Darkei Moshe* as the practical *halachah*, clearly indicating that the vast majority of *Klal Yisrael* have not practiced the custom of painting both sides of the *retzuos*.

There are, however, a number of sources that suggest that it is meritorious to dye the straps on both sides and that there were individuals throughout the generations who were meticulous about doing so. The Arizal is quoted[7] as having been strict in the matter.[8] The Radvaz and others[9] suggest that one be careful to follow the opinion of the Rambam to dye the straps black on both sides.

It should also be pointed out that there is a very practical advantage to dyeing the *retzuos* black through and through, including the reverse side. It is quite common that the blackness of the straps fades, chips, and cracks over time. Often this wear and tear is not noticed, or is noticed after many days of use without the proper blackness. Although it is easily repaired by repainting the faded or cracked parts (the ink or paint must be applied with the proper intent of *"lishmah"*), the days that the tefillin were worn without the *retzuos* dyed in every area have been lost.

---

2. See *Gemara* ibid. with *Rashi* for explanation.
3. *Rambam, Hilchos Tefillin* 3:14.
4. *Orach Chaim* 33.
5. Ibid.
6. Ibid. 21.
7. *Shaar Hakavanos.*
8. See *Chida* in *Machzik Berachah* 33.
9. See list of *Acharonim* brought in *Ohr Yisrael*, Volume 46, p. 104.

The precious mitzvah of *tefillin* is incumbent upon men every single day, and is often not fulfilled properly due to lack of knowledge or attentiveness. It is crucial to have the portion of the *retzuos* facing forward completely black at all times,[10] and even those who are aware of this *halachah* are often not careful to check the straps on a consistent basis.[11] If the *retzuos* are blackened throughout, there is very little chance that any part will become white even after extensive use. This dyeing process ensures that no one is caught off guard, discovering suddenly that the *retzuos* need another touch-up and that the mitzvah has not been fulfilled properly for some time.

It is important to note that even if one has *retzuos* that are dyed black on both sides, care should be taken to make sure the smooth, shiny side always faces the outside.[12]

Your historical question about why the *hiddur* has only become more popular recently is a valid one. If people were always able to dye the *retzuos* on both sides, why do we find that even the *gedolei haposkim* did not dye their *retzuos* on both sides?

I was told by experts in the field of *tefillin* that perhaps the *hiddur* is more prevalent today because of a combination of economics and technology. We now have the ability to perform the dyeing process in a faster, more efficient way, thus making the process more affordable than it was in years gone by. This factor, coupled with the relative prosperity of the *frum* community, has perhaps revived the age-old discussion of this aspect of possible *noi mitzvah*. These new *retzuos* are not much more expensive than the standard *retzuos*, and many are eager to spend a little more money for the possible gain in *hiddur mitzvah*.

One cannot, however, mitigate the *mesorah* of psak and *minhag Yisrael*. It is quite clear that the overwhelming majority of *poskim* rule that only the outer side of the *retzuos* must be dyed black. It is also very obvious that this has been the *minhag Yisrael* for many generations. You cannot go wrong by maintaining this *minhag* and purchasing for your son the same *retzuos* that both you and your father have.

It is important, though, to point out that the *tefillin* that you are

---

10. See *Beur Halachah* 33:3, *d"h Haretzuos Shechoros*.
11. See *Mishnah Berurah* ibid. 19.
12. See *Mishnah Berurah* ibid. 23 and *Beur Halachah d"h mibachutz*.

wearing, and certainly the *tefillin* that you will be purchasing for your son, are qualitatively superior to the *tefillin* your parents and ancestors wore. We are not discussing the *yiras Shamayim* of the *sofer* and the *kavanos* of *lishmah* by those who fashioned the *battim* and *retzuos*. It is obvious that in those areas we frequently cannot come even close to the *madreigah* of those of previous generations. We are only discussing *hiddurim* in the physical properties of the *tefillin* today, and it is clear that their quality surpasses those of yesteryear, again due to improved technology and economics.

HaGaon HaRav Wosner, *shlita*, of Bnei Brak, writes in *Shevet Halevi* 9:16 that those individuals who opt to purchase *retzuos* that are blackened on both sides will be blessed for their exemplary display of exactitude in *hiddur* and *noi mitzvah*. However, this should not necessarily be legislated as a new practice for the masses, writing, *"If individuals do this, may they be blessed; but I do not see a reason to do this as a halachic ruling."*[13]

As mentioned above, one should not feel any halachic or social pressure to buy *retzuos* that are dyed black on both sides. If one wishes to do so in order to avoid losing the precious mitzvah of *tefillin* for even one moment due to the fading or chipping of the dye, as happens often with our standard *retzuos*, there would be benefit in doing so. One would then also have the benefit of fulfilling the opinion of the Rambam and others.

Wishing you *hatzlachah* on your decision. *Mazal Tov* and much *nachas* on the upcoming bar mitzvah.

---

13. אם יחידים ינהגו כן, תבוא עליהם ברכה, אבל להנהיג דרך הוראה לא ראיתי צורך.

Scratching the Surface: A Close Look at a Tefillin Issue

An important matter relating to the kashrus of *tefillin* resurfaced several years ago. The issue concerns an important detail involving the painting of the *tefillin shel rosh*. Although the problem is not new, it is now known that the percentage of *tefillin* affected by it is much higher than was previously believed. The controversy involves *charitzim mezuyafim*. Literally translated, a *charitz* is a line, groove, or scratch. *Mezuyaf* means *fake* or *forged*.

When creating the four compartments of the *tefillin shel rosh* (into which the four *parshiyos* are placed), there are three natural *charitzim* separating each compartment from the adjoining one The division of these *charitzim* should preferably extend down to the base (*titurah*) of the *tefillin*.

If the *charitzim* between the *battim* are not recognizable from the outside, the *tefillin* may be rendered *pasul*.[1]

When the *battim* are formed, they are placed in a press in order to shape a perfect square. This press generates thousands of pounds of pressure. As the compartments are forced together, the *charitzim* become less recognizable. When painting the *bayis* at the end of production, these *charitzim* can disappear from view completely, thereby making the *bayis shel rosh* indistinguishable from the *bayis shel yad* (which has only one compartment for the one *klaf* that is placed in it).

Since the *charitzim* must be clearly visible in the finished *shel rosh*, the original *charitz* must be detected and re-defined. Should the *battim* painter instead proceed to engrave lines into the paint without ensuring that they correspond exactly to the original spot of the *charitzim* underneath, the *tefillin shel rosh* will be *pasul*. This is because the final lines

that are etched into the *shel rosh* are not actually enabling the four sections to be independently recognizable. The divergent paths of the real and fake *charitzim* can be clearly seen once the *tefillin* have been properly checked for this problem. This is the opinion of the leading *Gedolim* in *Eretz Yisrael*, including HaGaon HaRav Yosef Shalom Elyashiv, *shlita*, HaGaon HaRav Shmuel Ha Levi Wosner, *shlita*, and others, in accordance with their understanding of the majority of *Acharonim*.[2]

Although there are *poskim* who rule leniently on this issue *bedi'eved*,[3] all agree that the requirement of clear division between the *battim* is halachically necessary *l'chatchilah*.

---

1. *Gemara Menachos* 34b; *Shulchan Aruch Orach Chaim* 32:40 with *Mishnah Berurah* 188; see *Sefer Zichron Eliyahu*, authored by *HaRav* D. Morgenstern and *Harav* E. Gittman, pp. 43-46.
2. See *sefer Zichron Eliyahu*, ibid.
3. See *sefer Zichron Eliyahu*, p. 45, quoting the *teshuvah* of *Maharam Mintz*.

Incidentally, one reason the problem of *charitzim mezuyafim* has not always been obvious is because the supervision over making the *battim* is done at the *battim macher*, when the *battim* are initially produced. The final painting and line-etching is often outsourced to people who specialize in painting *tefillin*. Since the prevalence of this problem was discovered, this "weak link" has generally been addressed.

It is rare for a *battim* painter to completely overlook the natural *charitzim*. When false *charitzim* are discovered, it is common to find only part of the *charitz* scored into the paint in disregard of the actual division between the *battim*.

There is a dispute among contemporary *poskim* concerning a

charitz that corresponds to the actual division for *most* of the *shel rosh*. If the *charitzim* are done correctly along most of the top and sides of the *shel rosh*, Rav Elyashiv rules that the *battim* need not be replaced (they are valid *bedi'eved*).

There is an innate desire to want perfectly straight, equidistant lines on the exterior of the *shel rosh,* since the *tefillin* are more aesthetically pleasing when etched in a uniform way. Although the *tefillin* might appear more beautiful that way, the real *hiddur* in fulfilling the mitzvah of *tefillin* is in following each halachic detail exactly as it is required. The natural *charitz* will not always be 100-percent straight, because animal hides are natural products and do not always conform exactly as one wishes them to. Although this does not present any halachic problem, the fact remains that many consumers are not pleased if they receive a brand-new *shel rosh* with a wavy *charitz*. It is important to inform the customer that the real *charitz* is a natural division, which need not be a perfect line. During recent mass checking of *tefillin* in *Eretz Yisrael*, a frighteningly high number of *tefillin* (over 10 percent) were discovered to have *charitzim metzuyafim*.[4]

Although it takes only a few moments to check for false *charitzim*, the *bedikah* requires proper tools and experience, because *battim* can be ruined if they are not checked properly.

Many consumers spend a great deal of money to purchase a superior pair of *tefillin*, and they expect to receive a product with many *hiddurim*. They should certainly be given *tefillin* that fulfill all the basic halachic details mentioned in the *Gemara* and agreed upon by the *poskim*. The purpose of this brief overview is to raise awareness of one such detail that is sometimes overlooked.

May all of *Klal Yisrael* be *zocheh* to fulfill the mitzvah of *tefillin* produced with superior *hiddurim* and absolute kashrus.

---

4. See *Teshuvos Mishkenos Yaakov Yoreh Deah* 17 for the obligation to check if a problem is *mi'ut hamatzui*. *V'tzarich iyun.*

Common Mezuzah Questions Answered

Q My first question is, how much time does one have before affixing mezuzos to the doorposts of a new residence?

My second question involves the mezuzos that I am taking from my rented apartment. My landlord mentioned to me that I may not take my mezuzos because the apartment is being rented to another Jew. I was surprised to hear that I cannot take my own mezuzos for use in my new house and would like to verify whether my landlord is halachically correct. If so, can I at least request compensation for the mezuzos I must leave behind?

Finally, in the event that the new tenant agrees to give me my mezuzos but only after after he puts up his

own mezuzos, I may have to borrow
mezuzos for my new home. Do I make
a berachah on borrowed mezuzos? If
I am required to make a berachah,
am I then required to make a second
berachah when I replace the borrowed
mezuzos with my own?

Outside of *Eretz Yisrael*, one who is renting a house or an apartment is obligated to affix a *mezuzah* after thirty days.[1] One should put up the *mezuzos* after nightfall following the thirtieth day. If the tenant signed a lease obligating him to stay more than thirty days, some opinions hold that one is obligated to affix *mezuzos* as soon as he moves in. A *berachah* should not be recited at that time.[2]

In *Eretz Yisrael*, even a renter is obligated to affix a *mezuzah* immediately.

When one purchases a house, there is an obligation to place the *mezuzos* on every doorpost as soon as he moves in.[3] If one is storing furniture or other belongings on the premises but has not yet moved in, a *mezuzah* should be placed, without a *berachah,* on the doorposts of the rooms containing the furniture.[4]

With regard to your second question, your landlord is indeed correct. It is prohibited to leave the house without *mezuzos* for even a short while, unless the new tenant will be a non-Jew, who is obviously not obligated in the mitzvah of *mezuzah*.[5] Aside from the halachic prohibition against removing the *mezuzos,* the *sefarim* also say that there is a danger involved in removing the *mezuzos*. Even if the new tenant indicates that he plans to replace the *mezuzos* in a timely fashion, the prohibition and danger still apply unless the new ones are put up at the very time the old ones are removed.[6]

---

1. See *Sdei Chemed, Klalim* 40:112-113.
2. See *Sdei Chemed* ibid.
3. *Tosafos, Avodah Zarah* 21 d"h *af.*
4. *Orchos Rabbeinu* 3, page 171, quoting *Chazon Ish.*
5. *Shulchan Aruch Yoreh Deah* 291:2.
6. *Pischei Teshuvah* ibid. 7.

One can request that the new tenant pay the market price for used *mezuzos*.[7]

You have the right to replace the *mezuzos* (as well as their cases) with a less-expensive version (as long as they are halachically kosher) before you leave. It is preferable to have the *mezuzos* taken down and checked before moving them to the new location, in deference to the opinions that a *mezuzah* should not be removed while it is still kosher.[8] Checking the *mezuzah* gives further halachic grounds for removing it.

Although usually it is common to have *mezuzos* checked twice every seven years by a qualified, experienced individual, it is sufficient in this instance for the homeowner to make a cursory check himself.[9]

To answer your final question, one does make a *berachah* on borrowed *mezuzos*.

When you remove the borrowed *mezuzos* to affix your own, there are those who rule that a new *berachah* must be recited.[10] Others rule that the replacement is merely a continuation of the same mitzvah (without a significant time lapse between) and therefore no new *berachah* is recited.[11]

Because I travel abroad on business quite often, I would like to know if it is permissible for my wife to put up mezuzos in the event I am not home.

It is permissible for women to affix *mezuzos*, since they are obligated in the mitzvah as well.[12] Minors should not put up *mezuzos*.

---

7. *Shulchan Aruch*, ibid.; see *Pischei Teshuvah* 8, cf. *Chovas Hadar* 1, footnote 51, concerning a tenant who refuses to pay.
8. See *Magen Avraham* 15:2.
9. See *Pischei Teshuvah Yoreh Deah* 291:3.
10. *Shut Shevet Halevi* 2:158.
11. HaRav Elyashiv, quoted in *Leket Halachos* 4, footnote 5; see also *Sefer Halichos Shlomo* on *tefillah* 4, footnote 10.
12. *Shut Chasam Sofer Yoreh Deah* 271.

When one removes mezuzos to check them, is there an obligation to make a new berachah upon putting them up again?

If one is able to check them and put them up again on the same day, no *berachah* should be recited.[13] If a *mezuzah* was found to be *pasul* and was subsequently replaced or repaired (usually, a *mezuzah* with a true disqualification cannot be repaired), a new *berachah* is required, even if it is put up the same day.

Can I change the type of room that the mezuzah is used for when I move to my new home? My specific question is in regard to moving a mezuzah from the children's bedroom of my old apartment to a guest bedroom in my new home.

One must make sure that the *mezuzah* is placed on a door that carries with it the same obligation or greater. Therefore, one should not take a *mezuzah* from a doorpost that has a definite obligation and place it in an area that has questionable status. It would be objectionable, for instance, to take a *mezuzah* from a doorpost with a door and place it on a doorframe without a door, since the latter requires a *mezuzah* only according to some opinions.

Moving a *mezuzah* from one bedroom to another would be no problem if both have proper doors.

---

13. *Leket Halachos* 4:1, quoting HaRav Elyashiv and HaRav Wosner.

*I have a doorpost that is very narrow
and does not have enough room for the
mezuzah to be placed on a slant. What
should I do?*

According to Rashi, a *mezuzah* is always placed vertically, whereas according to Rabbeinu Tam it is always placed horizontally. The Rema[14] rules that in deference to the opinion of Rabbeinu Tam, the custom is to put the *mezuzah* on a slant.

However, if that is not feasible, the *mezuzah* is hung vertically, following the opinion of Rashi.[15]

*At what height should mezuzos be
placed on the doorpost?*

Mezuzos should be put at the bottom half of the top third of the doorframe. One should measure carefully to ensure proper placement, since the bottom of the *mezuzah* should not be placed below the bottom of the top third.[16] Many people follow the opinions that the *mezuzah* may be affixed anywhere in the top third, as long as it is not placed within a *tefach* (about 3 or 4 inches) from the top.[17]

If the doorframe is very tall, one should put the *mezuzah* at average shoulder height.[18]

---

14. *Yoreh Deah* 289:6.
15. *Pischei Teshuvah*, ibid. 9.
16. *Shulchan Aruch Yoreh Deah* 289:2.
17. See *Nekudos Hakesef*, ibid.
18. *Shach*, ibid. 4.

Some of my doors have metal frames. Am I permitted to use tape to fasten the mezuzos, since it is sometimes more difficult to drive nails or screws into such frames?

One must affix the *mezuzah* to the door in a sturdy and permanent way. If nails cannot be used, strong, double-sided tape (or Duco cement or the like) can be used. Ordinary Scotch tape or masking tape should not be used because it will not hold the *mezuzah* in a permanent manner.

One should apply the double-sided tape or cement before making the *berachah*, in order to minimize the time lapse between the *berachah* and the *mitzvah*.[19]

Is it preferable to use clear mezuzah cases rather than wooden or other opaque types?

When possible, it is preferable to have the *shin-daled-yud* visible. This is accomplished by either using a clear *mezuzah* case or one that has a small window so that one can see the *Shem Hashem* of *shin-daled-yud*.[20]

If the *mezuzah* is in a room where people are not always dressed appropriately, the *mezuzah* should be covered with an opaque case.[21] The *Shem Hashem* of *shin-daled-yud* should be facing outward even when encased in an opaque *mezuzah* cover.

---

19. See *Shut Shevet Halevi* 2:158.
20. *Rema Yoreh Deah* 288:15.
21. *Chovas Hadar* 9:4.

I just bought nice mezuzah cases for my new home. What do I do with my old ones?

As one would do with *sheimos*, the cases, as well as the plastic covering the *mezuzah*, must be buried.[22]

If you are upgrading the actual *mezuzos* and the used ones are still kosher, it is appropriate to find another place to affix them or to donate them to a *mezuzah gemach*. As mentioned above, it is preferable to check *mezuzos* that are taken down and then move them to the new location, in deference to the opinions that a *mezuzah* should not be taken off while it is still kosher.[23] Checking the *mezuzah* strengthens the permissibility of taking it down. As mentioned above, although usually it is preferable to have *mezuzos* checked twice every seven years by a qualified, experienced individual, it is sufficient in this instance for the homeowner to make a cursory check.[24]

Is it permissible to walk into the house of a Jew who has not put up mezuzos?

It is halachically permissible to walk into such a house. It is important to prevail upon the resident to purchase *mezuzos* for the home, if one can do so graciously, without antagonizing the homeowner. Most Jews will accede to such a request if they are informed of the importance of the *mitzvah*, as well as the protection it affords.

---

22. *Shulchan Aruch Orach Chaim* 154:3; see *Mishnah Berurah* 14.
23. See *Magen Avraham* 15:2.
24. See *Pischei Teshuvah Yoreh Deah* 291:3.

Aside from the berachah I make on the mezuzah I am putting up in my new home, is there any other berachah I should make when I move in?

One who buys a home for himself and his family recites the *bera-chah* בָּרוּךְ אַתָּה ה' אֱלֹקֵינוּ מֶלֶךְ הָעוֹלָם, הַטּוֹב וְהַמֵּטִיב, *Blessed are You Hashem, our God, King of the universe, Who is good and does good.* This *berachah* is recited when two or more people reap the benefit of a valuable gift or purchase. If a single person purchases a home, the *berachah* of *Shehecheyanu* is recited.[25]

Although the common custom is to recite a *Shehecheyanu/Hatov Vehameitiv* upon buying a house even when a mortgage is being paid, there are *poskim* who rule that the house should be completely paid for before the *berachah* is recited.[26]

Similarly, one makes one of these *berachos* upon the purchase of a car. If the vehicle is bought for the use of two or more people, the *berachah* of *Hatov Vehameitiv* is recited. If a car is purchased for the exclusive use of one party, a *Shehecheyanu* would be recited.

The *berachah* of *Hatov Vehameitiv* or *Shehecheyanu* should be recited after one affixes the *mezuzos* in the new home.[27]

---

25. *Shulchan Aruch Orach Chaim* 223:3, 5 and *Beur Halachah d"h banah.*
26. See *Kaf HaChaim*, ibid. 18.
27. See *Aruch HaShulchan*, ibid. 6.

WAYS AND MEANS OF TEFILLAH AND TEHILLIM

How Loudly Should One Recite Shemoneh Esrei?

I have always recited Shemoneh Esrei quietly, saying the words with my lips only. My train of thought during Shemoneh Esrei was recently interrupted when I overheard someone in the row behind me whispering the words of his Shemoneh Esrei audibly. When I mentioned to him in a nice way that it is unnecessary to actually hear the words, he told me that I was in error and that the halachah states that one is obligated to say the words in a whisper that is loud enough to hear. He said that the words should be audible to the person davening and not to those around him, and he apologized for disturbing my kavanah.

Could you please clarify this halachah?

There are two opinions regarding the proper recital of the "silent amidah" we call *Shemoneh Esrei*. The *Shulchan Aruch*[1] rules that one must indeed hear the words of *Shemoneh Esrei*. The *Shulchan Aruch*, however, warns that it is prohibited to raise one's voice. Doing so shows a lack of *emunah*, as if to say that Hashem cannot hear our *tefillos* unless we say them loudly enough.[2]

The Beis Yosef,[3] however, brings a *Zohar* that suggests that one should not *daven Shemoneh Esrei* so that he can hear the words. Rather, the *Zohar* states, *Shemoneh Esrei* should be recited in complete silence.[4]

It is important to stress that even according to the *Zohar*, one must enunciate the words by exuding breath and forming the letters with his tongue and lips.

The *Mishnah Berurah* rules according to the *Shulchan Aruch* (based on *Magen Avraham, Gra, Shulchan Aruch HaRav,* and *Chayei Adam*) that one must recite *Shemoneh Esrei* in an audible tone. All *poskim* agree that even if one has not done so, however, he has fulfilled the obligation of *davening*.

All opinions agree that when *davening* in an audible whisper, one must not say the words loudly enough for others to hear, because it can disturb their *kavanah*.[5] If he is indeed disturbing others, he should move his seat or rely on the *Zohar* and whisper inaudibly.

It seems that you have not seen (or heard) people conducting themselves according to the ruling of the *Shulchan Aruch* and *Mishnah Berurah* on this matter, and your observation is not that surprising. This is because there are many who are accustomed to following the opinion of the *Zohar,* quoted above.

---

1. *Orach Chaim* 101:2.
2. See *Gemara Berachos* 31.
3. *Orach Chaim* 101:2, *Bedek Habayis*.
4. *Piskei Teshuvos*, ibid. 4, quoting *Eishel Avraham*, ibid. 3; and *Pri Chadash*, ibid. 2; see his footnotes 32,34.
5. *Mishnah Berurah* ibid. 6.

Remembering One's Name for the Yom HaDin

Some siddurim print a list of names with corresponding pesukim that one should say before the pasuk of "Yihiyu leratzon imrei fi" at the end of Shemoneh Esrei. Is the reciting of this pasuk a minhag that everyone should adopt? What if I cannot find a pasuk that begins and ends with the first and last letters of my name?

There are many sources indicating that it is proper to recite a *pasuk* beginning and ending with the first and last letters of one's halachic name.[1] Your halachic name is the one by which you are called up to the Torah and would therefore include your entire name, even if not commonly used.

The *Kaf HaChaim*[2] says that reciting the *pasuk* is a *segulah* to help the *neshamah* remember its name on the Yom HaDin after

---

1. Eliyahu Rabbah, *Orach Chaim* 122:2, *Kitzur Shelah, Os Kuf.*
2. *Orach Chaim* 122:11, quoting the *siddur Nehara Hashalem.*

death. Others say that reciting the *pasuk* helps mitigate the judgement in *Gehinnom*.[3]

Although there is no halachic obligation to recite the *pasuk*, it is certainly advisable to do so, based on these sources.

If you cannot find a *pasuk* that begins and ends with the first and last letters of your name, then it is advisable to search for a *pasuk* with your name in it. If such a *pasuk* cannot be found, you may recite two *pesukim*: the first *pasuk* beginning with the first letter of your name and the second ending with the final letter of your name.[4]

Another option is to find a *pasuk* that begins with the first letter of your name and also contains all the other letters of your name.[5]

---

3. See bracketed comment of *Rashi/Mefaresh* to the *Navi Michah* 6:9.
4. *Iyunei Halachos* by HaRav Z. Rabinowitz, page 178, cf. footnote 3, quoting *sefer Divrei Yosef*.
5. Ibid.

Maariv After Midnight

On occasion, I come home very late from a business trip, arriving just in time to catch the last minyan for Maariv at a local shul (1 a.m.). A friend mentioned that it might be prohibited to postpone davening Maariv until after chatzos (halachic midnight) and suggested that I daven without a minyan while I am traveling. Is my friend correct?

As we will explain, your friend is half-right.

There is a *mitzvah d'Oraisa* to recite *Shema* sometime during the night. All things being equal, one should try to recite *Shema* as soon as possible after nightfall, for one should always do mitzvos with alacrity and zeal (*zerizim makdimim lemitzvos*). As well, one may not begin a meal with bread or get involved in any lengthy project before one has recited *Shema*.[1] *Chazal* mandated that one recite *Shema* before *chatzos*, when possible, in order to prevent people from failing to fulfill the mitzvah. If a person willfully delays

---

1. *Shulchan Aruch Orach Chaim* 232:2.

its recitation, he has violated this Rabbinic enactment.[2] However, if one was not able to recite *Shema* before *chatzos*, he is still obligated to do so until the morning.

If your itinerary will bring you home after *chatzos* but you will still have a *minyan* for Maariv when you arrive, the following should be done: You should recite *Shema* upon nightfall, and then *daven* Maariv later with a *minyan*.[3] There is no problem with reciting *Shema* again with its *berachos* before *Shemoneh Esrei*, just as one would do when *davening* with a *minyan* before *chatzos*. It is no different from reciting *Shema* before Shacharis in a case when one knows that he will be *davening* Shacharis after *zman Krias Shema* (but before *sof zman tefillah*).

I would like to commend you on your *mesirus nefesh* for *tefillah b'tzibbur*, even at one in the morning. It is important to point out that if the *minyan* is within an 18-minute round trip from your home – or your route home – it is not merely a commendable practice, but actually a halachic obligation. Although this is clearly the *din*, not everyone is so punctilious about the all-important mitzvah of *davening b'tzibbur*. You therefore deserve a hearty *yasher koach* for fulfilling this crucial aspect of *tefillah*. Your conduct will encourage your friends to do so as well.

---

2. *Rabbeinu Yonah*, beginning of *Masechta Berachos*, *Mishneh Berurah* 235:27.
3. See first *Halichos Shlomo* in *Tefillah* 13, footnote 51 for alternative views. See also *sefer Ishei Yisrael* 28: 15 concerning the scenario in which davening Maariv is possible before *chatzos*, albeit without a *minyan*.

A Woman's Obligation to Daven When Time Is Limited

If I am not able to daven fully due to my responsibilities toward my children, is there a minimum that I can say to fulfill the mitzvah of tefillah?

If you find that your time is limited due to the many mitzvos you perform in taking care of your children, you should daven an abbreviated Shacharis. One can fulfill the basic obligation of *tefillah* with the recital of a portion of *davening* that contains *shevach, bakashah, and hoda'ah* (praise, request, and thanksgiving).[1] An example of such a *berachah* would be *Birkas HaTorah* or *Birchos Hashachar* ending with the *Yehi Ratzon*. If one has more time, one should *daven* the *Shemoneh Esrei* of Shacharis.

If time is available for more than this bare minimum, a woman should attempt to recite the following portions of *tefillah*:[2]

▸ *Baruch She'amar, Ashrei,* and *Yishtabach* (the entire *Pesukei*

---

1. See *Rambam Hilchos Tefillah* 1:2.
2. See *Mishnah Berurah Orach Chaim* 106:4;70:2.

D'Zimrah should be recited when possible).

- ▸ [It should be noted that a number of *poskim* maintain that women are exempt from *Pesukei D'Zimrah* and therefore give *Krias Shema* and its *berachos* precedence over *Pesukei D'Zimrah* when there is not sufficient time for both.]
- ▸ First *pasuk* of *Shema*.
- ▸ *Emes V'yatziv* through the *berachah* of *Ga'al Yisrael* — in order to attach the *berachah* of *Ga'al Yisrael* to *Shemoneh Esrei* (*semichas geulah l'tefillah*).
- ▸ *Shemoneh Esrei* of Shacharis.
- ▸ *Tefillas* Minchah (women have not accepted *tefillas* Maariv as an obligation).

An attempt should be made to recite *Birkas Krias Shema* before the fourth (halachic) hour of the day (otherwise known as *sof zman tefillah*. The *zman tefillah* fluctuates throughout the year, and can be found in any *zmanim* calendar).

Although women are not normally restricted by time for the mitzvos that they do, some *poskim* rule that *Chazal* mandated the recital of *Birkas Krias Shema* only within the context of *zman tefillah*, and reciting these *berachos* after the *zman* would entail a *berachah levatalah*.[3] Although this *halachah* seems to be referring to men, as it is among the *halachos* of reciting *Krias Shema* in the proper time (which is certainly only obligatory for men), there are *poskim* who assume that if women will be reciting *Birkas Krias Shema*, they must recite it within the proper time as per the original framework of the *takanah*.[4]

Others argue that women can recite *Birkas Krias Shema* even after the fourth hour (until *chatzos* — halachic midday). This is because, regarding these *berachos*, women are not bound by the same time constraints as men are.[5] Another reason women might have until midday to recite *Birkas Krias Shema* is that there are opinions that rule that even men may recite these *berachos* until

---

3. See *Shulchan Aruch Orach Chaim* 58:1 with *Mishnah Berurah* 25 and *Beur Halachah d"h Korah belo birchoseha*.
4. HaRav Shlomo Zalman Auerbach quoted in *sefer Halichos Beisah* Chapter 5, end of footnote 9.
5. HaRav Yisroel Belsky, *shlita*.

chatzos if they were unavoidably prevented from doing so earlier.[6]

The common practice seems to be that many women do say *Birkas Krias Shema* after the official *zman* due to their extremely busy schedules. Although they have a halachic basis for doing so, one should preferably avoid the issue when possible.

The above list is for those with various levels of time constraints due to their busy schedules. One who has the time and ability to *daven* the entire Shacharis should certainly do so.

If a woman does manage to recite *Shemoneh Esrei* on a fairly consistent basis and makes a critical mistake (such as forgetting *Ya'aleh Veyavo* on Rosh Chodesh or *Vesein Tal Umatar* during the winter), *Shemoneh Esrei* should be repeated. If she recites *Shemoneh Esrei* only occasionally due to her busy schedule, she should repeat it with the condition that if it is not necessary *al pi halachah* to do so, the *tefillah* will be a *tefillas nedavah* — a voluntary prayer.[7]

Under normal circumstances it is prohibited for men or women to eat before *davening* in the morning.[8] Women (or men) who feel weak are permitted to have a snack or a drink before they *daven*.[9] It is preferable, when feasible, to recite a basic *tefillah* or *berachah* that incorporates *shevach, bakashah,* and *hoda'ah* (*Birkas HaTorah* or *Birchos Hashachar*; see above) before partaking of food.[10]

---

6. See *Beur Halachah* ibid.
7. See *Yabiya Omer* 6:18.
8. *Shulchan Aruch Orach Chaim* 89:3.
9. *Shulchan Aruch* ibid. with *Beur Halachah d"h vechein ochlin umashkin lirefuah.*
10. *Sefer Halichos Beisah*, Chapter 2, footnote 10, in the name of HaRav Shlomo Zalman Auerbach.

Dealing With Toddlers During Davening or Bentching

Someone once mentioned to me that while saying Shemoneh Esrei or Birchas HaMazon one is not allowed to hold a child or a baby. I was wondering if this applies to a mother as well. It is often difficult to bentch or daven when the baby is crying, and I know that the mitzvah of taking care of children exempts me from other mitzvos. However, I feel that I have the time to daven, and my child would be content if I hold him while I do so. What should I do?

While reciting *Shemoneh Esrei* or *Birchas HaMazon*, one is not allowed to hold a child (or anything else besides a *siddur* or a *bentcher*).[1] This *halachah* applies to men and women (even to busy mothers).

If your baby is crying and you need to *bentch*, you should calm or distract the baby before beginning *Birchas HaMazon*. Generally speaking, the limit for *bentching* is 72-minutes from the time you finished eating (the details regarding that limit are beyond the current discussion). If that time frame is quickly approaching and there is no one to watch the baby, you may take the baby on your lap and even hold the baby if necessary in order to *bentch*.

One may not interrupt *Shemoneh Esrei* for a crying baby (unless the baby is in danger). In the event that one cannot concentrate *at all* while listening to the baby crying, one can give the baby a pacifier or a toy and then resume *Shemoneh Esrei*. If the pacifier or toy does not suffice, one may hold the baby and finish *Shemoneh Esrei*. One should not bring such children to shul, where they will disrupt others.

I am wondering what to do if I am davening Shemoneh Esrei and my toddler walks into the room with a dirty diaper. May I continue to daven? Should I stop while reciting Shemoneh Esrei?

If a toddler walks into the room with a full diaper, one may not continue to *daven*.[2] This would apply to *bentching* or the reciting of any other *berachah* as well. One can signal for the child to be led from the room, and if that is not possible, one must walk to a different room (or at least 8 feet away from where the odor is no longer discernible) to finish the *Shemoneh Esrei*.

1. *Shulchan Aruch Orach Chaim* 91:1-2; ibid. 191:3; see also ibid. 183:8 with *Mishnah Berurah* 30 on similarities between *Shemoneh Esrei* and *Birchas HaMazon*.
2. *Shulchan Aruch Orach Chaim* 79:1-2.

Krias Shema al Hamittah — in Camp and Elsewhere

As camp is right around the corner, I would like to discuss a she'eilah that my friends and I discussed one late night last summer.

Many of the kids in our bunk do not say the berachah of Hamapil when saying Krias Shema al Hamittah due to the concern that they will be forced to talk (or be involved in other mischief) before they finally fall asleep in the wee hours of the night (or morning). I say "forced" to talk because in camp, even if one really wants to go to sleep, the ability to actually do so is often beyond one's control.

I have the same issue at home, because I share a room with two lively siblings. I am often skeptical about my chances of falling asleep without interruption, and therefore I have been reluctant to say the Hamapil with Shem Hashem. Would you please guide me as to the proper procedure for these and similar situations?

Your situation is very common, and a clarification of the issue is indeed in order.

The *Gemara* in *Berachos* (60b) states that one must recite *Krias Shema* and the *berachah* of *Hamapil* before going to sleep, and this *halachah* is brought in *Shulchan Aruch*.[1] The Rema[2] rules that one should not eat, drink, or talk after *Krias Shema*, but should attempt to fall asleep immediately (see there for the reason one should not interrupt even after the reciting of *Krias Shema* alone, which is aside from the greater issue of talking or eating after reciting *Hamapil*, as we will explain).

The *Beur Halachah*[3] quotes the *Chayei Adam* that even if one does not fall asleep right away, it is not a *berachah levatalah* because the *berachah* was enacted as praise to Hashem concerning our ability to sleep at night, thereby enabling us to be refreshed so that we can wake up the next day invigorated for a new day of *avodas Hashem*. The *berachah* is therefore recited on the *minhago shel olam* (the general practice of the world) of sleeping, and does not refer to the specific sleep activity of the individual reciting the *berachah*. It is therefore not a *berachah* said in vain if that individual does not fall asleep immediately (unlike *berachos* on food or mitzvos, where an interruption after the *berachah* may deem the *berachah* a *berachah levatalah* and may necessitate a new *berachah*).

---

1. *Orach Chaim* 239;1.
2. Ibid.
3. Ibid. *d"h samuch lemitasan.*

The *Beur Halachah* disagrees with the *Chayei Adam* and concludes that if one is in doubt whether he will be able to fall asleep, he should not recite the *berachah* of *Hamapil*. Following his reasoning in the *Beur Halachah,* the Chofetz Chaim in *Mishnah Berurah*[4] warns against interrupting after reciting *Hamapil,* even if one is thirsty or has something important to say. This is because the *Mishnah Berurah* understands that the *berachah* of *Hamapil* (like most other *berachos)* must connect immediately with the action referred to in the text of the *berachah*.

Although all agree that it is preferable not to interrupt after reciting *Hamapil* or after reciting *Krias Shema* (while speaking after *Krias Shema* can be rectified simply by repeating *Krias Shema* again, *Hamapil* cannot be repeated a second time, due to its form as a *berachah*), most *poskim* agree with the position of the *Chayei Adam* that if one does not fall asleep at all, *Hamapil* was not said in vain.[5]

That being said, one who uses the bathroom after *Hamapil* must recite *Asher Yatzar*. One must also *daven* Maariv or count *Sefiras HaOmer* if he neglected to do so prior to *Hamapil*.

I would also think that if one has a great need to make a *berachah* on a drink or to speak to someone concerning an urgent matter, it would be permitted to do so, even after reciting *Hamapil*. Similarly, if a parent asks a question that requires a verbal response, the child should respond in a respectful way rather than trying to convey a complex message with hand motions or charades. If the answer is a simple yes or no, a nod or shake of the head would suffice.

If the parents are demanding that a chore or other action be performed after the recital of *Hamapil*, the mitzvah of *kibbud av va'eim* should be fulfilled if the parents will not understand or appreciate the child's objection based on the halachic issue involved. Although *kibbud av va'eim* is normally pushed aside when it contradicts *halachah*, in this scenario the mitzvah of *kibbud* and *yirah* would take precedence if the child's inaction would upset or irritate

---

4. Ibid. 4.
5. See *Eliyahu Rabbah* ibid. 3; *Beur HaGra Orach Chaim* 432, d"h *Venohagim*; *Aruch HaShulchan* 239: 6; *Kaf HaChaim* ibid. 7; *Tzitz Eliezer* 7:27; *Yechaveh Daas* 4:21; HaRav Shlomo Zalman Auerbach quoted in *Halichos Shlomo* 13:15.

them. Your obligation toward your parents is no less urgent than the need for a glass of water when you are thirsty, and we have shown above that there is room to be lenient and interrupt for such a need.

As you can see, according to most opinions there is clearly a halachic requirement to recite *Birkas Hamapil* every night, even if one will not fall asleep. One should make a strong attempt to go to sleep shortly thereafter without any interruption. The requirement and benefit of *Birkas Hamapil* should not be cast aside for the sake of some extra schmoozing or troublemaking in camp.

If you know from past experience that the 11 o'clock "lights out" will not be adhered to, simply wait as long as you have to until quiet falls over your bunk and then recite *Hamapil*.

Although there are some *poskim* who rule (based on Kabbalistic sources) that after *chatzos* (halachic midnight) one should not say *Hamapil* with *Shem Hashem*,[6] most *poskim* — especially those who follow Ashkenazic *minhagim* — rule that *Hamapil* can be recited with *Shem Hashem* the entire night.[7] Therefore, unless you have a specific family or community *minhag* to the contrary, *Hamapil* should be recited even after *chatzos* (keep this in mind when you get to your bunk at 3 a.m. after winning color war).

If you are traveling on an overnight trip and you feel that there is a good chance that you'll be able to sleep for at least a half-hour, *Hamapil* should be recited. If you wake up and then sleep again a few hours later, there is no requirement to recite *Hamapil* again, as the *halachah* requires only one *Birkas Hamapil* per night.

The *berachah* of *Hamapil* is a *takanas Chazal* like any other *berachah* and must be treated as such. Please share this *halachah* and its parameters with your parents, friends, siblings, and bunkmates so that this somewhat neglected mitzvah can be revitalized.

May we all benefit from the protection that the entire *Krias Shema al Hamittah* gives us. We will reap much reward for carefully treasuring the *berachos* and *tefillos* that *Chazal*, with their *ruach hakodesh*, have given to *Klal Yisrael*.

---

6. *Shaarei Teshuvah* ibid. 1, quoting *Teshuvas Lachmei Todah; Kaf HaChaim* ibid. 8.
7. *Birkei Yosef* quoted in *Shaarei Teshuvah* ibid.; see *Teshuvos Vehanhagos* 1:198.

Reciting Tehillim at Night

I was told that there might be a problem with saying Tehillim at night. Is this indeed an issue, and would it make a difference if I had much more time available at night and could therefore say many more kapitlach?

The *Be'er Heitev*[1] quotes the Arizal, who said that one should not recite *pesukim* (verses) of *Tanach* at night without *mefarshim* (commentary) based on *Torah shebe'al peh* (the Oral Law). The *Mishneh Berurah* quotes the *Pri Megadim,*[2] who allows the reading of *pesukim* at night.

The Chofetz Chaim points out that even according to the Arizal, it is not actually prohibited to recite *pesukim;* rather, it is preferable to learn *Torah shebiksav* (the written word; i.e., reading *pesukim* from *Tanach*) only during the day, whereas *Torah sheba'al peh* (Oral Law; e.g., *Gemara, medrash,* and commentaries) can be learned day or night. A possible source to restrict the learning of *Torah shebiksav* to the daytime is the *medrash*[3] stating that while Moshe Rabbeinu was on Har Sinai, Hashem taught him *Torah shebiksav* only during the day.

---

1. *Orach Chaim 238:2.*
2. *Mishneh Berurah,(Shaar Hatziyun 238:1; Pri Megadim, Mishbetzos Zahav, ibid. 1.*
3. *Pirkei DeRabbi Eliezer 46.*

Since *Tehillim* is part of *Torah shebiksav*, some rule that it should not be recited at night.[4] Others claim that the stringency of the Arizal is not applicable to the recital of *Tehillim* because *Tehillim* is recited as a *tefillah* and praise to *HaKadosh Baruch Hu*, and is not said in the same manner as one would learn *pesukim*.[5] These *poskim* point out that there are sources that seem to indicate that Yaakov Avinu and Dovid HaMelech recited *Tehillim* at night (although it is possible that their recital took place only after midnight, and the restriction may not apply at that time).[6]

Many authorities[7] agree that on Shabbos and Yom Tov (and possibly Thursday night[8]) one need not refrain from the recital of *Tehillim*. One may also recite the *pesukim* of the weekly *parashah* for the mitzvah of *shenayim mikra* (reviewing the *parashah*) on Friday night (and Thursday night).

A frequent scenario occurs when a group of women gather to form a *Tehillim* group, and the only time convenient for all is in the evening, after the little ones are put to bed. There is firm basis to allow (and even encourage) the group to meet at night to recite *Tehillim* if a daytime meeting would attract fewer participants or result in less *Tehillim* being recited due to time constraints.

In summation, if all things are equal, it is better for *pesukim* from Torah or *Tehillim* to be recited by day in deference to the Kabbalistic teachings. It is imperative to recognize that there is absolutely no clear-cut prohibition against learning or reciting *pesukim* at night without commentaries, and it is certainly less than unanimous that this stringency would apply to the recital of *Tehillim*.

Therefore, if it is nighttime and one has the choice between undertaking an unconstructive activity or studying or reciting *pesukim*, the person should certainly study or recite *pesukim*. In addition, if it is better for the person to recite *Tehillim* at night, there are certainly many authorities that have no objection.

---

4. *Teshuvos Yosef Ometz*, 54.
5. *Tzitz Eliezer* 8:2, *Be'er Moshe* 4:22.
6. See *Kaf HaChaim Orach Chaim* 237:9, who permits the reciting of *Tehillim* after *chatzos* (halachic midnight).
7. See *Kaf HaChaim* ibid.
8. See *Taamei Haminhagim, Lekutim* 153.

V'Achalta v'Savata u'Veirachta — Eating and Bentching

Washing and Wealth

I have seen some people use a large amount of water when they wash for bread. Is there a reason to use more water than is halachically necessary?

The *Gemara*[1] quotes Rav Chisda as saying that washing with a large amount of water is a *segulah* for prosperity. The same *Gemara* comments that not washing with enough water to cover the entire hand properly can result in poverty.[2] Some sources indicate that even washing with the exact amount of water needed can result in poverty if more water was readily available. This is because one is taking a chance that the washing will not be done properly.[3]

Some authorities[4] state that washing with more water than necessary is only an advantage and *segulah* if one does so to assure that the entire hand will be covered without any doubt. Using more water than that is pointless and merely a waste of resources. Others argue that in areas where there is an abundance of water, it is definitely advantageous and a *segulah* to wash with large amounts of water, even beyond that needed to cover all parts of the hand.[5]

---

1. Shabbos 62b; see *Zohar HaKadosh Parashas Lech Lecha* for a similar statement.
2. *Gemara*, ibid., according to the explanation of *Derishah* 160:2.
3. *Ran,* Shabbos ibid.; *Yam Shel Shlomo Chulin* 8:16; *Teshuvas HaRashba* 7:535; *Shulchan Aruch HaRav* 158:14.
4. *Eishel Avraham Butchatch* 161; *Kitzur Shulchan Aruch* 40:4.
5. *Nemukei Orach Chaim* 158.

As with any *chumrah,* it should not be carried out at the expense of others. If there is a limited amount of water available, it is preferable that one wash only with what he needs. There is a well-known story that Rav Yisrael Salanter was asked why he did not use a large amount of water to wash his hands, and he explained that if he did so, the young servant girl would have to work harder to bring additional water.

It is important to note that like all *segulos,* there is no guarantee that the desired blessings will be forthcoming immediately (or at all) for every individual. One's *aveiros* can block the fulfillment of a particular *berachah* or *segulah.*

One must also bear in mind that blessings can take various forms. When the Steipler Gaon, *zt"l,* was asked why he was not wealthy although he had had the *zechus* to be a *sandak* at so many *brissos,*[6] he replied that he was indeed very wealthy, for he had merited to have a son like Rav Chaim (Kanievsky, *shlita*).

One must likewise perform *mitzvos* because that is what Hashem has asked of us and not solely to attain wealth and prestige.

---

6. See *Rema Yoreh Deah* 265:11, which states that being a *sandak* is a *segulah* for *ashirus.*

Talking After Washing

I was always under the impression that if one talks after washing before eating the bread, there is an obligation to wash again.

It recently happened to me at a simchah, and those seated near me were of the opinion that there is no need to wash again. Who is correct?

You are certainly not alone in assuming that there is a need to wash again. Your mistaken assumption is based on a very prevalent misconception. Most people erroneously believe that any extraneous talking between the *berachah* of *Al Netilas Yadayim* and the *berachah* of *Hamotzi* requires one to wash again, whereas talking is permitted between washing and the recital of *Al Netilas Yadayim*. As we will explain, the opposite is true.

The *berachos* for most *mitzvos* are recited immediately before the mitzvah is performed (*oveir l'asiyasan*). One of the notable exceptions is the *berachah* of *Al Netilas Yadayim*, which is recited after the hands are washed. The *berachah* is not recited beforehand because at that time the hands are often in a ritually unclean state. One avoids that problem by saying the *berachah* after the hands are washed.[1] By reciting the *berachah* before drying the hands, however, it is still considered to have been recited before the completion of the washing, because the drying process is part of the mitzvah. The mitzvah is complete only when the residual ritually impure water is removed. (This applies even when washing with a *reviis* of water.[2]) The hands must also be dried so that the bread does not become wet and unappetizing.[3]

One must be careful not to talk between washing and the *berachah* so that the *berachah* can be attached to the performance of the entire mitzvah. If one did interrupt before reciting the *berachah*, the hands should be washed again and a *berachah* should then be recited. However, due to the dispute involving this scenario,[4] it is preferable to first touch one's shoes to ensure that washing again is required according to all opinions.[5]

After reciting *Netilas Yadayim* and drying the hands, it is preferable for one to make *Hamotzi* as soon as possible.[6] When feasible, there should be no interruption (talking or any other activity) at that time. One should attempt to recite *Hamotzi* in the time it takes to walk 22 *amos* (a time range between 12 and 30 seconds).[7]

However, if one did wait for an extended period of time (e.g., at a large Shabbos meal where many people must wash[8]), or even if one talks accidentally, there is *no requirement* to wash again. This is because the requirement to make *Hamotzi* immediately after one has finished washing is not an absolute requirement, but rather an important code of conduct when possible. One should therefore not interrupt or delay needlessly.[9]

This being the case, one should answer *amen* to a *berachah* he hears while he is waiting to make or hear *Hamotzi*.[10] Some even have

1. *Shulchan Aruch Orach Chaim* 158:11.
2. See *Mishnah Berurah*, ibid. 43 and *Chazon Ish* 24:30 *d"h keshenotel*.
3. See *Mishnah Berurah*, ibid. 45.
4. See *Oneg* Yom Tov 18; *Shulchan Aruch* 165:1; and *Mishnah Berurah* 3.
5. *Kaf HaChaim* ibid. 85.
6. *Shulchan Aruch* and *Rema Orach Chaim* 166:1.
7. See *Piskei Teshuvah*, ibid., footnote 2.
8. See *Shulchan Aruch Orach Chaim* 165:2 concerning who should wash first.
9. *Tur*, ibid., quotes the *Yerushalmi* that states that one who is careful to make *Hamotzi* without interruption or delay will be protected during that meal.
10. *Kitzur Shulchan Aruch* 41:2.

a custom to recite *Mizmor leDavid Hashem Ro'i*. (This is a *tefillah* for *parnassah*. The *Zohar* in *Parashas Beshalach* states that one should *daven* for sustenance before eating. Others recite it after *Hamotzi*.[11])

While we are on the topic, it should be pointed out that after reciting *Hamotzi* one should actually swallow the bread before talking. Aside from the dangers of talking while eating,[12] one may not interrupt between the *berachah* on any food and the eating of that food, just as one may not delay the performance of a mitzvah after reciting the *berachah* for that mitzvah. If one did converse before swallowing, it is questionable whether he is required to repeat the *berachah*.[13] Some *poskim* rule that if nothing at all was swallowed prior to the interruption, one must recite the *berachah* again.[14] Others hold that due to the halachic doubt concerning this matter, one should not repeat the *berachah*.[15] One should certainly avoid getting into such a predicament by ensuring that at least a small amount of food is swallowed before any interruption is made.

A meal is often a wonderful opportunity for positive social interaction and conversation and, of course, Torah discussion — but all at the right time and in a halachically acceptable way.

---

11. See *Magen Avraham* 166:2 and *Mishnah Berurah*, ibid. 3.
12. See "Talking While Eating," page 85.
13. *Magen Avraham* 167:16.
14. *Elyah Rabbah*, ibid. 7; *Kitzur Shulchan Aruch* 50:6.
15. *Aruch HaShulchan*, ibid. 13 and *Kaf HaChaim*, ibid. 45.

Talking While Eating

I have learned the Gemara that says that one is not allowed to talk during a meal, and I have seen that it is brought down in the Shulchan Aruch as well.

Yet I notice that many are not careful not to converse while eating and was wondering what basis there is to be lenient.

You have correctly noted that the *Gemara*[1] states that one should not converse during a meal because of the danger involved. Talking while eating might result in food entering the windpipe (trachea) instead of the food pipe (esophagus). This ruling is indeed cited as *halachah* in *Shulchan Aruch*.[2]

The fact is that most people do talk as they eat, and the commentators suggest that perhaps the original danger is no longer applicable. This is because in the times of the *Gemara* people would recline while eating, as opposed to modern times, when people eat sitting upright.[3]

---

1. *Taanis* 5b.
2. *Orach Chaim* 170:1.
3. *Elyah Rabbah* ibid. 1, in the name of the *Prishah*.

Others[4] do not agree with this explanation since people would recline by leaning to the left (as we do on the night of the Pesach Seder), and the *Gemara* does not seem to be concerned with food going down the wrong pipe when people recline on their left side.[5]

Some *poskim*[6] suggest that although it is not safe to talk while eating, since the masses are doing it, Hashem protects them ("now that it had become common practice, we apply the verse 'Hashem guards fools'").[7]

Many classical *poskim*, however, do not cite any leniency at all. Although they do not allow conversing while one is actually eating, they do permit talking between courses. They point out that indeed it is a mitzvah to recite *divrei Torah* during the meal and the opportunity to do so is while the person is being served.[8]

One who wishes to be strict and not talk at all while eating is to be commended, as that seems to be the halachic position of many *poskim,* but one should do so without calling undue attention to himself and in a way that does not offend others. Although most people are lenient on this issue and they have on whom to rely, extreme caution is in order. *Chazal* were very meticulous when it came to many issues of health and safety, and it is prudent to bear in mind their direction on these issues.

---

4. *Shaarei Teshuvah* ibid. 1.
5. This is because the esophagus is on the left and the trachea is on the right, so the food will naturally go toward the esophagus.
6. *Shaarei Teshuvah* ibid.; *Aruch HaShulchan* ibid. 2.
7. See *Gemara* Shabbos 129b for an application of this principle.
8. *Magen Avraham* ibid. 1; *Mishnah Berurah* ibid. 1.

Just Desserts

I am aware of the halachah that if one eats a very large amount of cake, cookies, and the like, there is an obligation to wash, make Hamotzi, and bentch. in certain situations, this may apply even if one eats a small amount of these mezonos baked goods with a large quantity of other food in a way that satiates just as a regular meal would.

Does this halachah extend to the common scenario in which an entire meal consisting of non-mezonos items is eaten (such as a dinner consisting of meat and potatoes), and then one wishes to have a piece of cake or several cookies for dessert? Do we assume that the mezonos dessert combines with the non-mezonos meal to require bentching afterward?

Let us first elaborate on the halachic status of baked *mezonos* items (referred to halachically as *pas haba'ah b'kisnin*) and their status as a snack or a meal.

If cakes, pies, cookies, and other foods of this type are eaten as a snack (and in small quantities that reflect their snacklike status), the *berachah rishonah* is *Mezonos*, and the *berachah* afterward is *Al Hamichyah*. If, however, these foods are eaten in place of a meal (or in such large quantities that they resemble a meal), one must wash, make *Hamotzi*, and *bentch*.

There is a dispute concerning the amount of baked *mezonos* requiring *Hamotzi* and *bentching*. Some say that the amount is the equivalent of the size of four eggs, and others say that it is equivalent to the amount of food eaten during an "average meal."[1] The size of an "average meal" depends on the person's age and gender, so the "average meal" of women, children, and the elderly is smaller than that of adult males.[2]

It is important to point out that one can eat as much non-baked *mezonos* as he desires without any obligation to *bentch*. It is only baked *mezonos* products (resembling bread) that require washing and *bentching* when eaten in sufficient quantity. Therefore, even a full meal of meat and potatoes will require only a *Borei Nefashos* afterward. In fact, even the consumption of a large amount of pasta will require only an *Al Hamichyah*. Although pasta is *mezonos*, it is not a baked *mezonos* product that resembles bread, and therefore it can never attain the status of bread requiring *bentching*.

The *Magen Avraham*[3] rules that we also treat *mezonos* as bread when it is eaten in place of bread (*kava alav se'udaso*) in conjunction with a full meal, and the amount eaten is equivalent to the amount of bread one would eat with such a meal. According to this opinion, although one did not have a very large quantity of baked *mezonos* (*pas haba'ah b'kisnin*), we look at the combined quantity of all the food (non-*mezonos* and *mezonos*) consumed at the meal to judge whether or not washing and *bentching* are required. As long as most people would be satiated by such a meal, we view the baked *mezonos* as a

---

1. *Mishnah Berurah* 168:24.
2. See *Beur Halachah*, ibid. *d"h af al pi shehu kovei'a.*
3. *Mishnah Berurah* 168:13.

bread substitute, applying all the *halachos* of eating regular bread.

It should be noted that many authorities do not accept the *Magen Avraham's* opinion that other foods can combine with the *mezonos* foods to obligate the person to *bentch*.[4]

Additionally, it seems that the *Magen Avraham*[5] was referring to *mezonos* products eaten with other foods in lieu of bread.[6] In your scenario, the main meal did not involve the *pas haba'ah b'kisnin*; you merely wanted to have cake or cookies for dessert. This being the case, the *Magen Avraham* would likely agree that you should not *bentch*.

The Chazon Ish (34:4) discusses your question concerning *mezonos* (*pas haba'ah b'kisnin*) combining with the rest of the meal, and seems to conclude that it does not combine to assume the status of bread and therefore does not require *bentching*, even if eaten after a large meal. The *sefer Mekor Haberachah* (page 113-114) reaches the same conclusion.

You may therefore continue to have your cake and eat it too. Enjoy! (And don't forget the *al hamichyah!*)

---

4. See *Aruch HaShulchan*, ibid. 17 and *Kaf HaChaim*, ibid. 47, who question the assumption that other foods combine with *mezonos* to give it a status of bread. See also *Shulchan Aruch HaRav*, ibid. 8, who agrees that other foods combine with *mezonos*, but only if a minimum of the volume of four eggs of *mezonos* is eaten as part of that meal.

5. Ibid.

6. See *Mishnah Berurah* ibid., who seems to understand the *Magen Avraham* in this way: "*Im achalo im basar o devarim acheirim shemelaftim bo hapas sagi keshe'ocheil shiur she'acheirim regilim lisbo'a mimenu keshe'ochlim gam kein devarim acheirim.*" (Cf. *Igros Moshe Orach Chaim* 3:32.)

Bentching With Bread
on the Table

After finishing my tuna sandwich at work, a co-worker remarked that I must have some bread on the table for bentching. I have never heard of this halachah and I'm wondering if it is actually a requirement. If so, am I required to leave a sizable piece, or would the crumbs suffice?

The *Gemara*[1] states that if one does not leave bread on the table, he will not see a *siman berachah*. There are a number of reasons suggested to explain this *halachah*. Rashi (ibid.) says that the bread should be left on the table so that if poor people enter they will have food immediately available. Another reason advanced[2] is to show thanksgiving to Hashem for showering us with abundance. We show this by displaying food left over after we have had our fill.

The *Zohar* in *Parashas Yisro* states that it is prohibited to *bentch*

---

1. *Sanhedrin* 92a.
2. See *Mishnah Berurah Orach Chaim* 180:2, quoting *Levush*.

while sitting at an empty table because the blessings from Hashem are secured when they attach themselves to a tangible object already in existence.

During the famine at the time of the *Navi* Elisha,[3] the widow of Ovadiah HaNavi beseeched Elisha to save her from the creditor who had come to take her two children as slaves in lieu of payment.

Elisha asked her what she had in her house, and she replied that she had only a small flask of oil. Elisha instructed her to borrow as many empty vessels as possible, and to pour oil from her flask into the empty vessels. She filled all the empty vessels with the miraculous new oil, which was then sold to repay the creditor and support her and her sons.

The obvious question is: If Elisha was performing an open miracle, why was there a need to start off with a small flask of natural oil? The answer given by the *Zohar* is that Hashem showers blessing by increasing the natural product that already exists. When we *bentch*, we thank Hashem for the food He has given us and we ask for success in all areas of sustenance. It is therefore important to have bread in front of us as we make this request, so that the blessing will be fulfilled to the fullest extent.

The *Shulchan Aruch,* based on the *Gemara* in *Sanhedrin,*[4] rules that one should not remove the bread before *bentching.* One need not bring a new slice of bread, as pieces of bread are sufficient. (One should not bring a whole loaf unless pieces are not available.[5])

Although *Shaar Tziyon*[6] adds that it is preferable that the crumbs not be too small, so that there is an honorable amount to give a poor person who might ask for food. In contemporary times it is rare for a poor person to come and ask for a piece of bread; it would therefore seem that even small pieces can satisfy the requirement of leaving bread on the table.[7] This leniency might not apply, however, to crumbs that are insignificant in size. If the crumbs are so small that no one would bother eating them, leaving them on the table would not be a

---

3. *Melachim* II 4:1-7.
4. *Orach Chaim* 180:1-2; *Sanhedrin* ibid.
5. See *Mishnah Berurah* ibid.
6. *Shaar Tziyon* ibid. 3.
7. See *Yalkut Yosef,* page 237.

sign of thanksgiving to Hashem and might not be large enough for the blessing to "take hold."[8]

As you can see from these sources, your co-worker is correct in his assertion that one must leave some bread on the table for *bentching*. However, it would be sufficient to have crumbs (sizable) from your tuna sandwich to fulfill this *halachah*.

If you forget and dispose of the crumbs before *bentching*, you should find some bread to place on the table. In doing so, you will display *hakaras hatov* for *Hakadosh Baruch Hu's* abundance, as well as help yourself merit the fulfillment of the *berachos* that you are requesting in *Birkas HaMazon*.

May Hashem shower you with continued sustenance, *shefa*, and *berachah*.

---

8. See *Piskei Teshuvos* ibid., footnote 4, quoting *sefer Etz HaSadeh*.

Bentching While Distracted

Q *My brother habitually stacks the cups and collects the cutlery while he bentches. I felt intuitively that this is not the proper way to talk to Hashem, and I told my brother so. Although he admitted that it was not the best thing for his kavanah, he claimed that it was not officially prohibited to perform minor activities while bentching. Are there halachic sources indicating that his habit is actually forbidden?*

A Your intuition is correct, as it is indeed prohibited to do any "work" while *bentching*.[1] The *Kaf HaChaim*[2] cites the specific example of clearing off the table and insists that one must look only at the *bentcher* (or *bentch* with eyes closed), with the hands stationary.

The *Shulchan Aruch* (183:8) quotes the opinion that *bentching* is

---

1. *Shulchan Aruch* 191:3.
2. Ibid. 5.

similar to *Shemoneh Esrei*, and therefore one is not allowed to interrupt the reciting of *Birkas HaMazon* to speak even due to fear of or in honor of a powerful or important person ("*mipnei hakavod umipnei hayirah*"), just as one is not allowed to interrupt *Shemoneh Esrei* for such reasons. This would mean that if your boss asks you an important question while you are *bentching*, it is prohibited to respond, despite the adverse consequences that may result.

According to the *Mishnah Berurah* (ibid. 30), a further proof that *Birkas HaMazon* is comparable to *Shemoneh Esrei* is found in the *halachah* that *bentching* must be recited while in a stationary position. This is in contrast to *Krias Shema*, which, the *halachah* states, one can recite while walking (with the exception of the first *pasuk* or, at most, until after the *pasuk* of *al levavecha*), and we are indeed more lenient about responding to people whom we fear or honor, during *Krias Shema*. (This leniency does not apply in our times; it is beyond the scope of this response to explain the reason.)

Based on the above comparison to the *halachos* of *Shemoneh Esrei*, many *poskim*[3] claim that one may not interrupt even to say a *davar shebi'kedushah* (e.g., "*yehei Shemai rabbah*, *Kedushah*, *amen* of *haKeil haKadosh*) if one is reciting *Birkas HaMazon*. (See, however, *Piskei Teshuvah* 183:16, which quotes *Aruch HaShulchan* 183:8 and other *poskim* who seem to disagree. There is a further dispute over whether one may interrupt while reciting the fourth *berachah* of *hatov vehameitiv* or if answering is permitted only after the fourth *berachah* — see *Aruch HaShulchan*, ibid., and *Kaf HaChaim*, ibid.)

Based on the above, it is clear that *Chazal* took a firm stand concerning any unnecessary interruptions during *Birkas HaMazon*. This is probably due to the fact that the recital is an explicit *mitzvah d'Oraisa*, as well as a fundamental expression of *hakaros hatov*, appreciation, to Hashem for our basic food and sustenance.

If it helps as an impetus for *kavanah* while *bentching*, mention to your brother that *bentching* properly is a *segulah* for good *parnasah*. The *Mishnah Berurah* (185:1) quotes the *Sefer HaChinuch*, which says that one who is meticulous with the mitzvah of *Birkas HaMazon*

---

3. E.g., *Kaf HaChaim* 183:45 and *Yabia Omer* 1:11.

will be blessed with ample sustenance in an honorable way. Financial incentives should not be necessary when performing *mitzvos*, but *mitzvos* done with ulterior motives will (hopefully) lead to their proper fulfillment *leshem Shamayim*, for the sake of Heaven ("*mitoch shelo lishmah, ba lishmah*"). Many need that motivating factor to progress toward the desired goal.

A Berachah on
Chewing Gum

*I was taught that when I am cooking,
if I merely taste the soup or any other
dish to see if there is enough salt,
etc., a berachah is not required. If this
is true, why do we make a berachah
on chewing gum, since it is merely a
small amount of flavor that one tastes,
without actually swallowing any food?*

There is a dispute in *halachah* concerning one who, while cooking, tastes the food to determine what, if anything, may need to be added.

The *Shulchan Aruch*[1] records an opinion that if one is merely tasting the food, even up to the amount of a *reviis*, no *berachah* is required, even if the sample is swallowed. It then quotes a second opinion that holds that a *berachah* is required for any amount that is swallowed, even if it is strictly for sampling purposes. This second opinion agrees that if the sample is *not* swallowed, a *berachah* is *not* required, even if a large amount is tasted.

---

1. *Orach Chaim* 210:2.

Rema[2] *paskens* that one should not recite a *berachah* even when swallowing a sample because of the rule of *safek berachah l'hakel* (when there is halachic doubt concerning the recital of a *berachah*, we refrain from making the *berachah* to avoid possibly transgressing the severe prohibition against saying Hashem's Name in vain).

The *poskim* are divided concerning the final *psak* on this matter.[3] The *Chayei Adam* therefore suggests that if a person wishes to taste the food to determine the flavor, an effort should be made to actually swallow some of the sample with the intent to benefit from the food. This would certainly constitute eating that requires the recitation of a *berachah*.

As you can see, there are opinions that a *berachah* is required when one swallows even a minute amount of food, even when there is no intent to "eat." When one eats any amount of food for its taste (not merely testing a sample), a *berachah* is required according to all opinions.

This crucial point has a direct bearing on your question concerning chewing gum. While the gum base is not edible, the consumer enjoys chewing the gum to extract the flavor. Although it is a minute amount, this flavor is ingested and clearly requires a *berachah rishonah* (*shehakol*). However, the *berachah achronah* (*borei nefashos*) is not recited, as the small amount of flavor does not constitute the proper *shiur.*

It is also important to note that although it contains only a small amount of flavoring and sweeteners, chewing gum always requires a reliable *hechsher.* There are many complex processes involved in the manufacture of gum (even possible issues concerning the gum base itself), and the ingredients that give the gum its flavor must be verified and certified kosher by knowledgeable agencies.

---

2 *Rema* ibid.
3 See *Mishneh Berurah*, ibid. 19.

Berachos for Toddlers

I have a bright 3-year-old toddler, and I would like to begin teaching him to say berachos before eating. Should I mention Hashem's Name when I say the berachah with him and answer "amen"?

The age of *chinuch* begins at approximately 6 or 7,[1] depending on the development of the child.[2] There is a dispute among the *poskim* concerning answering *amen* to the *berachah* of a child who is not yet at the age of *chinuch*.

Many *poskim* rule that one should not answer *amen*.[3] Others point out that the common *minhag* seems to be that training for *berachos* does begin in some form before the age of 6 or 7.[4]

Even though the age of *chinuch* has not been reached, it is common practice at home and in schools to accustom children to saying *berachos* from an early age.[5] The parents may therefore begin the training at that time by helping with the recital of the *berachos*. Since

---

1. *Mishnah Berurah, Orach Chaim* 269:1.
2. Ibid. 343:3.
3. Ibid. 215:16; see *Yabia Omer* 2:13:11.
4. *Sefer Chanoch LaNaar* page 40, footnote 4.
5. See *Rabbeinu Yonah, Berachos*, third *perek* 11b.

the child has not officially reached the age of *chinuch*, one should not answer *amen* to the *berachah* unless the child will hear the *amen* (for example, if the child is reciting the *berachah* while you are in a nearby room). It is then considered part of the overall process of helping children become accustomed to mitzvah observance.

However, if the child is of the official age of *chinuch* (6 or 7 years old), any adult who hears the *berachah* must answer *amen* even if the child does not hear him. This is because at the age of *chinuch*, the child's recitation has the status of a valid *berachah* and *amen* must be said even if not for *chinuch* purposes.[6]

If your 3-year-old is sufficiently advanced to practice the recital of *berachos*, particularly if this coincides with your child's understanding the concept of saying "thank you" for things, you may begin the training. It is preferable to prompt a child with the beginning of Hashem's Name rather than saying the entire *Shem Hashem* yourself. If a mere prompt isn't sufficient, one may pronounce the entire *Shem Hashem* in order to teach the child how to recite a *berachah* correctly.

Please bear in mind that there is certainly no obligation to begin before the age of 6. It is merely an option that has the support of some contemporary *poskim* and that seems to be a common *minhag*. The age at which you begin will very much depend on the development and temperament of your child, so it is best to revisit the issue as each child approaches the threshold of his or her education.

---

6. HaRav Elyashiv, *shlita*, cited in *Sefer Chanoch LaNaar*, loc cit.

Offering Food to Nonreligious Jews

Relatives of mine who are not yet Torah observant come to visit me a few times a year. It's proper for a host to offer food to guests, and these relatives expect to be served dinner whenever they come. I once heard in a shiur that one may not offer food to anyone who will not recite a berachah. How do I keep this halachah without offending my relatives?

It is indeed *assur* to offer food to anyone who will not recite a *berachah* before eating as well as a *berachah acharonah* (i.e., *bentching, Al Hamichyah, Borei Nefashos*).[1] This is based on the prohibition "*Lifnei iver lo siten michshol* — Do not place a stumbling block in front of a blind man." In this context, the blind man is the unfortunate person who is not aware of the obligation to keep *mitzvos* and in particular to recite *berachos*. Even if he has access to his own

---

1. *Rema, Orach Chaim* 169:2.

food and will be eating without a *berachah* anyway, there is still an *issur d'Rabbanan* of being *mesayei'a yedei ovrei aveirah* (aiding and abetting others to sin) by giving them food that they will eat without reciting *berachos*.

If you are eating with these relatives, you can simply tell them that you will be making the *berachos* out loud and they should answer *amen* at the conclusion of each. Even if they are not amenable, you can still take care of their obligation by reciting the *berachah* out loud, for as long as they hear the words they are *yotzei* the *chiyuv berachah*.

This *eitzah* is more practical than most believe it to be. Friends and relatives who visit are obviously on good terms with their host, and are usually amenable to what they view as a minor inconvenience at worst. Most Americans are familiar with the concept of "grace" before or after the meal, and therefore you will, in the worst case, be regarded by them as religiously zealous but not as a foolish or peculiar person.

If for some reason you are unable to eat with your guests, you should attempt to give them a *bentcher* or *siddur* with a transliteration of the proper *berachos* and politely request that they recite them when appropriate.

If you have attempted to implement these ideas and have met with serious resistance, it is permissible to offer food when it is socially expected. The reason given is rather compelling and would probably be accepted by the Rema as well.

The *halachah* forbidding placing food in front of one who won't make a *berachah* is based on the *lifnei iver/mesayei'a yedei ovrei aveirah* prohibitions. These *issurim* teach us that we have a moral obligation to help others perform *mitzvos* and steer clear of *aveiros*. We may not tempt others with food if it will cause them to perform *aveiros* through eating it.

However, if by not offering food we will push these nonreligious people further away from *mitzvos* by causing them to hate those who are *frum*, we will be violating *lifnei iver* in a more serious way. It is therefore more effective to treat them as guests should be treated and have them walk away from the experience with a positive view of *frum* people, their *middos,* and the Torah way of life.[2]

One must be very careful before applying these leniencies, as we usually rule that one may not perform or condone any prohibition for the sake of *kiruv.* In our case, the leniency is based on the fact that it is prohibited to cause someone to sin; if, as a result of our insistence that they recite *berachos,* they will ridicule Torah and *mitzvos,* we have caused much more harm.

Another reason for leniency when the guests object to reciting or listening to *berachos* is as follows: The *Gemara*[3] states that every Jew is obligated in the mitzvah of *hochei'ach tochiach es amisecha* (one must reprove a fellow Jew), and consequently, must do everything possible to help his fellow with the performance of *mitzvos* and aid him in avoiding *aveiros.* However, one is absolved from this mitzvah of giving *mussar* to others if the recipient reacts with anger and rejection.

There are three opinions concerning how vehement the reaction must be to absolve one of further obligation. According to one opinion, if the person became enraged after he was rebuked, no further rebuke is in order. According to the second opinion, the person must continue to offer rebuke until the one being rebuked curses him. The third opinion requires one to continue his rebuke until the other person becomes physically violent.[4]

If you are taking a nonreligious Jewish client to a business lunch, you should first contemplate using one of the suggestions mentioned earlier. If you have a genuine concern that the client, potential client, or business partner will react adversely, to the extent that you might lose the deal (or the client), you are not obligated to mention the *berachos* issue. This is because one is not obligated in the mitzvah of *hochei'ach tochiach* if it will cause a significant loss of money, just as one is exempt from it when faced with the possibility of being rebuked, cursed, or hit.[5]

This does not mean that one can arbitrarily do an *aveirah* or bend

---

2. *Igros Moshe Orach Chaim* 5:13; *Minchas Shlomo* 1:35; *Teshuvos v'Hanhagos* 1:483; cf. HaRav Akiva Eiger *Yoreh Deah* 181:6.
3. *Arachin* 16b.
4. See *Rambam Hilchos Deios* 1:7 and *Semag, Mitzvos Asei* 11.
5. *Igros Moshe, Orach Chaim* 5:13.

the *halachah* in the face of possible loss of money. However, there are specific, isolated instances in *halachah* where one is not obligated to perform a mitzvah if it will entail a loss of money. One must certainly consult with a competent *posek* before applying any leniency due to monetary concerns.

Whether at home or in a business setting, every encounter with another *Yid* is a chance to create a *kiddush Shem Shamayim*. This is certainly true if the Jew you are spending time with has had little or no exposure to Orthodox Jews and Torah-true *Yiddishkeit*. Such encouters often engender situations that involve numerous issues of *halachah* and *hashkafah*, and it is crucial for a person to prepare himself beforehand, best discussing the issues with a Rav. This will ensure that he will best use the opportunity to make a lasting, positive impression and influence others through the beauty of Torah and *mitzvos*. If one does his homework thoroughly, he can be successful — spiritually and commenrcially — without compromising any halachic or hashkafic principles.

BERACHOS

100 Berachos a Day for Women

Is there an actual obligation to recite one hundred berachos each day, or is it a stringency? Are women likewise obligated to recite one hundred berachos a day?

The *Gemara*[1] states that there is an actual obligation to recite one hundred *berachos* each day (*"Chayav adam levarech me'ah berachos bechol yom"*). There is a dispute among the *Rishonim* as to whether this obligation is *mi'd'Oraisa* (originating in the Torah) or *mi'd'Rabbanan* (a Rabbinic ordinance),[2] but all agree that it is indeed an obligation. The *Shulchan Aruch*[3] rules that it is an obligation to recite a minimum of one hundred *berachos* every day.

Most *poskim*[4] rule that women are not obligated to recite one hundred *berachos* each day. This is because many of the *berachos* that

---

1. *Menachos* 43b.
2. See *Sdei Chemed maareches* 8: *Klal* 34; *Midrash Rabbah Parashas Korach* 21:18 indicates that it was an enactment of David HaMelech.
3. *Orach Chaim* 46:3.
4. *Teshuvas Shevet Halevi* 5:23; *Sefer Halichos Beisah* 13:1 in the name of HaRav Shlomo Zalman Auerbach *zt"l*; *Sefer Rigshei Lev* in the name of HaRav Yosef Shalom Elyashiv, *shlita*, and HaRav Chaim Pinchas Scheinberg, *shlita*.

constitute the one hundred are *berachos* that only men are obligated to recite (e.g., the *berachos* of *tzitzis, tefillin, tefillas* Mussaf). Although it is possible for women to achieve the one-hundred mark by reciting *berachos* on various foods, there is no way for them to attain the quota on a fast day. It is therefore obvious that women are not fundamentally included in this obligation.

Several *poskim* obligate women to recite one hundred *berachos* each day because it is not a time-bound *mitzvah (mitzvas asei shehazeman gerama)*, which women are exempt from performing. They suggest that women seek opportunities to fulfill the quota of one hundred *berachos* by reciting various optional *berachos* during the day.

It would seem that even if women are not obligated to fulfill the quota of *berachos* each day, it is meritorious for them to do so when possible. One should not, however, recite extra *berachos* when they are not at all necessary. Reciting Hashem's Name in vain is a serious offense, and one must be well versed in *hilchos berachos* to be able to determine when and where a *berachah* should be recited.

A Close Call and Bentching Gomel

As I was crossing the street the other day, I was startled to hear the screeching of brakes and the loud honking of a horn. As I looked to my left, I saw a car come to a halt within two feet of where I was standing. I was quite angry with the driver, whose reckless driving could have severely injured or even killed me, and I felt quite faint after I realized how close he had come to hitting me.

Having survived a potentially dangerous situation, I would like to say Birkas Hagomel at the earliest opportunity. However, some friends have claimed that not every close call requires one to bentch gomel and that a she'eilah should be asked.

I remember a similar incident many years ago when my vehicle slid on a patch of ice and swerved off the road onto the shoulder, almost hitting the guardrail. Baruch Hashem, I was not hurt, although I did bentch gomel at that time. Was that the correct thing to do?

The parameters concerning when to *bentch gomel* are complex and need to be examined in conjunction with the specific situation at hand.

The *Gemara*[1] states that four people must say *Birkas Hagomel*: one who crosses an ocean, one who travels through a desert, a seriously ill person who recovers,[2] and one who is released from prison.

The *Shulchan Aruch*[3] records a dispute regarding this list. One opinion rules that the list given in the *Gemara* is not exhaustive in nature. Rather, if one is saved from any situation of danger, *Birkas Hagomel* is required. The second opinion argues that the four examples given in the *Gemara* are the only cases for which *Chazal* mandated the reciting of *Birkas Hagomel* (possibly due to the fact that they were the most common situations encountered at that time).

Although the *Shulchan Aruch* rules that one should recite *Birkas Hagomel* without *Shem Hashem* upon encountering any danger that is not on the official list, the *Mishneh Berurah paskens* that common custom (at least among Ashkenazim) is to make the full *berachah* with *Shem u'Malchus* when delivered from any serious danger.

When discussing the halachic definition of an imminent life-threatening danger, one must examine the cases found in halachic literature. The *Shulchan Aruch*[4] quotes the *Teshuvas HaRivash* (the first opinion quoted above, requiring a *Birkas Hagomel* after surviving any serious danger) as ruling that one who survives any one of the following scenarios is required to *bentch gomel* : being buried under a

---

1. *Berachos* 54b.
2. See *Rema* 219:7.
3. *Orach Chaim* 219:9.
4. *Shulchan Aruch* ibid.

collapsed wall, being trampled or gored by a wild ox, being confronted by a lion, or being held up by a robber.

The common thread in all these cases is the fact that the person was actively in a situation in which many people lose their lives.

The *mechaber* even uses the words *"lemi shenaaseh lo nes"* — someone for whom a miracle was performed. Although the *Shulchan Aruch* is not referring to an open miracle, the fact that the escape is even referred to as a (hidden) miracle indicates that the situation is a life-threatening ordeal. The classic cases, traversing a wilderness or ocean, surviving serious illness or ancient prisons, were circumstances wrought with danger. A person who actually has a wall fall on him or encounters a wild ox or a ferocious lion or a robber has also survived — and not merely escaped — a potentially deadly experienced.

In contrast to these examples, we have the common occurrence of automobiles being driven by aggressive operators who stop within very close range of pedestrians, as in your case. Although certainly a potential danger, one can safely assume that most drivers do ultimately stop before colliding with pedestrians or other cars. Although we hear of many accidents that cause horrific injury and even death, there are many more close calls that result in a temporary fright but nothing more.

A car stopping short of its potential victim is similar to a wall that fell and almost buried a nearby pedestrian. It is clear from the *Shulchan Aruch* that the obligation to *bentch gomel* is only when the wall actually falls on the person. Although the examples involving the lion and the robber do not indicate that the person was actually attacked, this is because people who are confronted by lions or gangsters are generally in serious danger at the time of the confrontation. They are therefore required to *bentch gomel* when they survive the experience. The wall or car that came close to hitting you would not necessarily constitute a *sakanah* — a definite and present danger. Or they do present a danger, but the person was not actually engaged in any way.

If, while walking down 34th Street in Manhattan, you were to hear a loud crash behind you and realize that somebody had thrown a metal bar from the roof of the Empire State Building, narrowly missing you, a *Birkas Hagomel* would not be required. Similarly, when your car slid on the ice onto the shoulder of the road, stopping short of the guard-rail, there was no *chiyuv* to *bentch gomel*. This is despite the fact that had your car hit the rail, *chas veshalom*, it would have constituted a most serious, life-threatening situation.

Some time ago, I was asked a similar question with regard to a man who was in an elevator that suddenly dropped two or three floors. *Baruch Hashem*, the person was fine and inquired about his obligation to *bentch gomel*. The answer was that, due to many factors, no *gomel* was required. First, the elevator did not crash to the ground floor and therefore the person was not even injured by an impact. Second, all elevators have safety devices that kick in when the cables snap. In addition, braking systems on the elevator car grab on to the rails running up and down the elevator shaft. Some clamp the rails, while others drive a wedge into notches in the rails.

Even if the safety features completely fail, the elevator would not fall freely; friction from the rails along the shaft and pressure from the air underneath the elevator would slow the car down considerably. As well, most cable elevators have built-in shock absorbers at the bottom of the shaft that would cushion the impact. So even if the elevator had fallen to the bottom, chances of survival were very good. Therefore, *Birkas Hagomel* would not be recited because it possibly was not a life-threatening situation.

As mentioned above, the *halachos* of *Birkas Hagomel* are complex and depend on the careful assessment of the facts, which must be applied to the halachic principles involved. One must bear in mind that in regard to reciting *berachos* there is a general rule in *safek berachos lehakel*: when there is legitimate halachic doubt, we do not say the *berachah* with *Shem Hashem*, due to the severity of the transgression of mentioning the Name of Hashem in vain.

Besides the possible doubts concerning the presence of a clear, life-threatening danger, there is an overriding doubt in the application of any *Birkas Hagomel*. As mentioned above, there are opinions that rule that any situation not specified in the *Gemara Berachos*[5] does not qualify for a *Birkas Hagomel*. None of the cases discussed here are

---

5. *Berachos* ibid.

in the category of the four situations listed by *Chazal*. Although many *pasken* that *Birkas Hagomel* is recited when one is saved from any dangerous situation, the dispute is certainly another *safek* (doubt) for a *posek* to consider before rendering a halachic decision.

Rainy Day Questions

I am a bit confused concerning the sequence of berachos that should be made during a thunderstorm. I have heard that one berachah should be made on thunder and lightning, and others have told me that they require two distinct berachos. Can these halachos be clarified?

These *halachos* are extremely pertinent, and I will briefly outline the parameters.

The *Gemara Berachos*[1] indicates that when one sees lightning or hears thunder, he can either recite the *berachah* בָּרוּךְ אַתָּה ה׳ אֱלֹקֵינוּ מֶלֶךְ הָעוֹלָם, עוֹשֶׂה מַעֲשֵׂה בְרֵאשִׁית. *Blessed are You, Hashem, our God King of the universe, Who makes the work of Creation* or בָּרוּךְ אַתָּה ה׳ אֱלֹקֵינוּ מֶלֶךְ הָעוֹלָם, שֶׁכֹּחוֹ וּגְבוּרָתוֹ מָלֵא עוֹלָם, *Blessed are You, Hashem, our God King of the universe, for His strength and His power fill the universe.*

Common practice, however, is to recite the *berachah* עוֹשֶׂה מַעֲשֵׂה בְרֵאשִׁית, *Who makes the work of Creation*, on lightning and

---

1. *Berachos* 59a. See *Tosafos d"h Rava.*

שֶׁכֹּחוֹ וּגְבוּרָתוֹ מָלֵא עוֹלָם, *for His strength and His power fill the universe,* on thunder.[2]

This is because Hashem's strength and power are more acutely felt and understood when experiencing the boom and roar of thunder. If one recited either *berachah* for thunder or lightning, he has still fulfilled the requirement, and there is no need to recite any further *berachah*.

If one sees the lightning and hears the thunder at the same time, he should recite the *"Oseh maaseh bereishis"* to cover both (here as well, if one recited *"Shekocho ugevuraso malei olam,"* the obligation is fulfilled).

One should recite the respective *berachos* on the thunder and lightning if they do not occur at the same time (*toch kedei dibur,* the time it takes to say, *"Shalom alecha, rebbi"*).[3] It makes no difference whether he sees the lightning and then hears the thunder or vice versa.

One makes the respective *berachos* on thunder and lightning only once a day if it is the same storm. If the storm ended and the clouds completely dispersed, one should recite a new *berachah* if a second storm occurs. This scenario is somewhat unlikely, so one must make certain that it is a completely new storm front rather than a continuation of the previous storm after a bit of sunlight between cloudbursts.[4]

If a new day begins and the storm from the previous night is still raging, one does recite the *berachos* again.[5] Although the night is usually the start of the halachic 24-hour day, for the purpose of the *berachos* on thunder and lightning, the morning is considered the start of a new day (this is similar to the requirement of reciting *Birchos HaShachar* each morning).[6]

One must be careful to recite the *berachos* on thunder and lightning immediately after seeing the lightning and hearing the thunder. One should therefore commit the *berachos* to memory so that he can recite them immediately after the occurrence. If one could not say it within two to three seconds, he should wait for the next bolt of lightning and clap of thunder and recite the *berachos* at that time.

---

2. *Taz Orach Chaim* 227:1.
3. See *Mishnah Berurah Orach Chaim* 208:12.
4. *Shulchan Aruch Orach Chaim* 227, *Mishnah Berurah* ibid. 8.
5. *Mishnah Berurah* ibid.
6. *Az Nidberu* 6:32.

SHABBOS DO'S AND DON'TS

Adding Time to Shabbos and Yom Tov

*What is the proper time for men
to accept Shabbos and Yom Tov
upon themselves?*

It is a mitzvah to accept the *kedushah* of Shabbos early, as well as
to extend Shabbos past the absolute required time. This mitzvah — and
our discussion of its parameters — applies to Yom Tov as well.

The exact amount of time needed to fulfill the mitzvah of *tosefes
Shabbos* (adding on to the Shabbos) is not precisely spelled out in the
Gemara.[1] Some explain that the amount of time needed to fulfill this
mitzvah has no minimum *shiur*.[2] There is, however, a maximum *shiur*:
the maximum amount of time one may add on to the beginning of
Shabbos is from *plag haMinchah*, which is 1¼ halachic hours (each
hour being ¹⁄₁₂ of the day) before the end of the day. Any "acceptance"
of Shabbos before *plag haMinchah* is invalid.

Many rule that a little more than the bare minimum is required.[3]

---

1. *Tosafos, Beitzah* 30a, *d"h Deha*.
2. *Tosafos, Rosh Hashanah* 9a *d"h V'Rabbi Akiva*, states that even a *mashehu* —a tiny amount — is
   sufficient.
3. *Mishnah Berurah* 261:22; see *Igros Moshe Orach Chaim* 1:96, where approximately two minutes
   is indicated.

Other opinions[4] range from 4 or 5 minutes to 12 minutes.[5] It is commendable, when feasible, to accept Shabbos 18 or 20 minutes before sunset, in order to fulfill the mitzvah of *tosefes Shabbos* according to all opinions in the *Rishonim*. Let us explain:

The *Sefer Yerei'im* holds that Shabbos actually begins ¾ of a *mil* before sunset. What does this mean? A *mil* is a distance of about a kilometer (about ⁶/₁₀ of a mile); some say the average person covers this distance on foot in 24 minutes, while others say 18 minutes). Using the 18-minute measure for a full *mil,* covering ¾ of a *mil* would take 13½ minutes. An 18-minute addition prior to the beginning of Shabbos would thus leave 4½ minutes for *tosefes Shabbos.*[6]

The 20-minute *tosefes Shabbos* custom is based on the assumption of a 24-minute *mil*, ¾ of which is 18 minutes, plus 2 minutes of *tosefes Shabbos.*

This is a basis for the prevalent *minhag* for women to light Shabbos candles 18 to 20 minutes before sunset.

It is interesting to note that although it is a commendable custom, most men, including prominent *rabbanim* and *poskim*, have not adopted the 18-to-20-minutes-before-sunset rule for accepting Shabbos, for a variety of reasons. The most obvious one is that most men are able to *daven* Minchah only right before Shabbos, and one should avoid officially accepting Shabbos before he has *davened* Minchah. [If one is *davening* in a shul that schedules Minchah very close to sunset, he should verbally accept Shabbos after the silent *Shemoneh Esrei* in order to fulfill the important mitzvah of *tosefes Shabbos*. He should still answer *amen* and say *Kedushah* and *Aleinu* of Minchah even after such an acceptance of Shabbos.]

It is important to bear in mind that with a little foresight and preparation, the mitzvah of *tosefes Shabbos* (which, according to some opinions, is even a *mitzvah d'Oraisa*) can be fulfilled.

It is well known that there are two primary opinions in the *Rishonim* concerning the halachic definition of *shekiah* (sunset). Each person

---

4. See *Piskei Teshuvah* 261:2 for various opinions on the matter.
5. 4 minutes: *Avnei Nezer* 498; 5 minutes: *Minchas Elazar* 1:23; to 12 minutes: *Siddur Yaavetz, Cheder Shishi.*
6. *Sefer Minhag Yisrael Torah*; see there for other explanations of the various customs.

must ascertain his own family and community *minhag* in regard to the time of *shekiah*, as it pertains to the latest time for *davening* Minchah and the proper time for Maariv. It is, however, certainly commendable to fulfill the mitzvah of *tosefes Shabbos* according to all opinions.[7]

One can usually, without much difficulty, accept Shabbos before the first *shekiah* (the earlier opinion of sunset), because one is keeping Shabbos anyway by refraining from *melachah*. Even if one's *minhag* is to begin Minchah only after the earlier *shekiah*, he can still fulfill the mitzvah of *tosefes Shabbos* by accepting Shabbos before Minchah, relying on the opinions that rule this to be an acceptable practice.[8] This leniency may be relied upon only by individuals who clearly have a family *mesorah* to daven Minchah after *shekiah*.

May we all be *zocheh* to benefit from the *kedushah* and *berachah* of Shabbos and Yom Tov, and merit to usher in these most important days in a timely fashion.

In my haste to light the neros this past Erev Shabbos, I forgot to daven Minchah. I am careful to daven Minchah every day and I was quite disturbed when I realized that I had accepted Shabbos without doing so. What should I have done in this situation?

As you have assumed, a woman should try her utmost to *daven* Minchah on Erev Shabbos before lighting the candles.[9] This is because she is accepting Shabbos with her lighting and should not be reciting *tefillas* Minchah of Erev Shabbos after officially bringing in the Shabbos.

If she is running late and must light the *neros Shabbos*, she should

---

7. *Mishnah Berurah Orach Chaim 261:23.*
8. See *Shulchan Aruch HaRav, seder Hachnasas Shabbos; Teshuvas Chasam Sofer, Ohr HaChaim 65; Orchos Chaim 261:1.*
9. *Magen Avraham 263:19.*

make a verbal condition that she is not accepting Shabbos (this particular time) with her *hadlakas neros*.[10] Although under normal conditions one should accept Shabbos with the lighting of the *neros*, when there is a pressing need we allow for the making of such a condition.[11] She may then *daven* Minchah and afterward accept Shabbos.

If she already lit the *neros* and only then realized that she forgot to *daven* Minchah, she should *daven* Maariv twice, the second *Shemoneh Esrei* "making up" for the omitted Minchah.[12]

This would apply only to women who *daven* Minchah on a regular basis. Women who do not *daven* Minchah consistently do not have the option to make up for Minchah by reciting *Shemoneh Esrei* twice at Maariv. In such a case, the woman who truly desires to *daven* Minchah on Erev Shabbos but has already lit the *neros* should ask her Rav for direction, as there are various opinions on this matter.[13]

It is important to point out that a single man who is living alone (or a married man who is not with his spouse for Shabbos) must light *neros Shabbos* before he goes to shul on Erev Shabbos. Men do not accept Shabbos with *hadlakas haneros* and may continue to perform *melachos* until they accept Shabbos.[14] They may therefore *daven* Minchah after *hadlakas neros*.[15]

---

10. *Kaf HaChaim* ibid. 35.
11. See *Mishnah Berurah* ibid. 44.
12. *Mishnah Berurah* ibid. 43. The *Mishnah Berurah* is not necessarily disagreeing with the suggestion of the *Kaf HaChaim* concerning the making of a stipulation before *hadlakas neros*; rather, it is referring to a different scenario in which a stipulation is no longer an option. See *Halichos Beisah*, Chapter 14, footnote 169.
13. See *Shulchan Aruch HaRav, seder Hachnasas Shabbos; Teshuvas Chasam Sofer, Ohr HaChaim* 65; *Orchos Chaim* 261:1.
14. *Mishnah Berurah*, ibid. 42.
15. See *Shaarei Teshuvah Orach Chaim* 678: and *Mishnah Berurah* ibid. 2 concerning *davening* Minchah before *hadlakas neros* Chanukah on Erev Shabbos — *v'yesh lechalek*.

Omitting a Candle

Q *I was recently zocheh to have a healthy baby girl, and we spent the first Shabbos after the birth at my mother's house. I lit only two candles, as per my minhag when traveling (I assume that my understanding of the minhag to light only two when away from home is correct — please let me know). The following Shabbos, I began lighting three candles at home (the additional one for the new addition to our family). On the third Shabbos I forgot the extra candle and lit only two candles, as I had been doing through the first year of my marriage.*

I am aware that when one forgets to light Shabbos candles. there is a special kenas (penalty), that they light an additional candle every Erev Shabbos

*from that time on. Since I forgot to
light only one out of three, does this
penalty apply to me? I would like to
add that part of the reason I forgot to
light the extra candle was due to the
rush and pressure of a very busy Erev
Shabbos with our new baby, and so it
was not due to gross negligence that
the mitzvah was not performed exactly
as I had intended.*

You are correct regarding the *minhag* to light only two candles while traveling (one for "*shamor es yom haShabbos lekadesho*" and one for "*zachor es yom haShabbos lekadesho*"). Although there is certainly no prohibition to kindle as many candles as one desires even while traveling, the *minhag* to light two has a basis.[1]

Regarding your question of the application of a *kenas* for the scenario you described, there is firm basis for being lenient.

The *Beur Halachah*[2] cites that the Pri Megadim applies the penalty if even one candle was forgotten, but he disagrees and rules that no penalty is warranted as long as at least one candle was lit (and in your case, two out of three were kindled).

One might add that it is quite possible that even the Pri Megadim would agree that no penalty would apply in your specific case. This is because your forgetting was not due to any negligence but rather due to the fact that you were not accustomed to lighting the third candle for the new addition to your household (it was only the second week that you would be lighting the additional candle). One could infer this from the words of the Pri Migadim; he states, "even if she forgot only one candle from the candles she *usually* lights ...."

Although your case was not one of negligence, it was not an unforeseeable circumstance either. The *poskim* rule that we do *not* apply the penalty of lighting an additional candle when the woman missed

---

1. See *She'arim Metzuyanim Behalachah* 75:13.
2. *Orach Chaim* 263 d"h *Sheshachechah*.

lighting because of an *oness* (i.e., she was under duress). An example of this would be her need to attend to a family member who is ill at the time when she is supposed to light the *neiros*.[3] The fact that you were pressed for time would not be labeled "*oness*," because it is common for any household to be rushed and pressured right before Shabbos. The halachah would not differentiate between a rushed Erev Shabbos due to a recent birth, a family *simchah,* or the pressure of readying the children for Shabbos.

Although you need not light any added candles in this case (due to the fact that *hadklakas neiros* was performed, albeit without the usual number of candles), in the future, a strong commitment should be made to begin *hadlakas neiros* punctually and with peace of mind. You will then merit to perform correctly the special mitzvah that is your responsibility and *zechus.*

It should be noted that it is proper for the husband to participate in the mitzvah of candle-lighting by preparing the candles.[4] Preparing the candles in advance has the added benefit of enabling the wife to welcome the Shabbos Queen in a calmer and more pleasant atmosphere.

---

3. See *Shemiras Shabbos Kehilchasah* 43:5, last paragraph.
4. *Mishnah Berurah* 263:12.

Lighting Shabbos Candles When Eating Out

My wife and I will be eating out for the Friday-night seudah and returning home to sleep. Should she light Shabbos neiros in our host's home or in my house?

If she lights at home, can she travel by car to the host's home after she lights, if she has in mind not to accept Shabbos with her candle-lighting?

Your wife should light at home.[1] She should make sure to stay at home until it is somewhat dark in order to have some benefit from the candles before she leaves (this is not necessary if the candles will still be lit when you come home, later in the evening).

A woman should not travel in a car (or do any other *melachah*) after candle-lighting. There is a halachic dispute regarding whether a

---

1. *Chovos Hadar*, page 93, footnote 46.

woman may make a condition not to accept Shabbos with the kindling of the Shabbos lights.[2] Although there is room to be lenient and to make such a condition, it should be done only when necessary and not just for the sake of convenience. The Magen Avraham[3] proves that one may not take advantage of making such a condition under normal circumstances.

His evidence is the practice of reciting the *berachah* for candle-lighting after the mitzvah is performed rather than *before* the mitzvah is performed, as with most *mitzvos*.[4] The reason for this custom is that reciting the *berachah* may constitute an acceptance of Shabbos, so it would be forbidden for her to kindle the lights afterward.

If a woman could simply stipulate that she does not accept Shabbos with the *berachah*, we should have her declare that she does not accept Shabbos upon herself until after the lighting, and then have her recite the *berachah* before the lighting. The Magen Avraham concludes from here that stipulating that she dos not accept Shabbos with the *berachah* is a step to be used only sparingly, when it is truly a necessity.

2. *Shulchan Orach Chaim* 263:10.
3. *Orach Chaim* 263:20.
4. *Shulchan Orach* and *Rema* 263:5.

Using Alarm Clocks
on Shabbos

After I had arrived late to shul Shabbos morning for the fifth consecutive week, my friend suggested that I set an alarm clock to ensure that I wake up on time. He explained that a small travel clock would ring for only 15 or 30 seconds, at a volume that would not wake the rest of the family. I was surprised to hear of this possibility and I am wondering if it is indeed permissible to preset such an alarm for Shabbos morning.

You are fortunate to have good friends who can offer practical advice. The *Gemara* in *Shabbos* (18a) rules that there is no prohibition to activate machinery before Shabbos, even if it continues to function on Shabbos. However, there is a dispute regarding this *halachah*.

The *Shulchan Aruch* (252:5) rules that one may activate a mill just before Shabbos, even if it makes noise while grinding wheat on Shabbos.

The Rema (ibid.) states that the custom is, whenever possible, to forbid the ongoing use of any machinery that makes noise. This *gezeirah* was made because the noise generated (*hashmaas kol*) can be considered similar to *maaris ayin* (i.e., people might hear the noise and think that the machinery had been activated on Shabbos). The Rema comments, however, that the ongoing use of a clock that chimes (e.g., on the hour) is permitted, because people realize that a clock is usually set and running before Shabbos. Some *poskim*[1] extend this last ruling of the Rema to apply to using an alarm clock for Shabbos morning.

HaGaon HaRav Moshe Feinstein, *z"tl*, in *Igros Moshe*,[2] disagrees with the application of the Rema to the case of an alarm clock. He states that, unlike the chiming clock, the alarm clock is often set *each night* just before one goes to sleep; therefore, the *gezeirah* of *maaris ayin* (the suspicion that it might have been set on Shabbos) is still relevant. Rav Moshe rules, however, that it is permitted for a different reason. If the volume of the alarm is low enough that it cannot be heard outside the room, it would not be considered *hashmaas kol* (making noise) at a level that is forbidden.

Most small alarm clocks will indeed not be heard outside the room. It would, therefore, be permissible to use one of these preset alarms on Shabbos. If you habitually make use of the "snooze" option during the week, or if you are used to turning off the alarm manually (which could be problematic if it is an electric clock), consider covering the button to ensure that it is not inadvertently pressed on Shabbos.

I would suggest that it would be prudent to use the alarm clock if past experience has shown that you cannot wake up on time without it. You might also consider purchasing a second alarm clock, so that you are able to arrive on time for *shiur* (or *chavrusa*) on Shabbos afternoon after a nap.

It is important to bear in mind that we are speaking of using a regular alarm setting, such as the standard "beep-beep." It might not be music to your ears when you first hear it, but it will wake you up! It would certainly not be proper *kavod Shabbos* to preset a radio- or

---

1. See *Shevet HaLevi* 1:47.
2. *Orach Chaim* 4:70.6.

tape recorder-alarm clock so that you could wake up to a human voice or to a short clip of your favorite *nigunim*. This same would apply to an alarm clock with a prerecorded voice message and music clip. Doing so would entail *zilzul Shabbos* — belittling the sanctity of Shabbos (this ruling is based on personal communication with HaRav Shlomo Miller, Rosh Kollel of Kollel Avreichim Toronto). It could also lead to the use of various other means of technology that do not befit the honor of Shabbos.[3]

In summary, it is permissible to preset a low-volume alarm clock to ring on Shabbos. For many late risers, it may even be a mitzvah. In order to preserve the sanctity and spirit of Shabbos, one must be careful not to use settings such as music, radio, or prerecorded voice messages.

---

3. See *Shemiras Shabbos Kehilchasah* 31:25 and *Teshuvas Az Nidberu* 3:30 concerning preset tape recorders.

Berachah Acharonah After a Shabbos Kiddush

As I finished enjoying some cake and cookies served at the kiddush during a recent family simchah, I was called to wash for the Seudas Shabbos that was to take place in the adjacent room. I proceeded to recite al hamichyah before going to the seudah. A guest questioned my assumption that I was required to make a berachah acharonah immediately prior to eating a seudah. He assumed that my bentching after the seudah would have covered my al hamichyah. Was he correct? How can I avoid the she'eilah next time?

Many *poskim* say that one must make an *al hamichyah* before washing for the next *seudah*. This is because *bentching* does not exempt an earlier requirement to say *al hamichyah*.[1]

---

1. See *Aishel Avraham me'Butshetsh Siman* 208:17. See also *Shulchan Aruch* O.C. 208:17 with *Mishnah Berurah* 75 for a discussion concerning one who erroneously recited *Bircas Hamazon* instead of *al hamichyah*. The *Mechaber* in *Shulchan Aruch* rules that he must recite *al hamichyah*. The *Mishnah Berurah* cites *Acharonim* who say that, he is exempt from *al hamichyah*. All opinions seem to concur that , intitially, one should generally not use *Bircas Hamazon* to fulfill his obligation

Other *poskim* contend that the cake was eaten to satisfy the requirement of *kiddush bemakom seudah,* and therefore the actual *seudah* is merely a continuation; one can therefore rely on the *bentching* to cover the *Al Hamichyah.*[2]

Another mitigating factor in not requiring the *berachah acharonah* of *Al Hamichyah* is the well-known question concerning the *berachah* on *pas haba'ah b'kisnin.* In *halachah,* the cake, cookies, or crackers eaten at the kiddush are called "*pas haba'ah b'kisnin,*" which means a snacklike food that *Chazal* say carries with it a *berachah* of *Mezonos. Chazal* mandated a *Borei Minei Mezonos* for foods eaten primarily as a snack, even though they are made from the same grains used to make bread. There are three opinions in the *Rishonim* as to what constitutes the definition of *pas haba'ah b'kisnin.*[3] It is either a) a pocket-type pastry filled with fruits and/or other sweeteners and baked together as such; b) any dough with ingredients such as honey, oil, milk, and various sweeteners (our standard cookies and cakes); c) a brittle, crunchy *mezonos* snack (cracker, hard pretzel, etc.). Some *Acharonim* contend that there is no dispute and that **all three** are *pas haba'ah b'kisnin,* since any food eaten as a snack will meet *Chazal's* conditions for *Borei Minei Mezonos.* Others say that it is, indeed, a three-way *machlokes* and that each opinion carries with it the *safek* (doubt) whether it is *mezonos* or *hamotzi.* It is for this reason that, although most *poskim* say that we make a *berachah* on desserts that are *Shehakol* or *Ha'etz* (such as chocolate or fruit), we do not make a *berachah* on cake and cookies even when eaten solely as dessert. This is because each category of *pas haba'ah b'kisnin* is a *safek birchas hamotzi/mezonos* and is therefore possibly covered by the *Hamotzi* made at the beginning of the meal.[4]

Following this line of reasoning, if one had cake at the kiddush, it is possible that an *Al Hamichyah* should **not** be made, as the *berachah acharonah* will be covered by the *bentching.* This is due to the possibility that the cake might require *Hamotzi* and *Bircas Hamazon.*[5]

---

to recite *al hamichyah.*

2. *Aruch HaShulchan* O.C. 176:8.
3. *Shulchan Aruch* O.C. 168:7.
4. See *Biur Halachah* 168 *d"h T'unim.*
5. Indeed, we enjoy cake/cookies all week with a *birchas mezonos* and an *al hamichyah* without

Proper procedure would be to avoid the issue by simply finishing your kiddush cake and make an *Al Hamichyah* **some time before** the *seudah* is to begin, thereby avoiding any questions and disputes.

If one does not have time before the meal, the *al hamichyah* should not be recited, relying on the above *poskim* that *pas haba'ah b'kisnin* might possibly have the status of bread and therefore will be covered by the *bentching* after the meal. If one, however, had lukshen kugel, then *al hamichyah* would be recited before the meal. This is because kugel made out of noodles is not similar to bread (due to the fact that it is cooked, not baked), and is therefore not *pas haba'ah b'kisnin*. Since it was eaten separate from the meal, it would not be covered by the *bentching* of the *seudah* that follows.

In conclusion, you have *poskim* to rely on for the recital of your *al hamichyah* immediately before the meal. In the future, however, I would apply the rule *safek berachos lehakel* (loosely translated: "when in doubt, leave it out"), due to the dispute in the *poskim* concerning the *berachah acharonah* in this particular situation.

---

giving any thought to the above dispute. Rest assured, however, that there is no issue with the *berachos* of *mezonos/al hamichyah* on cake and cookies and the like when eaten out of the context of a regular meal. It is beyond the scope of our discussion to explain why this is so.

Davening for Personal Issues on Shabbos

There was a story in Hamodia about using the koach of Shabbos to daven for a yeshuah. I remember learning that we're not supposed to daven for personal requests on Shabbos. Please clarify. Along the same lines, I say Tehillim and the Yehi Ratzon for a list of cholim. What should I say on Shabbos? Is the halachah regarding Yom Tov any different?

To properly answer your question I must provide an overview of this interesting topic.

There are many sources that prohibit *davening* for personal needs on Shabbos and Yom Tov. The *Gemara* in *Shabbos* (12b) states that when going to visit the sick, one should say the abbreviated *tefillah*, "*Shabbos hi milizok urefuah krovah lavo, v'rachamov merubin v'shivsu beshalom* — Today is Shabbos, which prohibits us from crying out, but recovery will come soon. His mercies are many, and may you rest on Shabbos peacefully."

Although *Chazal* tell us that one must *daven* for the ill person in order to fulfill the mitzvah of *bikur cholim*,[1] a formal *tefillah* asking Hashem to send a *refuah* is permitted only on weekdays. Due to the sanctity of Shabbos and Yom Tov one must curtail the standard request for recovery.

A second source is the *Yerushalmi*[2] that states that one cannot ask for personal needs on Shabbos. Rav Chiya bar Rav is quoted as saying that this does not, however, include the standard parts of any *berachah* or *tefillah* that is part of the regular *nusach* of Shabbos and Yom Tov. The example given is *"re'einu zuneinu parneseinu* — tend us, nourish us, sustain us,"* which appears in the third *berachah* in *Bircas Hamazon*. Since these requests are made by everyone each time *bentching* is recited, they do not fall under the prohibition of making personal requests on Shabbos.

The *Magen Avraham*[3] explains that we say *Havdalah* (*Atah Chonantanu*) in the *berachah* of *Chonen Hadaas* in *Shemoneh Esrei* because this is the first *berachah* in which we make our requests. Since one may not make personal supplications until Shabbos is over, we say *Havdalah* in this *berachah*, allowing us to continue with our regular supplications during the rest of *Shemoneh Esrei*.

Various reasons are given to explain why *Chazal* prohibited personal prayers on Shabbos and Yom Tov.

Some explain the prohibition based on the *pasuk, "Mimtzo cheftzecha vedabeir davar"*:[4] one should not pursue his affairs or speak of them on Shabbos. This prohibition refers primarily to business or weekday affairs. However, *Chazal* understood this to also prohibit *tefillos* that are dedicated to one's weekday problems and needs, such as livelihood or health.[5]

The Reishis Chochmah[6] explains that we should refrain as much as possible from *sichah beteilah* (idle talk or discussions of matters not befitting the *kedushah* of this special day) on Shabbos,[7] and that is why one

---

1. *Rema Yoreh Deah* 335:4.
2. *Shabbos* 15:3.
3. *Orach Chaim* 394:1.
4. *Yeshayah* 58:13.
5. See *Yerushalmi Shabbos,* end of *perek* 15.
6. *Shaar Hakedushah, perek* 14.
7. See *Yerushalmi,* ibid.

should not *daven* for things that do not pertain to the holiness of the day.

Others explain[8] that one must enter Shabbos with a mindset that all his work is finished and he is to maintain that happy and serene state of mind throughout Shabbos. If one were allowed to *daven* for private needs, it indicates that he still needs things taken care of, which detracts from the tranquility, *simchah,* and *oneg* and may in fact lead to a sense of sadness and worry.

However, there are scenarios in which one *is* allowed to *daven* for personal needs on Shabbos.

We mentioned above (from *Shabbos* 12b) that when visiting a sick individual one may say a brief *tefillah* with the disclaimer of *"Shabbos hi milizok"* — that we cannot cry out in the conventional way since it is Shabbos. It is based on this *Gemara* that we have the *minhag* today to make a *mishebeirach* — with the addition of that phrase — on Shabbos during the reading of the Torah.

One may also say *Tehillim* for a sick person on Shabbos. However, one should not recite the prayer for the sick, in order to differentiate between the Shabbos *Tehillim* and the weekday recital, which includes the standard *tefillah* for the ailing.

It is permissible to *daven* for personal success in spiritual endeavors, for the whole purpose of Shabbos *and* Yom Tov is the pursuit of greater levels of *ruchnius.* One may therefore *daven* for success in learning Torah, improvement of *middos,* and success in *chessed* activities.[9]

To answer your question about *davening* for a *yeshuah,* I would say the following: If the matter concerns an ongoing issue that will likely continue after Shabbos, one should limit his request for help to the weekdays. If it is an emergency that must be taken care of on Shabbos, it would be permissible to *daven* for the specific need even on Shabbos.

Other exceptions to the basic prohibition of personal *bakashos* are the *tefillos* of Rosh Hashanah and Yom Kippur (most of the verses of *Avinu Malkeinu* relate to *gashmius*). There are sources in *poskim*[10] stating that it is permissible, and even commendable, to beseech Hashem for all personal needs during the *Yamim Nora'im.*

---

8. See *Korban Ha'eidah* on *Yerushalmi,* ibid.
9. See *Shaarei Teshuvah* 268:2; also *Minchas Elimelech,* Vol. 1, page 13.
10. See *Orchos Rabbeinu* Vol. 2, page 181, in the name of the Chazon Ish.

Davening for personal needs is certainly consistent with the theme of Yom Kippur and is a major part of its *tefillos*. Although the main theme of Rosh Hashanah is to declare *Malchus Shamayim* and *daven* that all of *Klal Yisrael*, as well as the nations of the world, accept Hashem's sovereignty, one is allowed to add personal requests as well.

See *Mateh Efraim* 584:25, who rules that the *mishebeirach* on Rosh Hashanah should be said as a *mishebeirach* would be said during the week. There is no need to add the disclaimer of *Yom Tov hi milizok*; even if Rosh Hashanah falls on Shabbos, one need not add *Shabbos/Yom Tov hi milizok*. This is because the usual personal *bakashos* are permissible on Rosh Hashanah.

Although we omit the recital of *Avinu Malkeinu* when Rosh Hashanah or Yom Kippur fall on Shabbos (with the exception of during *Tefillas Neilah*), it is only to remind us of *kedushas Shabbos*, and we leave it out to show that under normal circumstances personal requests are prohibited.[11]

Shabbos and Yom Tov are a time for spiritual pursuits and personal introspection. They are a time to focus on Torah and *chinuch*, as we have more time to learn and more time for our families. We also have time to *daven* at a slower pace and with more *kavanah*.

The *Zohar*[12] says that the day of the Shabbos is the day for the *neshamah*. We therefore sing the praises of Hashem with *tefillos* such as *Nishmas*, declaring that every *neshamah* must bless the Name of *HaKadosh Baruch Hu* on this special day.

If we focus on the incredible themes of the *tefillos* of Shabbos and Yom Tov, we will be *zocheh* to see the fulfillment of our request, "*Retzei na bimenuchasenu ... kadsheinu bemitzvosecha ... vetaher libeinu le'avdacha be'emes* — May You be pleased with our rest, sanctify us with Your commandments ... and purify our heart to serve You sincerely."

---

11. *Aruch HaShulchan* 619:8.
12. *Vayakhel* 245:2.

Is Snow Muktzeh, and Other Questions

My 7-year-old son enjoys making snowballs, and he would like to spend some time doing so in our fenced-in backyard on Shabbos afternoon. I have always understood that this is prohibited, but I would like to verify the halachah before I tell him that he can't do it.

You have taken care of any carrying issues by indicating that your son would be playing in your backyard, which is an enclosed area. We do not have to deal with the hashkafic issue of whether such activity is appropriate on Shabbos, as your child is only 7 years old, and the *Shulchan Aruch* rules[1] that a child who finds activities such as running and jumping pleasurable may do on Shabbos. As your child matures, he will, we hope, appreciate the sanctity of Shabbos and understand that making and throwing snowballs is not in the spirit of this special day.

With that said, there are a number of halachic issues that affect the making of snowballs on Shabbos.

Is snow *muktzeh*? Most *poskim* seem to indicate that, contrary to

---

1. *Orach Chaim* 301:2.

popular belief, snow is not *muktzeh*.[2] There are, however, those who rule stringently and declare snow to be *muktzeh*.[3] If one is touching snow merely for fun, there might be reason to find a different recreational activity. However, since most *poskim* rule leniently on the *muktzeh* aspect, I would not disappoint your young son based on this issue alone.

The more serious prohibition involved would seem to be the *melachah* of *boneh*, construction. The *Shemiras Shabbos Kehilchasah*[4] indeed rules that one is prohibited to form a snowball because it is similar to "building."[5]

The making of a snowman would entail a similar prohibition due to its similarity to the *melachah* of *boneh*. Destroying the snowman would violate the *issur* of *soseir*.

Another possible issue is that of crushing snow. When one fashions a snowball, one must pack the snow tightly, and, as a result, some of it might melt. It is prohibited to cause water to drip from snow or ice (it is a safeguard *mi'd'Rabbanan* lest one come to squeeze fruits for their liquid,[6] and possibly because of the *issur* of *nolad*, creating a new object).[7] The *Shulchan Aruch* (320:11) indeed rules that one should preferably not touch snow or ice due to the above problem, and if one must handle snow or ice, it should be done with caution and without squeezing, so that liquid is not exuded.

To summarize: There are a number of possible prohibitions involved in making snowballs on Shabbos. As your child is at the age of *chinuch* (even though he is not old enough to be required to stop all active recreational activity), I would suggest that he find a different activity for his Shabbos-afternoon recreation.

---

2. *Teshuvas Be'er Moshe*, 1:20; *Shemiras Shabbos Kehilchasah* 16:44
3. See *Pri Megadim*, Introduction to *Hilchos Yom Tov* 3:29; *Igros Moshe, Orach Chaim* 5:22:37
4. Ibid.
5. See ibid. footnote 109, quoting the *sefer Menuchah Nechonah*, who prohibits throwing snowballs, and HaRav Shlomo Zalman Aueurbach, *z"tl*, who held that throwing a snowball made before Shabbos would be permitted despite the fact that the snowball is demolished upon impact. See there the basis to differentiate between the *melachos* of *boneh* and *soseir*, demolishing, as it applies to the forming and throwing of snowballs.
6. See *Shulchan Aruch, Orach Chaim* 320:9 with *Mishnah Berurah* 33.
7. See *Rema* 318:16 and *Mishnah Berurah* 320:35.

Q

Is it permitted to shovel snow on Shabbos (within an eiruv, of course)?

A

We have mentioned above that most *poskim* rule that snow is not *muktzeh*. Even according to the opinion that snow is *muktzeh*, moving the snow with a shovel would be permissible, as it entails *tiltul min hatzad,* indirect movement of *muktzeh*.[8] If the snow is still soft and has settled on a hard surface that will not be made smoother or leveled out as a result of the shoveling (the prohibition of *mashveh gumos,* leveling the ground), there is theoretically a basis to be lenient. However, one should seek a non-Jew to clear the snow.[9]

If the snow has already hardened, one should be extra diligent in attempting to find a non-Jew to clear the walkway rather than doing it himself. This is because there are opinions that rule that clearing frozen snow or ice is prohibited because of *binyan* (since the frozen snow or ice becomes a second layer of the walkway, moving it might entail *mashveh gumos*).[10]

If a non-Jew is not available and the hazardous condition will prevent exit from or entrance to the house, there might be room to be lenient to clear a small path. This would be permissible, of course, only within an *eiruv* or on a porch that is properly enclosed.

This should only be done as a last resort (if the hazardous condition cannot be remedied by pushing the snow aside with one's feet) and in consultation with your Rav. This is due to the intricacies of the halachic issues and the need for heavy exertion while shoveling, as well as the possible appearance of *uvda d'chol* (mundane activity).

Q

Is it permissible to salt the walkway in order to facilitate the melting of the ice?

---

8. See *Mishnah Berurah* 337:8 and *Shaarei Tziyon* ibid. 7.
9. Cf. *Mishnah Berurah* 320:36; *Teshuvos Mishneh Halachos* 4:45.
10. See *Magen Avraham Orach Chaim* 340:15 and *Teshuvas Har Tzvi* ibid.; see, however, *Machatzis HaShekel Orach Chaim* ibid. and *Mishnah Berurah* ibid., who are lenient on this issue.

The *Rema*[11] rules that if there is a great need (*bemakom tzorech*), one may cause a congealed or frozen item to melt on Shabbos despite the fact that liquid is created and the action is similar to the prohibition of *nolad* (creating a new object). Although it is prohibited to create liquid by squeezing ice or snow, merely placing an object near a source of heat is an indirect action and therefore permitted.

There is no halachic difference between placing an object near a source of heat and placing the melting catalyst near (or on) the ice or snow. It is, therefore, permissible to place salt on ice to remove a potential hazard of slipping on the walkway.[12] As mentioned above, the area in question must be enclosed (and a proper *eiruv chatzeiros* prepared if the area is shared by a number of neighbors) to permit the sprinkling of the salt.

Am I allowed to shake the snow from my coat and hat when I come home?

The *Shulchan Aruch*[13] rules that new garments that become wet should not be shaken to force out the wetness. This is due to the prohibition of *sechitah* (squeezing) and *libun* (laundering). (Our garments today are often in as good-as-new condition due to constant laundering and dry-cleaning. The *Aruch HaShulchan*[14] rules that a garment is still considered new if it does not appear to be old and worn and one is still particular about keeping it in proper condition.[15])

The *Beur Halachah*[16] rules that one may shake off snow because it merely sits upon the garment and is not absorbed in the fabric. If one lightly shakes the garment, only the snow that has not melted will be removed. *Caution, however, is in order, for it is difficult to measure*

---

11. *Orach Chaim* 318:16.
12. *Shemiras Shabbos Kehilchasah* 25:9, footnote 49; *Orchos Shabbos* 4, footnote 94.
13. *Orach Chaim* 302:1.
14. Ibid. 4.
15. See also *Mishnah Berurah* ibid. 1.
16. Ibid. *d"h min hatal she'aleha*.

the force needed to shake off the surface snow without dislodging the snow that has begun to melt into the fabric. Any vigorous shaking that will dislodge the melted snow that has been absorbed into the fabric would be prohibited as a form of *sechitah/libun*.

One may shake snow (or rain) from a plastic raincoat. This is because snow is not at all absorbed into the garment and there is therefore no prohibition of *sechitah* (squeezing).[17]

---

17. *Shemiras Shabbos Kehilchasah* 15:36.

Using Costco Trash Bags on Shabbos

Q *I am a frequent user of the thirteen-gallon drawstring garbage bags sold by Costco stores under their store brand. I have been using them all week, including Shabbos. Recently, a friend mentioned to me that one may have to open these bags before using them on Shabbos, because one rips apart the sides of the bag when unfolding it.*

Is this how the bags are made? If it is true, is there really a problem with opening them on Shabbos?

A There is a similar question regarding the use of disposable diapers on Shabbos. The ends of the diapers are often slightly stuck together, and one must separate them open to make them ready for use. The diapers pose no problem, because the parts became are not considered connected at all; they just became pressed together *unintentionally*[1]

---

1. See *Magen Avraham* 340:18.

due to friction during the cutting process and the pressure applied while packing the product.[2]

The garbage bags, however, are more problematic. This is because the seams are actually intentionally sealed together during manufacturing. I learned from company representatives that as part of the manufacturing process, the bags are left connected at the side seams after they are perforated. The perforation is done after the bags are partially folded and causes the seams to "stick" to the bag. This is done so that the bag can be easily folded one more time. Most of the time a consumer will need to tug slightly on the folds to unfold the bag before putting it in the trash can.

Based on this information, it seems that it is prohibited to open the bags on Shabbos. It is indeed a mitzvah to make others aware of this potential *chillul Shabbos*. Although it is not an issue with many other brands, those using the problematic brands (Glad Forceflex seems to have the problem as well) might not even notice the problem had it not been pointed out.

---

2. See *Sefer Lamed Tes Melachos*, page 846.

Getting to the Hospital for a Shabbos Birth

Q *We are preparing for the birth of a baby and there is a possibility that it will happen on Shabbos. I have a question concerning the proper mode of transportation. I was told by a friend that it is better to use a non-observant taxi or car service operator rather than to use a gentile taxi driver. I was very surprised to hear this and I am wondering if it is, in fact, the halachah.*

A The logic of what you were told runs as follows. If a non-observant Jew is, in any case, regrettably driving his taxi Shabbos, it might be better to use him for a medical emergency so that for the duration of the emergency. the driver will be credited with a mitzvah and not charged with violating the Shabbos.

Although this is a fascinating angle, it is far from simple. The Beis HaLevi on *Chumash*[1] says that a person who must violate the Shab-

---

1. *Bais HaLevi al HaTorah Parashas Shemos d"h vayaar.*

bos *b'oness* (under absolute duress) is not held liable for this violation only if he would never contemplate violating Shabbos under non-emergency conditions. One who would violate the Shabbos in any event is not protected when he happens to violate it while saving a life. In our example, the taxi driver falls into this latter category. Although we do not generally determine *halachah* based on a non-halachaic *Chumash* commentary, the Beis HaLevi does have many convincing proofs to support his position.

It is also not possible that the driver would not have been driving had you not called him. If he stays at his base, there might be little or no *chillul Shabbos* taking place. Thus, your call is not necessarily saving him from *chillul Shabbos*. You are running the risk of causing him to do more driving or writing once he is out for your call.

Therefore, despite the allure of saving a *Yid* from possibly violating Shabbos, it is better to call a gentile car service for the trip to the hospital. This is of course assuming that both taxi drivers will do the job with the same speed and alacrity. If time is critical, Hatzalah should be called or your husband should quickly grab his own car keys.

B'shaah tovah u'mutzlachas!

Ace Bandages, Ice, and Allergy Medicine on Shabbos

ACE BANDAGES AND ICE

1. Is it permissible to wrap an Ace bandage around a sprained wrist on Shabbos? (This has come up during my children's somewhat wild activities.)

2. Is there any problem with applying ice to a bump on the forehead on Shabbos to reduce swelling?

Ace bandages and ice are often used to heal or soothe conditions that usually would not be painful enough to cause someone to be a *nafal lemishkav* (one who, due to illness, is confined to bed or prevented from carrying on daily activities), and therefore should be prohibited for use on Shabbos. However, it is actually permissible to put on an Ace bandage — without making any permanent ties — or to use ice to reduce swelling from a bump or bruise.

This is because only medicines and treatments that normally involve (or could potentially involve) the grinding of ingredients were prohibited by *Chazal*, lest one come to prepare them on Shabbos in a prohibited way.[1]

The therapeutic value of an Ace bandage cannot be duplicated with

---

1. See *Shaar Hatziyun* 328:104.

pills or other types of standard medicines. The same logic and leniency can be applied to exerting pressure with a cold object to reduce swelling. Although there are many anti-inflammatory pills that one can take to help reduce swelling, it is the opinion of the medical experts consulted that the standard method of treating bumps and bruises to reduce swelling is with ice or another cold compress and therefore the prohibition would not apply.

An exception to this leniency is exercise on Shabbos. Although the therapeutic value of exercise is not normally accomplished by taking conventional medicines, it is still considered a standard weekday activity (*uvda d'chol*) and is therefore forbidden.

ALLERGY MEDICINE

I often suffer from allergies on Shabbos. Is it ever permissible to take allergy medicine on Shabbos?

One who has slight-to-moderate allergies should not take allergy medicine on Shabbos. If, due to an allergic condition or reaction, he feels ill to the extent that he cannot function (the halachic equivalent of the status of a *nafal lemishkav*), it would be permissible to take the allergy medication.

Some *poskim* are lenient in a situation in which the allergy causes an extremely embarrassing situation (such as a serious case of sneezing or runny nose), to the extent that it becomes a case of *kavod habrios* (basic human dignity).[2] One should consult a *posek* to clarify the parameters of this *heter* as applied to each individual case.

---

2. See HaRav Shlomo Zalman Auerbach, quoted in *Shemiras Shabbos Kehilchasah* 34, note 52.

Sleeping Pills and Handling Medication on Shabbos

Is it permissible to take sleeping pills on Shabbos?

Contemporary authorities question whether it is permissible to take sleeping pills on Shabbos. The question revolves around the following issues:

Chazal prohibited the medical treatment of a *michush b'almah* (a minor wound, ache, or pain). This is a *gezeirah* (precaution) to prevent the grinding of herbs and the like for medicinal purposes (*shechikas samemanim*, which is a form of the *melachah tochen*, grinding. (See our fuller discussion of this topic in "Ace Bandages and Ice on Shabbos" (page 144).

If lack of sleep were considered a sickness, taking pills for it would be considered a *refuah*, a medical treatment, which would be prohibited on Shabbos. Even if the *halachah* assumed that sleeping pills are not considered to be a "medicine," since they do not treat a medical "condition," perhaps they would be prohibited because they are in pill form, and therefore fall under the precautionary *gezeirah* against grinding (*shechikas samemanim*).[1]

As there is no clear consensus in the *poskim* about taking sleeping pills on Shabbos, one should rely on the lenient positions only at a time of great need.[2]

In the situation of a *choleh shenafal lemishkav*, a person who is so ill that he or she must or should be in bed, medicine can be taken. This is permissible even if one is not a *choleh sheyeish bo sakanah*, a person with a life-threatening illness. It is only one who has a *michush b'almah* — a mild illness or uncomfortable condition, such as a slight headache — who is prohibited from taking medicine due to this *gezeirah*. You should consult your Rav if you feel that your condition may fall into this category.

I have been told that since taking medicine is usually not permitted on Shabbos, medicines have no use and are therefore muktzeh. However, when my husband was sick with the flu, he had to take Tylenol on Shabbos. Is it permitted for anybody in the house to bring medicine to the person who is not feeling well, or must the infirm person get it himself due to the muktzeh prohibition?

Since it is normally prohibited for a person who is not ill to take medicine on Shabbos (unless he has the status of a *nafal lemishkav*, as explained above), any medicines that had not been set aside for use

---

1. See *Tzitz Eliezer* 9:17:2:40; ibid 8:15:15:17, quoting *Mirkeves Hamishneh*; *Shulchan Shlomo* 328:57. See also *Magen Avraham* 328:45, who assumes that the use of *samemanim* is prohibited in every case, even for something other than healing an illness. The *Taz*, ibid: 27, seems to disagree.
2. *Shemiras Shabbos Kehilchasah* 33:16.

on Shabbos has a status of *muktzeh* as a *kli shemilachto l'issur*, an item used for purposes that are prohibited on Shabbos.[3]

Muktzeh that has a status of *kli shemilachto l'issur* may be moved when the *muktzeh* item is needed on Shabbos, and it may be used for a permissible application (just as a hammer may be used to open a coconut if no completely non-*muktzeh* item is available). Therefore, medicine that is needed on Shabbos may be moved by anyone bringing it for the *choleh* as well.

If the person was already sick before Shabbos started, the medicine that is normally taken for his particular ailment is not *muktzeh* at all and may be moved for every reason, even not for immediate use.[4]

---

3. *Shemiras Shabbos Kehilchasah* 33:4; *Shulchan Shlomo, Hilchos Shabbos* 308:9.
4. *Shulchan Shlomo* 318:7.

Vitamins on Shabbos

*Is it permissible to take vitamins
on Shabbos?*

As with all medical *she'eilos* on Shabbos, a Rav should be consulted for detailed applications of the *halachos* involved. Below is merely an overview.

Please see our discussion beginning on page 146 concerning the sources and reasons for the prohibition of taking medicines on Shabbos.

There is a dispute in the *poskim* whether vitamins are included in the prohibition against taking medicine on Shabbos. Many rule that vitamins should not be taken on Shabbos.[1]

HaRav Moshe Feinstein[2] rules leniently and permits one to take vitamins that are merely intended to strengthen the body of a healthy person.[3]

Due to the aforementioned dispute in the *poskim*, it is preferable when possible to avoid the question by scheduling the taking of vitamins immediately before and after Shabbos. If there is a need to take the vitamins at a specific time each day, one may rely on the lenient opinions.

Generally, a child may take vitamins that are necessary for growth or the preservation of health where it is medically indicated. This is because

---

1. See *Mishnah Berurah* 328:120; *Shulchan Shlomo* Vol. 2, page 213; and *Shemiras Shabbos Kehilchasah* 34:20.
2. *Igros Moshe Orach Chaim* 3:54.
3. *Shemiras Shabbos Kehilchasah* ibid. — second view; see *Eglei Tal Meleches Tochein* 47, who contemplates a lenient view as well.

young children have a status of *choleh sh'ein bahem sakanah* — one who is ill with a *non*-life-threatening illness. Similarly, expectant mothers are usually permitted to take prenatal vitamins and the like where it is needed to aid her health and the well-being of the unborn child.[4]

---

4. *Shemiras Shabbos Kehilchasah* 36:1;37:4.

Exercise on Shabbos

*Is it permissible to do stretching
exercises after I wake up on Shabbos
morning?*

The *Shulchan Aruch* rules[1] that one may not exercise or massage strenuously on Shabbos. Doing so falls under the general prohibition of applying *refuos* (medicine or other actions that provide relief from mild illness or discomfort) on Shabbos.

This prohibition is a *gezeirah* (enactment) by *Chazal* to prevent one from violating the *melachah d'Oraisa* (Torah prohibition) of *shechikas samamanim* (grinding medicines, which is prohibited as a form of *tochen* — grinding). In the time of *Chazal,* medicines were often made by grinding or pulverizing herbs and the like. Some medicines today are still manufactured using a process that would involve *chillul Shabbos.*

It is important to understand that even if all medicine could be made without violating any *melachah,* the *gezeirah* of *Chazal* prohibiting the taking of medicine or performing any related act of *refuah* would still be in full force. This is because decrees of *Chazal* are made as a *lo plug* (literally, no differentiating; no exceptions). This means that we are duty-bound to uphold the *gezeirah* even where the reason for it does not seem to apply.

---

1. *Orach Chaim* 328:42.

This is because *Chazal* could have other reasons for making the *gezeirah*, many of which are not known to us. Another motive for the across-the-board prohibition (*lo plug*) is the ever-changing world in which we live. *Chazal* understood that although the reason(s) might not apply in every era or to every circumstance, the *gezeirah* must stand guard to protect from *aveirah* in all eventualities. This "insurance policy" has saved many *Yidden* from transgressing unknowingly.[2]

The *gezeirah* with regard to healing prohibited only treatments that have some relation to grinding. The splinting of a broken limb, for instance, is not included.

Although vigorous exercise does not involve any grinding, since medicines are sometimes used to induce a patient to sweat, activities that yield this result are all included in the enactment.[3]

Only one who merely has a *michush b'almah* — a mild illness or uncomfortable condition, such as a slight headache — is prohibited from taking medicine due to this *gezeirah*. In the situation of a *choleh shenafal lemishkav,* a person who is so ill that he is in bed or would like to get into bed, medicine can be used.

In the event of a *choleh sheyesh bo sakanah,* a person with a life-threatening illness, it is a mitzvah to do whatever is needed to save the person, even actual *melachos d'Oraisah.*

Based on the above, a person with a sore muscle, back pain, or neck pain that is severe enough to prevent normal functioning would be allowed to exercise to relieve the condition. This is because without the exercise the person would have the status of a *nafal lemishkav* due to the severe pain involved.

We must now discuss whether stretching exercises are included in the *gezeirah* forbidding general exercise and the taking of medicine on Shabbos. The *Mishnah Berurah*[4] questions the permissibility of massaging the body to regain strength and dispel weariness, leaning toward the strict view that prohibits such action due to the *gezeirah* of *refuah.*

HaRav Shlomo Zalman Auerbach[5] ruled that upon awakening in

2. *Noda BeYehudah Tinyana* 49; *Toras Chesed Orach Chaim* 17; *Pischei Teshuvah Even Haezer* 13:4; and *Tzitz Eliezer* Volume 8-15, 15:4.
3. *Mishnah Berurah* 328:130.
4. *Orach Chaim* 328:130.
5. *Shulchan Shlomo* Volume II, page 219 footnote 2.

the morning, it is nevertheless permissible to perform simple stretching exercises that loosen up the body. HaRav Auerbach posits that this type of exercise is not considered "healing"; rather, it releases the natural stiffness of the body that occurs after a long sleep (*leshachrer es haguf*). He explains that massaging the body to regain strength is prohibited because exertion is necessary to accomplish that goal.

A morning stretch, however, merely speeds up the process of relieving stiffness of the body. The body would naturally return to its normal agility without the exercise, albeit a short while later.

The *Shulchan Aruch*[6] rules that children and youngsters who enjoy running and jumping on Shabbos are allowed to do so because that is their *oneg Shabbos*. HaRav Auerbach applies this *halachah* as an additional reason to be lenient on the issue of morning exercise — if one has pleasure (*oneg Shabbos*) from the exercise. (Even adults have the previously mentioned allowance of running for *oneg Shabbos*.[7])

This *does not* imply that one may jog or involve oneself in any strenuous exercise or activity on Shabbos. *Oneg Shabbos* must conform to the spirit of Shabbos, and these activities would be a contradiction to the *kavod* and *kedushah* of Shabbos. We are permitting only morning exercises that stretch the limbs and enable the body to emerge from its lethargic state more quickly.

---

6. *Orach Chaim* 301:2.
7. See *Mishnah Berurah* ibid. 6.

Havdalah for and by Women

My husband recently began to travel overseas on business, and often his trips last ten days or more. On Shabbos I make Kiddush for my family, but am unsure what to do about Havdalah. I have two girls, 16 and 13, and three boys all under bar mitzvah. There is no adult male to be motzi us. What are my options?

The *Shulchan Aruch* (296:8) records a dispute concerning the obligation of women to recite *Havdalah*. The first opinion rules that women are obligated in *Havdalah,* as they are in *Kiddush*. This is based on the *pasuk, "Zachor es yom haShabbos lekadsho."*[1] *Chazal* learn that there is an obligation to "remember" Shabbos (on Shabbos) by reciting *Kiddush,* and to "remember" Shabbos when it departs by reciting *Havdalah*.

Women are normally exempt from time-bound *mitzvos (mitzvos asei shehazeman grama);* however, since women are obligated to keep Shabbos by abstaining from all *melachos* that are prohibited, they are bound to keep the positive *mitzvos* of Shabbos as well (*itkish zachor leshamor*). According to this opinion, the positive *mitzvos* of

---

1. *Shemos* 20:8.

Shabbos include the mitzvah of *Havdalah*, wherein we remember and honor the Shabbos as it departs. (There is a dispute in *poskim* if this obligation of *Havdalah* is *mi'd'Oraisa* or *mi'd'Rabbanan*.[2])

The second opinion rules that women are exempt from reciting *Havdalah*, as they are from any other time-bound mitzvah. Since *Havadalah* is recited after Shabbos, it is not part of their overall obligation to observe the Shabbos.

The Rema[3] rules that due to this dispute, women should not make *Havdalah* themselves; rather, they should try to hear a man make *Havdalah*. Although Ashkenazic women follow the custom of reciting *berachos* on the *mitzvos* that they voluntarily undertake and should therefore be allowed to recite the *Havdalah* themselves, the practice is discouraged when avoidable. This is because of the long-standing custom that women do not drink from the *Havdalah* wine unnecessarily. (This is based on kabbalistic sources and is not a halachic prohibition.) See *Magen Avraham*[4] for another reason that women avoid making *Havdalah* even though they normally recite *berachos* for other *mitzvos* that are not obligatory in nature.)

If a man hears *Havdalah* in shul after Maariv, it would be best for him to specifically have in mind not to fulfill the mitzvah of *Havdalah* in there, because if his wife is not truly obligated to make *Havdalah*, he would not be allowed to repeat it at home on her behalf.[5]

When your husband is away on business, you should attempt to go to a neighbor to hear *Havdalah*. If this is at all difficult or cumbersome, you may rely on the opinion ruling that women are obligated in *Havdalah*, and recite the *Havdalah* yourself. Although there is generally a *kabbalah*-based custom that women do not drink wine from *Havdalah*, you may drink from the wine or grape juice without fear of any repercussions, since halachically you must drink from the cup to fulfill the mitzvah of *Havdalah* properly. Some suggest that a woman in this situation make *Havdalah* on *chamar medinah*, other beverages that are suitable for *Kiddush* and *Havdalah*, rather than using wine

---

2. See *Mishnah Berurah* ibid. 34.
3. Ibid.
4. Ibid. 11.
5. *Mishnah Berurah* ibid., 36.

or grape juice.[6] (It is preferable to drink 4.5 ounces or slightly more of the beverage, so that you can recite the appropriate after-*berachah* without any doubt concerning the proper *shiur.*)

The *Beur Halachah*[7] questions whether women who are in a position where they must recite *Havdalah* themselves should recite the *berachah* on the candle (*Borei Me'orei Ha'eish*). Although the *berachah* on the *Havdalah* candle is part of the general *Havdalah* recitation, it is not really an integral part of the *Havdalah* obligation. The main *berachah* of *Havdalah* "remembers" Shabbos and contrasts the holiness of the Shabbos with the workweek that is being ushered in. It is a fulfillment of the obligation to remember Shabbos as it leaves, and as we have explained, women have this obligation as well (according to most *poskim*).

The *berachah* on the *ner*, though, is a commemoration of the gift of fire that was given to Adam HaRishon (and therefore humanity) on Motza'ei Shabbos. *Chazal* linked it with the other *berachos* of *Havdalah* so that it can be recited over the cup of wine as well. The *Beur Halachah* concludes that there is probably no obligation for women to include the *berachah* on the *ner* in their *Havdalah*. HaRav Moshe Feinstein, *zt"l*,[8] rules that even if one takes the position that women are not obligated in *ner*, they certainly may opt to recite the *berachah* of *Borei Me'orei Ha'eish*.

Although there are opinions that hold one can be *yotzei* the mitzvah of *Havdalah* over the telephone,[9] most *poskim* rule that one cannot fulfill the mitzvah of *Havdalah* over the phone.[10]

To summarize: If your husband is away and you cannot easily hear *Havdalah* from a neighbor, you should recite *Havdalah* yourself and drink the wine. When your son becomes bar mitzvah, he can assume this responsibility and make *Havdalah* for the entire family, thus avoiding many of the questions we have discussed. Until that time, you have the right and obligation to recite *Havdalah* for yourself and the rest of the family when no man is available to do so.

---

6. See *Shemiras Shabbos Kehilchasah*, 60:38, 45.
7. Ibid. *d"h lo yavdilu l'atzman.*
8. *Igros Moshe, Choshen Mishpat* 2, 47:2.
9. See *Tzitz Eliezer* 8:11 concerning microphone, radio, and telephone. See *Igros Moshe Orach Chaim* 4:91.
10. *Minchas Shlomo* 1:9, *Minchas Yitzchak* 1:37, and *Yechave Daas* 3:54.

Melaveh Malkah —
An Easy Mitzvah Not
to Be Skipped

I have had a bit of difficulty eating melaveh malkah after having eaten seudas shelishis late in the day, and I am wondering how important it is. Although I have no problem eating this seudah during the fall and winter months, during the spring and summer it is challenging to work up an appetite on such a short Motza'ei Shabbos.

The *Gemara* states that one should set the table in an elegant fashion on Motza'ei Shabbos in order to escort the Shabbos Queen.[1] The table should be set for this festive meal even if one is eating only a small amount. The *Gemara* is cited in *Shulchan Aruch*[2] and is quoted in many *halachah* and *Kabbalah sefarim* as being a very important

---

1. *Shabbos* 119b.
2. *Orach Chaim* 300.

aspect of *kibbud Shabbos*. It is also a source of *berachah* and *parnassah* for the week.[3]

As an example of the esteem in which the *melaveh malkah* was traditionally held, it is written that the Vilna Gaon was extremely careful to eat bread for the *melaveh malkah seudah* every Motza'ei Shabbos, without exception.[4] It states there that one Motza'ei Shabbos, the Gaon was ill most of the evening and still exerted himself to eat some bread toward the end of the night.

On a different Motza'ei Shabbos, upon hearing that his *talmid,* Rav Chaim Volozhiner, had fulfilled the mitzvah of *melaveh malkah* with cake due to illness, the Gaon told him to wash for bread immediately to fulfill the mitzvah properly. (One fulfills the mitzvah of eating only when it is not an *achilas gassah*. *Achilas gassah* is defined as a type of eating from which one derives absolutely no pleasure or benefit. It is obvious that the incidents involving the Vilna Gaon did not refer to forcing oneself to eat to the point that it becomes *achilas gassah*.)

The Vilna Gaon's rebbetzin had once taken upon herself to fast beginning right after Shabbos. The Gaon directed her to eat *melaveh malkah* and to fast instead at a permissible time.

Since the purpose of *melaveh malkah* is to bid farewell to Shabbos, one should attempt to fulfill the mitzvah as soon as he can after the conclusion of Shabbos. He should not become involved in any time-consuming activity that would delay the meal, since it is unusual to have a farewell dinner long after the guest has already left.[5]

If eating the *seudah* soon after Shabbos is not possible due to lack of appetite or another unavoidable delay, one should attempt to fulfill the mitzvah before *chatzos* (halachic midnight). If *chatzos* has passed, one should still eat the *seudah* any time during the night.[6]

One should attempt to eat bread during the *seudah*. If he is too full, cake or cookies (or any other *pas haba'ah b'kisnin* product) would be the second choice. The next choice would be *kneidlach,* or any other

---

3. *Shaarei Teshuvah* 300:1.
4. See *Tosafos Maaseh Rav.*
5. See *Shaarei Teshuvah*, ibid., quoting from the *talmidim* of the Ari *zt"l*, to the effect that the extra Shabbos *neshamah* does not depart until after the *seudas melaveh malkah*, and therefore it is not proper to involve oneself in activities prohibited on *Shabbos* until after he has eaten this *seudah*.
6. *Kaf HaChaim* 300:14.

type of cooked *mezonos*. If even that is too difficult, one should attempt to eat fruit.[7]

In the unlikely scenario that there is no food available at all (or in case of illness where the eating is not an option), one should at least consume a hot drink[8] or a cold beverage for the sake of *melaveh malkah*.

If possible, one should prepare a new dish for the *melaveh malkah* rather than eat leftovers from Shabbos.[9]

In deference to the *seudas melaveh malkah*, one should not over-eat during *seudah shelishis*. However, it is permissible to eat as much as one enjoys during the *seudah shelishis*, even if he becomes satiated to the point that he cannot eat *melaveh malkah* as soon as Shabbos departs. He is not obligated to detract from the *oneg Shabbos* of the Shabbos meals (or to eat *seudah shelishis* earlier in the day) in order to leave an appetite for an immediate *melaveh malkah*. This is because the obligation to eat three meals on Shabbos is more stringent than the obligation to eat *melaveh malkah*.[10] As mentioned, if one is still satiated from *seudah shelishis*, he should wait even until the late hours of the night to fulfill the mitzvah of *melaveh malkah* with bread.

Women are obligated in *seudas melaveh malkah* to the same extent as men are.[11] This is because they are included in all the mitzvos of Shabbos (including *seudah shelishis,* contrary to popular belief). Some have a tradition that proper fulfillment of the mitzvah of *seudas melaveh malkah* is a *segulah* for an easy birth.[12]

Some authorities[13] rule that one should remain in his Shabbos attire until after *Havdalah*. Others[14] suggest that Shabbos clothing not be changed until after *seudas melaveh malkah*.

Many have a *minhag* to sing *zemiros* and light candles at the *seudas melaveh malkah*, just as they do when Shabbos arrives.[15]

---

7. *Mishnah Berurah* 300:1, based on the *Magen Avraham*.
8. *Gemara Shabbos,* ibid., encourages one to eat hot bread and drink a hot beverage on Motza'ei Shabbos.
9. *Shaarei Teshuvah* ibid.
10. *Shulchan Aruch HaRav* 300:3; *Mishnah Berurah,* ibid.:2. See *Rambam, Hilchos Shabbos* 30:5, who can be understood to equate *seudas melaveh malkah* with the other meals of Shabbos.
11. *Machatzis Hashekel,* ibid.
12. *Piskei Teshuvos,* ibid., quoting the *Orchos Chaim Spinka*.
13. *Magen Avraham* 262:2.
14. *Kaf HaChaim,* ibid.
15. *Taz,* ibid.:1; *Mishnah Berurah,* ibid. 3.

As you can clearly see from the sources, eating the *seudas melaveh malkah* in an elegant, joyous atmosphere is an important aspect of *kevod Shabbos*. It is also a source of *berachah* for the week ahead. It is important to make time and to work up an appetite for this important *seudah*.

Some mitzvos are somewhat difficult to perform because of the constant battle we wage with our *yetzer hara*. However, *mitzvos* that require us to eat delicious food should not be among the more difficult. Everyone has a favorite dish, and the natural "*yetzer hara*" for food can be used as a tool in fulfilling this mitzvah. Although one should ideally fulfill all *mitzvos* completely *lishmah*, if he is having difficulty with *melaveh malkah*, he can rely on *Chazal's* principle that "*mitoch shelo lishmah ba lishmah*."

HALACHOS AROUND THE YEAR

Yom Tov Gifts
for One's Wife

My wife recently pointed out (in a nice way) that there is a requirement for every married man to give a gift to his spouse for each of the Shalosh Regalim (Pesach, Shavuos, and Succos). Although I will certainly try to accommodate, I was wondering whether it is a strict halachic requirement or simply good advice to enhance shalom bayis. If it is halachically mandated, what are the parameters and practical applications?

PART 1: THE HALACHIC REQUIREMENT

The *Shulchan Aruch*[1] rules that one is obligated to reach and maintain a state of happiness during Yom Tov. This obligation is incumbent on all adult males; there is a *machlokes* regarding whether women

---

1. *Orach Chaim* 529:2.

are obligated in this mitzvah just as men are.[2] The *Shulchan Aruch*[3] further explains that an adult male is obligated to bring happiness to those around him, such as his wife, children, and anyone in his care. To accomplish this, men should drink wine[4] and eat meat.[5] Women of the household should be given nice clothing or jewelry, and the children should be given snacks.[6]

_____ PART 2: THE PARAMETERS OF SPENDING

One should not limit one's budget for Yom Tov needs to the absolute necessities; rather, one should spend freely, in order to make the Yom Tov a joyous occasion for everyone. The *Gemara*[7] states that the exact amount of money a person will receive during the year is determined on Rosh Hashanah, with the exclusion of money spent for Shabbos and Yom Tov (and for his son's Torah education). Hashem will add to one's yearly allotment any money spent for the *kavod* and *oneg* (honor and enjoyment) of Shabbos or Yom Tov. The Gemara says that Hashem declares: "*Levu Alai va'Ani poreia* — Borrow from Me and I will repay," and, therefore, one should spend generously for Shabbos and Yom Tov needs.

However, spending with some discretion is advisable, for this "money-back guarantee" comes with certain restrictions.

The *Gemara in Pesachim* (112a) rules that one should eat a simple weekday diet on Shabbos (or even skip *seudah shelishis* if one cannot afford it) rather than to ask for support from others in order to have a festive Shabbos or Yom Tov meal (*asei Shabbascha chol ve'al titztarech labriyos*).

Tosafos[8] raises the question: If we are guaranteed by Hashem that He will repay any funds we borrow for Shabbos and Yom Tov ex-

---

2. See *Rosh Hashanah* 6b; *Rambam Hilchos Yom Tov* 6:17-18; *Raavad, Kesef Mishneh* and *Lechem Mishneh* in *Hilchos Chagigah* 1:1; *Teshuvos Rabbi Akiva Eiger siman alef.*
3. Ibid.
4. *Shulchan Aruch* 529:1.
5. *Mishnah Berurah* 529:11, based on *Rambam, Hilchos Yom Tov* 6:18.
6. *Rambam*, ibid.
7. *Beitzah* 15b.
8. Ibid., *d"h Levu Alai va'Ani poreia.*

penses, why should we not ask others for help — at least for loans that Hashem will repay?

Tosafos (according to our text) answers that the directives to borrow money (and Hashem's guarantee concerning repayment) applies only when we can realistically expect to pay it back based on our actual financial means (the guarantee assures us that the amount spent will not be counted toward our yearly budget allotment).

The loans discussed in *Beitzah* refers to a person borrowing due to a temporary slump in business income or because his assets are not currently liquid.[9] The *Gemara* in *Pesachim*, however, deals with a person who is indigent, and who would be borrowing funds that he would not be able to repay under natural circumstances. In this situation, the *Gemara* rules that one should make the most basic Shabbos rather than resort to borrowing money or accepting charity.

It should be noted, however, that once someone has fallen into circumstances where he is forced to depend on charity, the community must provide him with enough for three full Shabbos meals and two meals on each day of Yom Tov.[10]

Therefore, one should not overextend oneself to purchase gifts that are not affordable based on one's current or expected income. It is interesting to note that the Vilna Gaon suggests a different *girsa* (text) for the answer in *Tosafos*. This alternative version rules that Shabbos food should be kept simple only if there is no one willing to extend a loan. If the needy person can obtain a loan, then the money should be spent on fine Shabbos and Yom Tov cuisine .This is the case even if the recipient of the loan has no concrete financial plan concerning repayment. (It would appear that the lender must be notified of that risk.) This explanation assumes a higher level of *bitachon* and *emunah*, as well as *mesirus nefesh* for the *mitzvos* of *kavod*, *oneg*, and *simchah*.

If the word of caution concerning overspending might even apply to Shabbos and Yom Tov expenditures, one must certainly exercise restraint the rest of the year, even when spending money for so noble a cause as bringing happiness to your spouse and children. The *Beur*

---

9. See *Maharshal*, quoted in margin of *Tosafos*, ibid.
10. See *Mishnah Berurah* 242:1, *Shaarei Tziyun* 6.

Halachah[11] bemoans the current practice of overspending (and this was before the days of credit cards), and says that the purchasing of unnecessary luxuries is a terrible plague, and leads to embarrassment due to financial ruin as well as thievery to support one's lavish lifestyle (this is besides the massive amounts of time taken away from Torah learning in order to pay for the excessive expenditures).

Regarding year-round spending, the *Gemara* does tell us[12] that Rava advised the people of his city to spend money generously to buy gifts for their wives, for not only is it an important ingredient for a successful marriage, it is a *segulah* for wealth as well. Based on the above, a man must balance the desire to make his spouse happy with a realistic budget. A person must be generous, but within his means. It is important not to go broke trying to merit a *segulah* for wealth.

We must also entertain the possibility that the "money-back guarantee" for expenditures on Shabbos and Yom Tov would be ensured only if the spending was done for the sole purpose of the mitzvah. If the intention is just to enjoy good food and display expensive clothing, the guarantee might not apply.

_____ PART 3: PRACTICAL APPLICATIONS

The above sources teach us that there is indeed a halachic obligation to purchase items for your wife that will enhance her *simchas Yom Tov*. Although the *Shulchan Aruch* designates clothing and jewelry as gifts of choice, the list may not necessarily be limited to these items. Any gift that brings happiness during the Yom Tov may fulfill the requirement, even if the gift is usable only before Yom Tov (e.g., a new mixer or oven) in preparation for the needs of the *chag*. HaGaon HaRav Shlomo Zalman Auerbach would, on occasion, purchase kitchenware for his rebbetzin prior to Yom Tov. He is quoted as allowing the purchase of any item that enhances the wife's *simchas Yom Tov*, even if the item cannot be used on the Yom Tov itself.[13] However, HaGaon

---

11. *Orach Chaim* 529 d"h *Ve'al yetzamtzem behotzaas Yom Tov.*
12. *Bava Metzia* 59a.
13. *Halichos Shlomo,* page 210, footnote 4 in *Archos Halachah.*

HaRav Yosef Shalom Elyashiv, *shlita*, rules that one fulfills the mitzvah of bringing *simchah* to one's wife on Yom Tov only through the purchase of clothing and/or jewelry. It is advisable, therefore, to attempt to purchase clothing or jewelry, but if that is difficult, one may buy any item that brings happiness for the Yom Tov.

Many husbands point out that they are not in a position to purchase clothing and jewelry for their wives, because they do not know what to buy. They claim, and wives will frequently concur, that their taste in vendors and fashion would not necessarily be to their spouses' liking. They also complain that their choices of past gifts were not received with joy and excitement, but rather with surprise, bewilderment, and sometimes even tears. One husband commented that he came to the realization that he will never fully understand his wife, for despite her golden *middos* and constant display of *hakaras hatov* for the many things he does for the family, his gifts never seem to evoke a feeling of warmth and happiness. I informed him that many men grapple with this issue, and he need not be overly concerned. The art of gift-giving is acquired over time, and the learning curve is longer for some than for others (and in the meantime he should not cast blame on his wife).

I told him the story of a couple I know who have a wonderful marriage despite the debacle of his first attempted gift. This nice fellow bought a new anti-aging cream for his wife and couldn't understand why she was so upset when she received it. After crying for a few days, she told him, "It's the thought that counts, but in the future, please allow me to buy my own present."

If you feel that your wife would appreciate a gift that *she* can choose, either plan a shopping trip together, when she can choose her own gift, or simply tell her before Yom Tov that you would like her to buy something special for herself and that she will be your *shaliach* (messenger) to fulfill the mitzvah. Often the wife has full access to the family money reserve via her credit card, ATM card, and checkbook, and she purchases whatever clothing and kitchen appliances she might need throughout the year. Before Yom Tov, however, you should remind her to buy something special, so that it is bought especially to enhance *simchas Yom Tov* .She can even make the purchase at a convenient time during the year (like when it is on sale or when she is out shopping anyway) and first use the item for her *simchas Yom Tov*.

In conclusion, it is also important to remember the admonition of *Chazal* concerning the giving of *tzedakah* for the Yom Tov needs of the poor, as well as the great mitzvah of *hachnasas orchim* in inviting the lonely and forlorn members of the community for Yom Tov meals. To paraphrase the words of the Rambam:[14] When a person eats and drinks he is obligated to feed the stranger, the orphan, and the widow, as well as other poor and unfortunate people. One who locks the door of his courtyard and eats and drinks alone with his wife and children without giving food and drink to the poor and the embittered does not have the *simchah* of performing *mitzvos* but has only the *simchah* of the stomach.

Let us each focus on bringing *simchah* to our spouse and children on Yom Tov, and let us not forget the need and obligation to bring happiness to others as well.

---

14. *Hilchos Yom Tov* 6:18.

Yom Tov Candle-lighting Time

Q What is the proper time to perform the mitzvah of hadlakas neros for Yom Tov? One must obviously light Shabbos candles before Shabbos, as lighting on Shabbos would constitute chillul Shabbos. However, on Yom Tov, perhaps we have more time to light since it is permissible to kindle a flame on Yom Tov.

I am also confused about the time of lighting on the second day of Yom Tov. Should one light before sunset or after the second day of Yom Tov has arrived (after nightfall)?

Many women light *neros* before Yom Tov comes in, at the same time they usually light candles on Erev Shabbos.[1] Although the transfer

---

1. See introduction to *Tur Yoreh Deah* by the son of the *Drishah*. *Ba'er Heiteiv Orach Chaim*, end of Chapter 503 notes that the candles should be lit before Yom Tov so that the people do not come home to a dark house. Now that we have electric lights, this reason would not apply.

of fire is permitted on Yom Tov, this custom assumes that it is proper to light early so that one has completed all preparations for Yom Tov before it actually commences, just as one concludes all preparations for Shabbos (such as bathing, dressing, and setting the table) before Shabbos is accepted. It is considered an expression of *kavod* (respect) for Shabbos and Yom Tov to finish all preparations beforehand, even if one could continue preparing after dark without violating any *halachos*.

Other women have the custom of lighting after dark, right before the meal begins.

Some suggest that this custom developed due to the fact that the correct time to light Yom Tov candles on the second night is specifically after the second day has been ushered in, as we will explain below.

In order to prevent confusion and possible mistakes, a custom developed to perform the mitzvah of *hadlakas neros* after Yom Tov has been ushered in (after Maariv) even on the first day of Yom Tov.[2]

The candles of the second night of Yom Tov must be lit after nightfall. The reason one should not light shortly before the second night of Yom Tov as we do when lighting on Erev Shabbos (and for many, when lighting candles for the first day of Yom Tov) is because the advent of electricity obviates the need for candles to provide light in our homes in the late afternoon. Since the candles' light is not needed at that time, *hadlakas neros* is being done only for the second day of Yom Tov. It is therefore prohibited, as is any *melachah* done without authentic need. It would constitute *hachanah* from the first day of Yom Tov to the second as well.[3]

Families should light candles the first night of Yom Tov based on the family's *minhag*. One who is uncertain should consult their Rav for direction.

As mentioned, the proper time to light *neros* on the second night of Yom Tov is after dark.

---

2. *Mishnas Yaavetz* 34.
3. See *Mishnah Berurah* 514:33, which permits lighting in the late afternoon of the first day of *Yom Tov* because it adds necessary light in the house. That reasoning does not seem to be pertinent today, when electric lights sufficiently illuminate all areas of the home.

Practical Pesach Pointers

Q

When does the Rav sell my chametz when Erev Pesach is Shabbos? Are there any special provisions that apply to the sale on those years?

A

When Erev Pesach is Shabbos, *chametz* is sold on Friday. Although many Rabbanim sell *chametz* to the non-Jew before the sixth halachic hour so that no mistake is made other years, when Erev Pesach is on a weekday, the sale may be done until right before Shabbos.

A clause is put in the contract to indicate that the sale takes effect shortly before Shabbos. The *chametz* to be eaten on Shabbos should not be included in the sale.

Q

When is bedikas chametz performed when Erev Pesach is Shabbos? What are my options for chametz removal in those years?

When Erev Pesach is Shabbos, *bedikas chametz* is performed on Thursday night, and the *chametz*, except for that being kept for use over Shabbos, is burned before the end of the fifth halachic hour of the day on Friday morning.[1] The *minhag* is to maintain a schedule that is as close as possible to a weekday Erev Pesach, in order to ensure that people are accustomed to burning their *chametz* at approximately the same time every year.

Bitul chametz (declaration of nullification) should not be done until after the *chametz* is disposed of before the end of the fifth halachic hour on Shabbos.

Although the sale and destruction of *chametz* is performed earlier in the day in deference to the regular Erev Pesach schedule, one is still permitted to eat *chametz* the entire Erev Shabbos, just as he is permitted to eat *chametz* on Shabbos itself (until the *zeman issur achilas chametz*).

Laundry, haircuts, and nailcutting, although normally prohibited on Erev Pesach after *chatzos*, are not prohibited on Erev Shabbos when Erev Pesach is Shabbos. The *minhag* to treat the day like a regular Erev Pesach applies only to *biur chametz* and *mechiras chametz*, which if done late on a regular year violates a Torah prohibition.[2]

What can one eat during the Shabbos/ Erev Pesach meals?

Technically, one can eat *chametz* during the night meal and the morning meal, as long as he completes the *seudah* before the end of the fourth halachic hour of the morning. However, due to difficulty in ensuring that no *chametz* will be spread around the house, many opt to eat only a small amount of challah (or pita bread, which leaves fewer crumbs. One should make sure that the pita is *pas Yisrael*, for the custom on Shabbos and Yom Tov is to eat only *pas Yisrael*[3]).

---

1. *Beis Yosef* 444; *Mishnah Berurah* ibid. 9.
2. *Chikrei Lev* 88: see *Beur Halachah* 468:1.
3. See *Mishnah Berurah* 242:6.

One should eat at least the minimum: an egg-sized piece of chal-lah. The size of an egg is preferable to the size of an olive, because many *poskim* rule that one can only recite the *berachah Al Netilas Yadayim* when washing for bread if he will eat an amount equal to at least the size of an egg. The challah should be eaten over a tissue or napkin, and with the crumbs disposed of by flushing them down the toilet. The table is then cleared, the floor is swept, and the rest of the meal is served with a completely *kosher lePesach* menu. Any leftover *chametz* must be disposed of by the end of the fifth halachic hour of the day by flushing, as mentioned above. Leaving *chametz* in the garbage bin is problematic because it will then still be considered your property.

Those who are apprehensive about the prospect of dealing with even a small amount of *chametz* opt to wash *netilas yadayim* and recite *Hamotzi* on "Kosher for Pesach" egg matzos.[4] The egg matzah must be eaten by the end of the fourth halachic hour of the morning (which is the *sof zeman achilah* — check your local calendar for the exact time), and the remainder then put away with the *chametz*.

How does one fulfill the mitzvah of seudah shelishis on Shabbos that is Erev Pesach?

Regarding the obligation to eat *seudah shelishis* on this special Shabbos, there are two main opinions.

The *Rema*[5] suggests that one eat meat, fish, fruits, or vegetables in the afternoon in order to fulfill the mitzvah of *seudah shelishis* in its proper time. For those who eat *gebrokts*, some suggest that one

---

4. See *Beis Yosef* 444, which mentions this option but comments that it is difficult for the average person to make *matzah ashirah* [egg matzos] for this purpose. In the time of the *Beis Yosef* and until recently, egg matzos were not typically baked or mass produced; *Igros Moshe Orach Chaim* 1:155 also allows the use of egg matzos for the *Shabbos seudah*.

On Pesach, these matzos may only be used by the elderly or infirm.

Although one usually recites a *mezonos* on egg matzos, by basing his entire meal on them, he gives them the status of *hamotzi*, like other *pas haba'ah b'kisnin*. *Igros Moshe*, ibid., offers another reasoning for citing *hamotzi* on egg matzos in this situation.

5. Ibid. 1.

should have a *kneidel* to fulfill the mitzvah of *seudah shelishis*, for a *mezonos* product is more preferable than other types of foods for the fulfillment of this mitzvah. Although one may not eat matzah or most matzah products on Erev Pesach, these opinions maintain that is permissible to eat *kneidlach*[6] since they are cooked (cake made with matzah meal is not permitted).

If one is eating *kneidlach,* he should partake of these foods before the beginning of the tenth halachic hour of the day. If he has not fulfilled the mitzvah of *seudah shelishis* by that time, he should no longer eat *kneidlach* and must eat only other foods for the *seudah*. One should be careful with how much he eats, so that he should have a healthy appetitie for the matzah at the Seder.[7]

Other *poskim*[8] rule that one should split the morning *seudah* into two parts. The first part should contain the regular Shabbos menu, although one must leave room for the second meal. One *bentches* after the first meal and takes a break for about half an hour,[9] or less if he is pressed for time.[10] He should preferably take a walk or at the least leave the table between the meals.[11] He then washes again, says *hamotzi*, and eats an egg-size portion of challah.

By eating this second meal for *seudah shelishis* in the morning before the *issur zeman achilas chametz*, one has the advantage of being able to eat challah for *seudah shelishis*, which is the preferable way of fulfilling the mitzvah. The disadvantage of this method is that many *poskim* claim one cannot fulfill the mitzvah of *seudah shelishis* in the morning. If possible, it is suggested that one fulfill the mitzvah of *seudah shelishis* according to both opinions. He should split the morning meal and partake of permissible foods in the afternoon.

Is it permissible to prepare for the Pesach Seder on Shabbos in order to begin as promptly as possible?

6. See *Mishnah Berurah* 444: 8, *Shaar HaTziyun* 1.
7. See *Shulchan Aruch Orach Chaim* 471:1; *Magen Avraham*, ibid. 2.
8. See *Mishneh Berurah*, ibid. 8.
9. See *Igros Chazon Ish* 1:188.
10. *Shulchan Aruch Orach Chaim* 291:3 gives no minimum time that one must wait after *bentching*.
11. *Mishnah Berurah* 291:14.

One should attempt to complete his Seder preparations before Shabbos. It is very important to begin the Seder on Motza'ei Shabbos as soon as possible so that the children will be awake and alert enough to recite the questions in the *Mah Nishtanah* and to hear the answers as well.

Despite the importance of preparing for the Seder, the preparations do not override Shabbos. Therefore, when possible, one should prepare the matzos, the Seder plate, and whatever else is necessary on Erev Shabbos. One who is eating the Shabbos meals in a room other than the dining room will be able to set the dining-room table for the Seder before Shabbos, guaranteeing a prompt and tension-free start to the Seder.

One can sleep on Shabbos afternoon to prepare for the late-night Seder, but he should not say that he is napping for that specific purpose.

Women's Obligation to Recite the Haggadah

My wife tends to the needs of the Pesach Seder for our family each year and finds it challenging to read the entire Haggadah, or even most of it. Is there an obligation for women to read the Haggadah, or is it a minhag to fulfill when possible? If it is indeed an actual obligation, is there a bare minimum that is necessary to fulfill the mitzvah?

There is a dispute in the *Rishonim* and *poskim* concerning the level of obligation of women to engage in the mitzvah of *sippur yetzias Mitzrayim* (reciting the story of our redemption from Egypt) through the reciting of the *Haggadah*.

Rambam[1] exempts women from the Biblical obligation because it is a *mitzvas asei shehazeman gerama* (a time-bound mitzvah), from which women are exempt.

Sefer HaChinuch,[2] however, rules that women have a *mitzvah*

---

1. *Hilchos Avodah Zarah* 12:3.
2. *Mitzvah* 21.

mi'd'Oraisa (a Biblical obligation) to fulfill *sippur yetzias Mitzrayim* on Pesach night.

Some suggest that women are obligated to tell the story as an off-shoot of the mitzvah of matzah, which is called *lechem oni — lechem she'onim alav devarim harbeh* (a bread upon which much commentary and background is offered). Since women are obligated in the mitzvah of eating matzah,[3] according to this opinion they are also obligated in the mitzvah of relating the story behind it.[4]

The *poskim* assume that even if women are not obligated *mi'd'Oraisa* in the mitzvah of *sippur yetzias Mitzrayim*, there is at least a *mitzvah d'Rabbanan* to do so.[5] *Mishnah Berurah* 473:64 rules that to fulfill the minimum obligation properly, all women must hear (or recite) Kiddush and recite the *Haggadah's* discussion of the three primary mitzvos: *Pesach*, matzah, and *maror* (רַבָּן גַּמְלִיאֵל הָיָה אוֹמֵר, כָּל שֶׁלֹּא אָמַר שְׁלֹשָׁה דְבָרִים אֵלּוּ בַּפֶּסַח לֹא יָצָא יְדֵי חוֹבָתוֹ..., *Rabban Gamliel used to say, "One who has not said these three things on Pesach has not fulfilled his obligation…"*). The *Mishnah Berurah* adds that it is customary for women to join in the reciting of the ten *makkos* as well.

It goes without saying that, when possible, it is meritorious for women to join the Seder for the entire *Haggadah*, or at least for most of it.

---

3. *Rambam* ibid.
4. HaRav Yosef Shalom Elyashiv, *shlita*, in *Kovetz Teshuvos* 152,
5. *Shulchan Aruch Orach Chaim* 472:14 rules that women are obligated in all the *mitzvos* of the Seder night.

Counting Sefirah
Before Maariv

I often daven Maariv in a shul that has several minyanim. I occasionally arrive toward the end of the previous Maariv, at the time when the tzibbur is counting sefirah. Should I count sefirah with them, or should I wait until I daven Maariv and count sefirah after my own davening?

Based on the rule of *tadir veshe'eino tadir, tadir kodem* (the mitzvah of greater frequency precedes the mitzvah of lesser frequency), you should *daven* Maariv and then count *sefirah. Tefillas* Maariv has greater frequency than *sefiras ha'omer*, thus giving it halachic precedence in this situation.[1] Another reason to *daven* Maariv first is due to the recital of *Krias Shema*, which is a mitzvah *mi'd'Oraisa* and therefore supersedes *sefiras ha'omer*, which, according to many *poskim*, is a *mitzvah diRabbanan* in today's times.[2]

If one came to Maariv as the *minyan* was counting *sefirah* and there

---

1. *Beur Halachah* 489, *d"h achar tefillas Arvis*, in the name of the *Chok Yaakov.*
2. See *Beur Halachah* ibid. *d"h lispor ha'omer.*

was no other *minyan* afterward, some rule that one should count the *omer* with the congregation. This is because the advantage of counting the *omer* with the *tzibbur* (*Berov am hadras Melech*) outweighs the rule of *tadir veshe'eino tadir, tadir kodem*.[3] It also eliminates the risk of possibly forgetting to count later.

Others rule that even in such a circumstance one should count *sefirah* after Maariv, even if he will be saying it alone.[4]

---

3. *Minchas Yitzchak* 9:56; see *Piskei Teshuvos* 489, footnote 15 and 16 for a discussion of the position of the Chazon Ish on this matter.
4. *Teshuvos Vehanhagos* 2:248; see there the *Shaagas Aryeh*'s ruling that one should daven Maariv before *Kiddush Levanah* because of the rule of *tadir*, even when it was the last night that one could possibly recite *Kiddush Levanah*. Despite the risk of "losing" the *levanah*, the *Shaagas Aryeh* insisted that Maariv be recited first. *Sefer Shaarei Horaah* brings a similar *psak halachah* in the name of Rav Chaim Volozhiner.

Lechaim During Sefirah

My son is about to become a chassan, and we would like to make a lechayim or vort as soon as possible. Are there any halachic issues regarding making this type of simchah during sefirah?

One is allowed to mark the occasion of an engagement with a lechayim or even a meal or a vort during the days of *sefirah*.

However, dancing is prohibited even without the accompaniment of live music.[1] The custom to refrain from dancing applies even to a small, insignificant dance in a home setting, and even if only a few people participate.[2] Music is certainly prohibited as well.

---

1. *Magen Avraham* 493:1; *Mishnah Berurah* 493:3.
2. Rav Shlomo Zalman Auerbach quoted in *sefer Bein Pesach LeShavuos*, Chapter 15, footnote 1, based on his interpretation of *rikudim* and *mecholos*.

Reciting of Shehecheyanu
During the Days of Sefirah

*My family minhag is to keep the laws
of sefirah until shortly before Shavuos.
I am in need of a new suit, and I have
heard conflicting opinions concerning
the permissibility of reciting the
berachah of Shehecheyanu during the
days of sefirah. As I normally recite
Shehecheynu for such an expensive
purchase, am I allowed to buy the suit
and wear it during the sefirah?*

The custom is not to recite the *berachah* of *Shehecheyanu* during
Bein Hamitzarim, the three weeks between Shivah Assar B'Tammuz
and Tishah B'Av,[1] which is the period of national mourning for the
destruction of the *Beis HaMikdash.*

The days of *sefirah* are not as formal or stringent a time of mourning as the *Bein Hamitzarim* (the Three Weeks). Although the calamity
of the passing of 24,000 students of Rabbi Akiva has given rise to various customs of mourning and avoidance of *simchos*, the time period

---

1. *Shulchan Aruch Orach Chaim 551:17. See Mishnah Berurah 98.*

of *sefirah* still retains its distinguished place in the Jewish calendar. It is a time of preparation and excitement as we draw close to *kabbalas haTorah* with the Yom Tov of Shavuos. The *mefarshim* stress the holiness of the days of *sefirah* by pointing out that these days have a status, on an esoteric level, of a Chol Hamoed that connects two Yamim Tovim (Pesach and Shavuos), as well as a time of purification for *Klal Yisrael*.

This distinction between the Three Weeks and *sefirah* has led many *poskim* to rule that there is no prohibition to recite *Shehecheynanu* during the days of *sefirah*.[2]

Others have ruled that one should refrain from reciting *Shehecheyanu* even during the days of *sefirah*, in deference to the theme of mourning that is pervasive during these days.[3] Some rule that even according to these stringent opinions, one may recite *Shehecheyanu* on Shabbos; many opinions allow *Shehecheyanu* on Shabbos even during the Three Weeks.[4] Others are stringent even on Shabbos.[5]

Many *poskim* limit their leniency to reciting *Shehecheyanu* on new fruits. They suggest that one try to avoid the purchase of expensive clothing during *sefirah*, thereby avoiding the recital of *Shehecheyanu*.[6]

If you can delay the purchase of the suit till after *sefirah,* it may be meritorious to do so, and one may certainly be lenient if he needs the suit immediately. It would be advantageous to wear the suit for the first time on Shabbos and recite the *Shehecheyanu* at that time.

If a new suit is needed for Shavuos and must be purchased during *sefirah* in order to be tailored on time for Yom Tov, you may buy the suit and recite the *Shehecheyanu* on Yom Tov, when you wear it for the first time.

---

2. *Mishnah Berurah* 493:2, see the comment from HaRav Chaim Kanievsky brought in *sefer Bein Pesach LeShavuos*, Chapter 16, footnote 1, that *Mishnah Berurah* allows the recital of *Shehecheyanu* even *l'chatichlah*. See comment in footnote ibid. for an alternate understanding of the *Mishnah Berurah*'s position; *Kaf HaChaim* ibid. 4; *She'arim Metzuyanim Behalachah* 170:7; *Yabiya Omer* 3:26; *Tosafos Chaim* on *Chayei Adam* 131:12.
3. *Or Zarua* 493:1 in the name of *Rabbeinu Yerucham*; *Leket Yosher* page 97.
4. See *Mishnah Berurah* 551:98.
5. *Yafeh Lalev* 2:493:7.
6. See *Yabiya Omer* ibid.; *Tzitz Eliezer* 18:41.

Berachos on Beverages During the Night of Shavuos

Q *I am looking forward to spending the entire Shavuos night learning and attending shiurim. Like most people, I drink coffee and other non-alcoholic beverages throughout the night in order to remain awake and alert.*

I am confused about the proper procedure for the berachah rishonah (Shehakol) and berachah acharonah (Borei Nefashos). I do not bring the drinks to the table at which I'm learning. The soda, coffee, and cake are kept in the simchah hall, and I usually break for a quick drink every hour or so.

Should I recite Shehakol once at the beginning of the night and have in mind that it should cover all the drinks I take throughout the night, or make a new berachah each time I take a break?

If there is reason to make a berachah each time, I would assume a berachah acharonah (Borei Nefashos) should be recited after I finish the beverage. Is that correct?

It is well known that one can only recite *Bircas Hamazon* as long as he feels satiated from the meal.[1] The approximate time frame given is 72 minutes, although it actually depends on the size of the meal eaten, as well as on the individual's appetite and metabolism.

There is also a limited time frame for the recital of a *berachah acharonah* on all foods and beverages. This time frame, which will also depend on the amount consumed and the speed of digestion, can be considerably less than 72 minutes. It is therefore important to recite the *Borei Nefashos* as soon as the beverage is finished. One should then recite a new *Shehakol* on the next beverage later on in the night.

(Please note that one generally recites a *Borei Nefashos* on a drink only if at least three and a half ounces were consumed quickly. There is debate if this applies to hot drinks that are usually sipped slowly, like coffee or tea.[2])

Although there are many *poskim*[3] who rule that one can recite a *berachah rishonah* with the intent that it should cover food or drink for an extended period of time (as long as there is no very large gap of time, change of location, or *hesech hadaas* (distraction) between the various portions of food or drink), there are those who disagree and claim that once the food has been digested, a new *berachah rishonah*

---

1. *Shulchan Aruch Orach Chaim* 184:5
2. See *Mishnah Berurah* 210:1, *Shemiras Shabbos Kehilchasah* 54, footnote 96.
3. See *Shaar Hatziyun* 184:18.

is required, because we compare limitations of *berachah rishonah* to those of *berachah acharonah* and *bentching*.[4] Additionally, your Torah study may constitute *hesech hadaas*.

It is therefore prudent to avoid this dispute and make a separate *berachah* at each coffee and soda break. You will also have the advantage of reciting a *Borei Nefashos* in its proper time rather than reciting it at the end of the night, which would only cover the most recent beverage consumed.[5]

---

4. *Magen Avraham* 184:9.
5. *Halichos Shlomo, Moadim* 12:3, see footnote in *dvar halachah* #4.

Learning Torah and Chanukah Get-Togethers

Baruch Hashem, I have a very large extended family, as does my wife. Between us, we have yearly invitations to over fifteen Chanukah mesibos! Not only is it logistically impossible to attend every mesibah, but I have found that these family gatherings wreak havoc on my learning throughout Chanukah. Last year I missed every one of my nightly sedarim due to the daily Chanukah activities.

I feel it is unfair and hashkafically unbalanced when I receive a negative reaction from our families when I assert that I cannot attend every mesibah due to my learning schedule; yet when my brother-in-law the attorney says he cannot come because he has important clients to see in the evening, he is immediately forgiven. This is due to the fact that he is making money, whereas "all" I want to do is sit and learn!

Is there a mitzvah to attend these mesibos? Do I have an obligation to go, even at the expense of my learning?

A This question is one that applies to many people, and each situation must be dealt with with an understanding of the circumstances amd that remains true to *halachah* and yet sensitive to issues of family and *shalom bayis*. Every person should consult his rav or rebbi for guidance, and I would not attempt to offer a "one-answer-fits-all" response.

What I would like to do is explore some of the underlying issues.

Let's start by discussing whether there is a mitzvah to make a *mesibah* or a *seudah* during the days of Chanukah.

The *Shulchan Aruch*[1] rules that festive meals are not required during Chanukah, because *Chazal* did not institute a mitzvah of eating and drinking to commemorate the miracles that occurred. In this respect, Chanukah is unlike Purim. *Chazal* instituted a mitzvah to eat and drink on Purim to celebrate the miracle that we were saved from physical annihilation. The celebration of Chanukah focuses on the fact that Hashem saved us from spiritual annihilation, and therefore we celebrate and commemorate the miracle in a more *ruchniusdig* (spiritual) way, through *l'hodos ul'hallel*, expressing our gratitude and lauding Hashem through *tefillos, shiros, v'tishbachos* — prayer, song, and praises.[2]

The Rema[3] says that there is a mitzvah to have extra meals to commemorate the completion of the *Mishkan* in the time of Moshe Rabbeinu. (Work on the *Mishkan* was finished on 25 Kislev, although it was inaugurated in Nissan.) We are also commemorating the rededi-

---

1. *Orach Chaim* 670:2.
2. *Mishnah Berurah*, ibid.6.
3. Ibid.

cation of the *Beis HaMikdash* on 25 Kislev at the time of *nes Chanukah*. The Rema comments that the *minhag* is to make the meal a *seudas mitzvah* by adding songs of praise to Hashem and discussing the great miracle that occurred during this time.

The Maharshal[4] states that the Chanukah *seudah* be replete with a celebration of Torah learning, and advises that one should not cancel his set time to learn for the sake of a Chanukah *mesibah*. He bemoans the fact that there are those who gather for frivolous activities instead of sanctifying the time with *zemiros, tishbachos,* and other spiritual pursuits.

Even if the *mesibah* is a *seduas mitzvah*, one would have to carefully weigh the obligation to learn against his performance of other *mitzvos*. There is a general rule that one is allowed to interrupt Torah learning only in order to perform *mitzvos* that cannot be performed by others, such as *mitzvos* that are incumbent upon each individual to perform (*mitzvos sheb'gufo* — e.g., *tefillin*, matzah, *succah*) or any acts of *chessed* or community needs that will not be taken care of by others.[5]

Not only is the importance of *talmud Torah* greater than any other single mitzvah, but the sheer quantity of *mitzvos* that can be fulfilled through learning gives it precedence over any other mitzvah (according to the guidelines set forth above). The Vilna Gaon[6] explains that every single word of Torah is an independent mitzvah, and therefore hundreds of *mitzvos* can be fulfilled in a very brief period. *Talmud Torah* is therefore chosen over other *mitzvos* that can be performed in the same time frame, because one can accomplish so many more *mitzvos* in the same time frame.

It is certainly acceptable and commendable to attend and enjoy a Chanukah *mesibah*. In addition to the *mitzvos* of Chanukah, there are issues of *shalom bayis, chinuch habanim* (including the value of showing children the beauty and *simchah* of Chanukah). These are the factors that a rav or rebbi will balance against the the obligation of *talmud Torah*.

The contrast in their response to you and your brother-in-law the

---

4. *Siman 85: Beur Halachah, Orach Chaim, d"h v'nohagim lomar.*
5. *Yerushalmi Pesachim 3:7; Rambam Hilchos Talmud Torah 3:4; Shulchan Aruch 241:18.*
6. *Shenos Eliyahu, perek aleph, Pe'ah.*

attorney is indeed troubling. It is extremely unfortunate that there are still those in our community who understand a professional's absence from *mesibos* or *simchos* because of his professionial "obligations," but who are far less accepting when it comes to empathy for lost learning time. Learning with diligence should ideally be placed on the highest pedestal, but, at the very least, it ought to be considered at least as honorable an undertaking as earning money.

In general, people bear in mind that Chanukah is a time that is especially propitious for focus and success in Torah learning (this is especially true of *Torah Sheb'al Peh,* such as *Mishnayos* and *Gemara*[7]).

The Shelah HaKadosh[8] writes that the holy days of Chanukah are particularly conducive to *hasmadah* in learning. The Shelah bemoans the fact that many, unfortunately, take time from Torah learning and occupy themselves with spiritually empty activities.

The Kedushas Levi[9] writes that it is proper for every Jew to focus on diligent Torah learning "because it is during these days that *HaKadosh Baruch Hu* began to bestow upon us the special light of His Torah."

Chanukah is an auspicious time to focus on the *pasuk* in *Mishlei* "*Ki ner mitzvah v'Torah ohr.*"[10]

May *Hashem* help us all imbue ourselves and others with the light of Torah at the *mesibos* we do attend, as well as during all the days and nights of Chanukah.

---

7. See *Pri Tzaddik, Parashas Miketz.*
8. *Sof inyanei tefillah.*
9. *Derushim l'Chanukah, d"h yadua.*
10. Ibid. 26:3.

Purchasing a Home
During the Three Weeks

*I am going to contract for the purchase
of a home, and the (non-Jewish) seller
would very much like to close rather
quickly. The date he specified calls for
a closing around July 25, which comes
out during the Three Weeks.*

*I always assumed that it is prohibited
to purchase or build a home during
times of mourning such as the Three
Weeks and the days of sefirah, and
therefore I am reluctant to accede to
the seller's request.*

*My friend, however, mentioned to me
that his Rav allowed him to purchase
a home during sefirah. Is my entire
assumption concerning the prohibition
incorrect, or is there perhaps a*

difference between the days of sefirah and the Three Weeks?

The *psak halachah* that your friend received from his Rav is not incorrect. Many *poskim* rule that one may purchase a home, as well as do any repairs (including painting and extensions), during *sefirah*. These *poskim* maintain that we refrain from purchasing, building, or repairing a home (for the purposes of *simchah* or luxury) only during the Three Weeks preceding Tishah B'Av. Even during the Three Weeks these activities are permissible if the need is urgent and the work is for functional purposes.[1] Although we prohibit weddings, music, and dancing during the *sefirah* period, as we do during the Three Weeks, we do not apply many stringencies of the Three Weeks to the *sefirah* period.[2]

Others rule that one should avoid taking possession of a new home during *sefirah* because it is an activity that engenders extreme *simchah* and therefore contradicts the theme of mourning during *sefirah*.[3]

If all things were equal and a delay in the closing would not cause financial loss or other hardships, it would be better to take possession of a new home after the days of *sefirah*, thereby avoiding the dispute mentioned above. Your friend obviously had a situation where delaying his closing would have been difficult; hence, his Rav's ruling was in consonance with the ruling of most *poskim*.

As mentioned above, the laws of mourning for the period of the Three Weeks are more stringent than are the customs of mourning during *sefirah*. One should therefore make every attempt to avoid purchasing a home during that time. If the seller is not willing to compromise on the closing date and you risk losing the house, you may purchase it if it is being bought for the basic needs of the family. If the new house is not essential living space but a luxurious expansion, it would generally not be permissible to close during the Three Weeks.

---

1. See *Shulchan Aruch Orach Chaim* 551:2 with *Mishnah Berurah*.
2. *Yechaveh Daas* 3:30; *Tzitz Eliezer* 18:41; the *Satmar Rebbe*, zt"l, quoted in *Piskei Teshuvos* 493, footnote 6.
3. *Avnei Tzedek Yoreh Deah* 34; *Bais Mordechai* 30; see *Piskei Teshuvos* ibid., footnote 1, for other opinions that rule stringently on the matter.

Kriyah at the Kosel

I hope, i"yH, to go to Eretz Yisrael for Succos, and would like to have clarified the halachos of kriyah in Yerushalayim and at the Kosel. I have always assumed that there is an obligation, yet I have noticed that many people are not careful to do kriyah. Are there leniencies that I do not know about?

There is indeed an obligation to tear one's garment upon seeing the area where the *Beis HaMikdash* once stood.[1]

There are those who want to avoid this obligation and therefore transfer ownership of their shirt to an acquaintance until the following day. Aside from the question of whether this legal trickery (*ha'aramah*) is effective, it is certainly improper. One should never go out of his way to avoid having to perform *mitzvos*, and doing *kriyah* at the *Kosel* is a *mitzvah d'Rabbanan*. It is extremely ironic that a tourist who spends thousands of dollars traveling to *Eretz Yisrael* will resort to flimsy leniencies to save the minimal cost of a shirt (an inexpensive or old shirt can be used for *kriyah*). One should yearn to fulfill this precious obliga-

---

1. *Mo'ed Katan* 26a; *Shulchan Aruch* 561:2.

tion because it will set the emotional tone and proper frame of mind for the visit to the *Kosel.*

One who is visiting the *Kosel* for the first time, or after an absence of 30 days, must perform *kriyah.* Those who live in Yerushalayim on a consistent basis are exempt from *kriyah.*

Although there is an obligation to tear *kriyah* upon seeing Yerusha-layim (meaning certain sections of the Old City[2]) and *orei Yehudah* (cities that were part of the ancient kingdom of Judah), there is some disagreement about the parameters of this *halachah.*

According to HaRav Moshe Feinstein, *z"tl,* there is no obligation to do *kriyah* for these areas when they are under Jewish control.[3] HaRav Shlomo Zalman Auerbach, *z"tl,* rules that one must perform *kriyah* even in these areas of Yerushalayim.[4]

If one wishes to avoid this dispute, it is advised that when he travels to the *Kosel* for the first time, he should not look at the Old City from afar and instead perform the *kriyah* upon seeing the *Kosel.* If he extends the *kriyah* more than a *tefach,* it will cover both the *Kosel* and Yerushalayim.[5]

Kriyah should be done on the shirt and should begin on the left side (over the heart), under the collar, and go down approximately 3 to 4 inches (one *tefach*). One will need to start the tear carefully with a blade or pen point, but it should be continued by hand. Because of security concerns, it is probably better not to bring any small, sharp objects to the *Kosel* area; instead, it might be prudent to make a short incision before one leaves for the *Kosel.* If the *kriyah* cannot be completed with one's hand, it may be done with a blade.[6]

Before performing the *kriyah,*[7] one should recite the *pasuk,* בֵּית קָדְשֵׁנוּ וְתִפְאַרְתֵּנוּ אֲשֶׁר הִלְלוּךְ אֲבֹתֵינוּ הָיָה לִשְׂרֵפַת אֵשׁ וְכָל מַחֲמַדֵּינוּ הָיָה לְחָרְבָּה, *The Temple of our holiness and our splendor, where our fathers praised You, has become a fiery conflagration, and all that we desired has become a ruin.*[8]

---

2. It is not clear exactly which areas are actually part of the ancient city of Yerushalayim, but the area closest to *Har HaBayis* is certainly included.
3. *Igros Moshe Orach Chaim* 4:70,11.
4. *Minchas Shlomo Kamma* 73:10. חושבני דכל זמן שרואים עדיין בעיר הקודש והמקדש כנסיות של
נכרים וגם קברי עכו"ם וכו', ואין אנו יכולים למעקר למלחנא נוכראה, עדיין היא בחורבנה.
5. See *Shulchan Aruch,* ibid.; *Mishnah Berurah* 9.
6. See *Piskei Teshuvos* 561:4.
7. *Shulchan Aruch* ibid., with *Mishnah Berurah* 6, quoting *Bach.*
8. *Yeshayah* 64:10.

בָּרוּךְ דַּיַּן הָאֱמֶת. כִּי כָל מִשְׁפָּטָיו צֶדֶק וֶאֱמֶת. הַצּוּר One should also say,
תָּמִים פָּעֳלוֹ כִּי כָל דְּרָכָיו מִשְׁפָּט, קֵל אֱמוּנָה וְאֵין עָוֶל צַדִּיק וְיָשָׁר הוּא.[9] וְאַתָּה
צַדִּיק עַל כָּל הַבָּא עָלֵינוּ. כִּי אֱמֶת עָשִׂיתָ. וַאֲנַחְנוּ הִרְשָׁעְנוּ[10], *Blessed is the
true Judge, for all His paths are righteous and true. The Rock! —
perfect is His work, a God of faith without iniquity, righteous and
fair is He. And You are righteous in all that has come upon us, for
You have acted truthfully, while we have acted wickedly."*

It is best for a person to have these verses handy before arriving at
the *Kosel*.

Some suggest that one should refrain from eating meat or drinking
wine the day that one does *kriyah* at the *Kosel*.[11]

Kriyah is not done on Shabbos, Yom Tov, or Chol Hamoed. Although many do not do *kriyah* on Erev Shabbos or Erev Yom Tov
after midday,[12] many *poskim* question the validity of this practice.[13]
Some limit this leniency to one who is visiting the *Kosel* after *plag
haminchah* (1¼ hours before *shekiah*). Others maintain that it applies
only if one is already dressed for Shabbos/Yom Tov.[14]

It is not proper to go to the *Kosel* at a time of questionable obligation if one is doing so only to bypass the mitzvah of *kriyah*. Aside from
the hashkafic issues involved, it is somewhat questionable whether one
would then be exempted from *kriyah* on his next visit, even if it takes
place within 30 days.[15]

Women are obligated in *kriyah* (it may be advisable for them to bring
along safety pins to hold the tear closed for reasons of *tznius*). There is
no obligation of *kriyah*, even for *chinuch* purposes, for minors.[16]

Let us *daven* that these *halachos* will no longer apply in the very
near future. Until then, we must follow the dictates of *Chazal* by
mourning the *Beis HaMikdash* in a tangible way. Doing so will no
doubt be a catalyst for its rebuilding: *Kol hamisabel al Yerushalayim
zocheh v'ro'eh b'simchasah.*

---

9. *Devarim* 32:4.
10. *Nechemiah* 9:33.
11. Ibid.; *Mishnah Berurah* 4.
12. *Ir Hakodesh V'Hamikdash* 3:17:5.
13. See *Orchos Rabbeinu*, Vol. 2, page 149, quoting *Chazon ish*; *Igros Moshe, Yoreh Deah* 3: 52:4.
14. See *Teshuvos Vehanhagos* 1:334.
15. *Igros Moshe* ibid.; *Dinei Yerushalayim V'Hamikdash* 1:25; cf. *Minchas Shlomo* ibid.
16. *Orchos Rabbeinu* ibid. 154.

Pertinent Purim Questions

Q **Who is required to give machatzis hashekel on Erev Purim?**

A The *Rema* (694:1) rules that only males over 20 are required to give *machatzis hashekel*. This is because *machatzis hashekel* is given in the month of Adar as a remembrance of the requirement to give the half-shekel coin in the time of the *Beis HaMikdash* (the coins were collected during Adar since the new accounting year for the purchasing of *korbanos* in the *Beis HaMikdash* began in the month of Nisan), and the *Rema* is of the opinion that the obligation in the *Beis HaMikdash* applied only to males 20 years and above. Other *poskim* argue that any male from bar mitzvah age and up was obligated to give *machatzis hashekel,* and should therefore give the half-shekel before Purim as well. It has become customary for many to give *machatzis hashekel* for sons under bar mitzvah as well. If one began such a custom (or if one's father began giving a *machatzis hashekel* on his behalf), he must continue to do so every year.

It has also become common for many to give *machatzis hashekel* for their wives and daughters as well.[1] This *minhag* is based on the

---

1. *Kaf HaChaim* 694:27.

pasuk that indicates that giving *machatzis hashekel* is an atonement --- "*lechaper al nafshoseichem.*"[2]

When is the preferred time to have the Purim seudah when Purim falls on Erev Shabbos?

When Purim falls on a regular weekday, it is customary to have the meal in the afternoon (after Minchah). It is preferable to begin the *seudah* with enough time before sunset to ensure that most of the *seudah* is eaten on Purim day.[3] There are those who defend the practice of eating most of the *seudah* into the night of Shushan Purim.[4] One should follow such a practice only if one has a clear tradition to do so.

There are Kabbalistic sources suggesting that one should have the *seudah* in the morning. Some *poskim* suggest that when possible, one should partake of a *seudah* in the morning as well as in the afternoon.[5] When Purim falls on Erev Shabbos, all *poskim* agree that it is ideal to eat the *seudah* on Friday morning.[6] Although the earlier one begins in the morning the better it is, he should make a strong attempt at least to begin the *seudah* before halachic midday (*chatzos*). If one did not manage to begin the *seudah* before *chatzos*, he can still begin before the start of the tenth halachic hour.[7] If one was delayed even past this time, a minimal *seudah* can still be eaten.[8]

---

2. *Shemos* 30:16.
3. *Rema* 695:2.
4. See *Piskei Teshuvos*, ibid. 5.
5. *Kaf HaChaim* ibid. 23; *Pri Megadim* ibid. 5.
6. *Rema* ibid.
7. *Yad Ephraim* 695, quoting the *Maharil*.
8. See *Mishnah Berurah* 529 :8.

Q

How much money must one give for matanos le'evyonim? Can one use maaser money for the mitzvah?

A

One must give a minimum of one gift (either money or food) to two poor people on Purim. The *Ritva*[9] rules that each gift must be at least the value of one *perutah*. Others argue that a *perutah* is too small a sum and claim that it must be at least enough to purchase a meal the size of three eggs.[10]

Fortunately, it is not difficult to fulfill this precious mitzvah by giving a sum that can purchase a meal, according to the stringent opinions.

One cannot use *maaser* money for *matanos le'evyonim* or any other mitzvah (such as *machatzis hashekel*) that is obligatory in nature. After fulfilling the basic mitzvah of *matanos le'evyonim*, one can give additional *tzedakah* from *maaser* funds.[11]

Q

I read Megillas Esther for the homebound in my neighborhood. Is there a special berachah to recite before leining the Megillah for women? Should I make the berachah myself?

A

There is a dispute regarding the proper *berachah* recited on the *Megillah* when reading for women. Some rule[12] that the mitzvah is for women to **hear** the *Megillah* and not **read** it, and therefore the *berachah* for women should be *Lishmo'a Megillah* (as opposed to *Al Mikra Megillah* for men). Some have it as *Lishmo'a Mikra Megillah*, which is a slight variation of the *nusach*.[13]

Others rule that women have exactly the same obligation as men

---

9. See *Mishnah Berurah* 694:2.
10. *Shaarei Teshuvah*, ibid. 1, quoting *Zera Yaakov*.
11. *Mishnah Berurah*, ibid. 3, see *Piskei Teshuvos* ibid. 7.
12. *Rema* 489:2.
13. *Mishnah Berurah*, ibid. 8.

when it comes to *Megillah* reading, and therefore the *berachah* remains *Al Mikra Megilah*.[14]

If the man reading for women has already fulfilled his mitzvah of *krias Megillah*, and there are fewer than ten women listening, the women should make the *berachah* for themselves. If there are more than ten women present, some rule that one woman should recite the *berachah* on behalf of the others.[15] Others say that each one should cite the *berachah* on her own.[16]

Are married women obligated to give money for matanos le'evyonim and food for mishlo'ach manos?

Women are obligated in all the *mitzvos* of Purim since they were included in (and brought about) the *nes*. This rule would obligate women in the mitzvah of *mishlo'ach manos*.[17] However, the *Magen Avraham*[18] comments that the custom seems to be that married women fulfill the mitzvah through their husbands. Some explain that the woman fulfills the mitzvah even if her husband sent one *mishlo'ach manos* for them both.[19]

Others explain that even according to the lenient approach, the husband must send at least two gifts of *mishlo'ach manos* (one to each of two recipients), one from himself and one from his wife. He should let her know that the *mishlo'ach manos* is being sent, because according to the *sefer Menos Halevi*, the purpose of sending *mishlo'ach manos* is to increase friendship and camaraderie, and this can only take place if both the sender and the recipient are aware of the gift.[20]

The *Magen Avraham* concludes that women should be stringent in

---

14. See *Shaar Tziyun*, ibid. 16; *Yabia Omer* 1:44.
15. *Minchas Shlomo* 2:19:3.
16. See *Minchas Yitzchak* 3: 53-54.
17. *Rema* 695: 4.
18. Ibid. 14.
19. See *Aruch HaShulchan* 694:2, who allows the wife to fulfill the mitzvah of *matanos le'evyonim* through the gift that the husband gives to fulfill his mitzvah. He bases this on the concept of *ishto kegufo*. This lenient position would apply to our discussion of *mishlo'ach manos* as well.
20. *Sefer Halichos Beisah* 24: footnote 55. See there for an explanation of why it is not necessary to let one's wife know that money was sent on her behalf for *matanos le'evyonim*.

the matter and send their own *mishlo'ach manos* (to their friends) even if they are married (the husband should gift the food items to his wife for this purpose).

It is quite easy to perform this mitzvah according to all opinions, since most people send out several *mishlo'ach manos* packages anyway. The husband can therefore simply designate one as his wife's. However, those who are accustomed to relying on the lenient opinions certainly have a firm basis for doing so.

What should one do if he missed a word during the Megillah reading?

One must hear every single word of the *Megillah* in order to fulfill the mitzvah properly. If he missed a word due either to noise or lack of concentration, he must say it quickly in order to catch up to the reader.[21] He has still fulfilled the mitzvah even if it is necessary for him to read a few words or even a few sentences from a printed *Megillah* as he catches up to the *baal korei*, as long as at least 51 percent of the *Megillah* is being *leined* from a kosher *Megillah*.

While the *Megillah* is being publically read, it is best to listen to the *leining* while following along in a kosher *Megillah* scroll (a *klaf* without *nekudos*), if one knows how to pronounce the words properly and speedily. This is because it is a *hiddur mitzvah* to fulfill the mitzvah of *krias Megillah* in its entirety from a kosher *Megillah*, and in the event that one misses a word, he will be able to make it up out of a kosher *Megillah*, thus ensuring that it is completely read from a kosher scroll. If he is not sufficiently knowledgeable about the words and would lose precious time catching up with the *baal korei*, it is better to follow along in a printed *Megillah* with *nekudos* and punctuation. As mentioned, one has fulfilled the mitzvah of *krias Megillah* if more than 51 percent of the *Megillah* was heard as it was being read from a kosher *Megillah*.

---

21. *Mishnah Berurah* 690:19.

Q

Is it proper to remain seated while listening to krias Megillah?

A

Although the person reading the *Megillah* must stand, those listening have the choice of standing or sitting. It would be advisable to make the decision based on whichever position enables you to concentrate more fully.

The *berachos* must be said standing, and those listening must stand as well.[22]

---

22. *Shulchan Aruch, Orach Chaim* 690:1; *Shaar HaTziyun* 1.

CHAPTER EIGHT

KEEPING KOSHER

Cleaning Help and Complications in the Kitchen

I recently attended a shiur that dealt with the prohibition of bishul akum. I was surprised to learn that in the absence of a pilot light that was originally lit by a Jew, I may not allow my household help to turn on the fire and cook for the family. Our stove has no pilot light, and each time the oven is turned on it is a brand-new fire.

Our housemaid has been cooking delicious, elaborate meals for several years (under our close supervision due to kashrus concerns) and has been turning on the fire herself throughout this time.

In addition to changing the way we do things in the house, I am faced with two dilemmas.

*The first is concerning her frozen
dinners that are stored in my downstairs
freezer. We have a large supply of meals
that she has made for a rainy day. Must
I dispose of all this food or are there
halachic grounds to allow us to eat it?*

*My second dilemma concerns my
utensils. Must I kasher all the utensils
that came in contact with the hot meals
she produced?*

You are certainly correct concerning your newfound understanding of the laws of *bishul akum,* food cooked by a non-Jew. These laws apply to foods that generally are not eaten raw and that are *oleh al shulchan melachim* (food served at a royal or state dinner, or, according to many *poskim,* food normally served at weddings or other high-end dinners).

If a non-Jew cooks such a food, and a Jew did not have a hand in the cooking (e.g., he did not at least light the original fire or stir the food as it was cooking), the food is not kosher *mi'd'Rabbanan.* (The leniency of having a Jew light the fire is not sufficient for those who follow Sephardic tradition.)

Our Sages instituted this prohibition in order to prevent social interaction that could ultimately lead to intermarriage. *Chazal* understood that a common way of building a close relationship is over fine cuisine and good drink.

Shulchan Aruch[1] cites different opinions regarding whether this prohibition applies to foods cooked by a non-Jewish servant of a Jew. The logic of those who permit food by a non-Jewish servant is that there is no feeling of friendship and camaraderie (*kiruv hadaas*), as the servants have no choice but to follow orders given by the employer.[2]

Rema rules in accordance with the lenient opinion.

Even so, however, there is some question about whether this leni-

---

1. *Yoreh Deah* 113:4.
2. See *Teshuvas HaRashba* 68.

ency applies to employees or only to true servants.

A second mitigating factor that would allow a leniency in your case is that the cooking was done in a Jewish home, which would lead to less danger that it will lead to improper social interaction.[3]

In fact, we allow the food to be eaten only if both factors are met — the cooking was done by a worker, in a Jew's home — in a *bedi'eved* (ex post facto) situation such as yours. One is not allowed to rely on this ruling to allow a non-Jewish employee to cook.

Since you have a large supply[4] of food that was cooked by your maid in your house, you have the halachic right to be lenient and not throw out the food.

In a situation where the non-Jewish employee cooked food for himself or herself in the Jew's home, these leniencies would not apply. Such cooking is done on a voluntary basis, and therefore the food will always remain prohibited.[5]

Normally, utensils used for *bishul akum* must be kashered.[6] In your situation, the *halachah* is lenient and would not require kashering of the *keilim*. This is based on the same reasoning mentioned for permitting the food to be eaten.

It is generally not a good idea to allow the hired help to do *any* cooking in your house. The risk that you will forget to light the fire initially or that the person will cook food for herself (even a simple egg is considered a food that is *oleh al shulchan melachim*, a food fancy enough to grace the table of a king, a president, or an elaborate *bris*) makes her cooking a situation fraught with halachic dangers.

Although you mentioned in your question that the cooking was done under supervision of members of your household, it is important to bear in mind that once she is allowed to cook, she may do so even when members of the family are not there to pay careful attention to what is being done. This can compromise the kashrus of the entire household.

---

3. See *Shach Yoreh Deah*, ibid.
4. See *Chachmas Adam, Hilchos Maachalei Akum* 66:7.
5. *Shach Yoreh Deah* 113:20.
6. *Shulchan Aruch Yoreh Deah* 113:16.

Tevilas Keilim on Gifts

I received for mishlo'ach manos a beautiful serving tray with assorted cookies arranged on it. The accompanying note said that the glass tray was mine to keep for simchas Purim, and that the tray had already undergone tevilah (immersion in a mikveh).

Is tevilah by the original owner sufficient, or must I immerse the tray again?

A utensil bought for nonfood use does not require *tevilah*.[1] The Taz[2] therefore rules that utensils bought strictly for resale (a nonfood use) do not require *tevilah* before the sale. One should therefore not ask a store owner to *tovel* any item before it is actually acquired by the purchaser.[3] It might follow that a utensil bought for the sole purpose of gift-giving would be exempt from *tevilah* while still owned by the giver, and any *tevilah* by the original owner would be meaningless.[4]

---

1. *Shulchan Aruch Yoreh Deah* 120:8.
2. Ibid.
3. See *Teshuvos Minchas Yitzchak* 8:70.
4. *Sefer Tevilas Keilim* 8:6, with footnote 9.

Your scenario, however, is slightly different, in that the tray was actually used for food — to transport the cookies — by the original owner. The question is, would that be reason enough to obligate the purchaser to *tovel* the tray?

Although the Rema rules[5] that a utensil earmarked for nonfood use requires *tevilah* if it is used for food even on a temporary basis, one could argue that merely using the tray to transport the food to the intended recipient is not considered a "food use" by the original purchaser. It is simply a fancy way to package the item that is being given. Although food-storage utensils normally require *tevilah* (without a *berachah*[6]), perhaps that is only when they are purchased for one's own use.

Some suggest[7] that it is best for the gift-giver to transfer ownership of the utensil to the intended recipient before he immerses it. This can be done by handing the utensil to a third party (non-family member of the giver) who will acquire it on behalf of the person who will receive the gift.[8] This way, the immersion is valid according to all opinions.

Many *poskim* rule, however, that there is ample reason to assume that one is obligated to immerse the utensil before the *mishlo'ach manos* is sent.[9]

The reasoning is that a utensil purchased as a gift is the same as merchandise purchased for business use. This logic, in conjunction with the fact that the utensil is being used with food before it reaches the hands of the recipients, would trigger a *tevilas keilim* obligation immediately upon use for food.

---

5. *Yoreh Deah* 120:8. See *Darchei Teshuvah* ibid.: 68, quoting the *Pri Chadash*, who disputes *Rema*; see also *Aruch HaShulchan* ibid.:41 for a different understanding of *Rema*.

    It is important to note that a utensil earmarked for use with food requires *tevilah* before using it for food (it is a popular misconception that one can use it temporarily before *tevilah* is done).

6. See *sefer Tevilas Keilim* 11:16, footnote 13.

7. See *Mekor Chaim siman* 14.

8. Cf. Harav Shlomo Zalman Orbach, quoted in *Sefer Tevilas Keilim* ibid.

9. *Moria,* Tishrei 5755, pg. 122 quoting Harav Shalom Yosef Elyashiv; *Sefer Hilchos Purim,* quoting HaRav Shmuel Kamenetsky.

A Brewing
Controversy

*I recently bought the Keurig
coffeemaker, and was told that it is
not possible to tovel it because the
computer inside would be damaged.
Is one allowed to use the coffeemaker
without tevilah? Is there any other way
to resolve this?*

Since the advent of electrical food-preparation appliances, new
halachic dilemmas regarding *tevilas keilim* have arisen. This issue is
certainly relevant to the coffeemaker machine in question.

Halachah requires *tevilah* of all metal or glass utensils manufactured
by or purchased from a non-Jew and that are used in food preparation
or consumption. Most *poskim* are of the opinion that this obligation
is *mi'd'Oraisa* (originating in the Torah) regarding metal products but
mi'd'Rabbanan (a Rabbinic ordinance) for glass.

Ordinarily, the *tevilah* can be performed without much difficulty, but it
is a bit of a challenge with regard to an electrical appliance such as an urn
or a sandwich maker. Nevertheless, the consensus among contemporary

poskim is that, just like all other utensils, electrical items require *tevilah*.[1]

Experience has shown that, contrary to popular belief, immersing electric appliances in a *mikveh* will cause no damage *if one follows the proper precautions*. The item must be dried thoroughly after *tevilah* and allowed to dry further for a few days before use.

This question has come to the forefront once again with the popularity of single-cup coffee-brewing machines. Although made mostly of plastic, these coffeemakers have important components that are made of metal. The difference between these new coffeemakers and many electrical kitchen appliances of the past is that these machines will often cease to function properly if submerged in water.

Even if the coffee machine were to survive the immersion, the *tevilah* would not be acceptable. This is because without the aid of the electric pump, which does not operate when the unit is turned off, the *mikveh* water cannot reach all the metal used to heat the water. (This could be an issue for some other urns and coffeemakers as well.)

A number of possible *heterim* are discussed by the *poskim*. Not all are equally accepted, and some are more practical than others to implement. It must be borne in mind that the *Maharil Diskin* and others flatly reject the following options, although HaRav Shlomo Zalman Auerbach, *z"tl*, is quoted as saying that it may be relied upon in times of great need.[2]

One leniency involves the concept that it is not *assur* to own a utensil purchased from or made by a non-Jew, but there is a mitzvah to immerse the utensil before it is used. In the case of this particular coffeemaker, this mitzvah cannot realistically be fulfilled. Logic therefore dictates that there can be no such *obligation*, since Hashem did not give us *mitzvos* that we cannot perform. For this reason, these machines have no *chiyuv tevilah* and may be used after purchase as is.[3]

Another suggestion[4] is to use the coffeemaker without acquiring it. One would have to have in mind when purchasing it not to make an official *kinyan*, which would allow its use (since it had been paid for)

---

1. See *Shevet HaLevi* Y"D 57:3. *Igros Moshe* Y"D 1:57 requires *tevilah* on the actual utensil, not the part containing the wires, whereas *Minchas Yitzchak* 2:72 rules that the entire utensil must be immersed. That dispute is not relevant to the coffeemaker in question, whose electrical and computer parts are integrated.
2. See the *sefer Tevillas Keillim perek* 3, footnotes 15 and 16.
3. See *Minchas Shlomo tinyana* 68:2.
4. See *Ketzos HaShulchan* 8:146.

without halachically owning it. One who already owns such an appliance can *mafkir* it in front of three people and then continue to use it.

A similar option involves giving or selling the item to a non-Jew and then borrowing it back.

Although it is certainly *haaramah* (legal subterfuge) to employ these novel ideas, there is a halachic precedent for utilizing loopholes when *no other* alternative presents itself (*Mishnah Berurah* 323:34 quoting *Taz*, ibid. rules that this solution should *not* be relied upon for long-term use of the utensil). However, the moral question would remain: Should one rely on such a leniency merely to enjoy the luxury of a more delicious cup of coffee?

The most widely accepted solution to this problem is to have the item disassembled and then reassembled by a Jew.[5] The logic is that once the item has been disassembled, it no longer has the halachic status of a utensil. When it is reassembled, it is a new *keli* that has been created by a Jew and therefore does not requires *tevilah*. [One who uses this solution need not take the machine apart entirely — only to the point that an expert is needed to reassemble it (*maasei uman*). If it can be reassembled by an "ordinary" person (*maasei hedyot*), it has never lost the halachic status of a *keli*.] Every community has professionals who can readily perform such a service.

When the question involving these coffee brewers was recently presented to HaGaon HaRav Elyashiv, *shlita*, he was not prepared to endorse the logic that it does not require *tevilah* at all. HaRav Elyashiv was also not comfortable as a long-term solution with relying on the option of giving it to a non-Jew or having in mind not to officially acquire the item at the time of purchase.[6] The solution he most favored was to have the brewer "fixed" by a Jew, obviating the need for *tevilah*.

One must always carefully investigate the validity of any potential leniency and weigh the necessity of relying on *kulos*. Let us hope that when we wake up and smell the coffee, it will be percolating in a way that satisfies all the halachic requirements.

---

5. See *Teshuvos Vehanhagos* 1:450.
6. See *Mishnah Berurah* ibid.

Disposing of Food Not Bearing Reliable Kosher Supervision

I received an assortment of packaged foods and nosh on Purim. Some items did not have what I consider a proper kosher certification (hechsher). Should I simply dispose of these items, or is it better to give them to friends and neighbors who regularly eat them? I must make clear that all the items in question bear a certification, but I have been told that these particular certifying agencies do not have the highest standards in kashrus.

One must consider this question carefully, for on the one hand we are dealing with a prohibition of wasting (*bal tashchis*) if the food is thrown out unnecessarily. However, giving the food to friends and neighbors might entail a violation of *lifnei iver lo sitein michshol* (the prohibition of placing a stumbling block in front of a blind person. In our scenario, the "blind" people might be those who are unaware that the kosher certification should not be relied upon).

If you were privy to halachically reliable information that the certifications in question have a halachically substandard level of kashrus, then the food should not be eaten by any Jew. It would therefore be prohibited to give it away, even to a person who buys this product on his own. The food may be given to a gentile who is owed a favor, or from whom you might need a favor. This would include a neighbor, co-worker, subordinate, or employer with whom it is important to foster friendly relations.[1]

If your information does not have halachic validity, it simply falls into the category of *lashon hara* or *hotzaas shem ra.*

The scenario that is less clear from the halachic standpoint would be concerning a bona fide, respected *hechsher* that relies on certain leniencies that in, in the opinion of other *poskim,* should not be relied upon. (These disputes certainly come up concerning the production of certain nonstaple food items, which could include most of the nosh that you receive in your *mishlo'ach manos.*) The certifying kashrus agency might follow accepted *poskim* who do allow these leniencies, and they are entitled to their opinion.

To give proper direction on what to do with food bearing such *hechsherim,* we must examine a fascinating question concerning the exact parameters of *lifnei iver lo sitein michshol.* Can Reuven ask Shimon to perform an action (in our case, the act of eating) that Reuven holds is prohibited and Shimon holds is permissible (where both opinions have a solid halachic basis)?

HaRav Shlomo Zalman Auerbach[2] was asked if a Sephardi could ask an Ashkenazi to perform an action on Shabbos that the Beis Yosef (whom the Sephardim generally follow) prohibits but which the Rema (whom Ashkenazim generally follow) allows. Rav Shlomo Zalman replied that it depends on whether or not the person who is strict really assumes that it is actually prohibited. If it is due to custom (and one

---

1. See *Shulchan Aruch Yoreh Deah* 151:11 with *Shach* and *Taz* for parameters.
2. *Sefer Maor HaShabbos,* brought in *Sefer Lamed Tes Melachos, Hakdamah l'meleches Shabbos,* footnote 361.

must always follow his family and community custom) that one adheres to the stringent view, and he has no strong opinion or concrete proof that the lenient view is incorrect, there will be no issue of *lifnei iver*. This is because objectively there is no "stumbling block" when all involved are merely following their communal customs and the guidelines of their *poskim*.

If, however, the request to perform an action is coming from a person who really believes that the action is prohibited, it would be *lifnei iver* to make the request, despite the fact that the person asked would regularly perform this action without compunction, relying on his *minhag* and *poskim*.

According to Rav Shlomo Zalman, it follows that it would be prohibited to give the food to your friends and neighbors only if the leniencies used by the certifying agencies were the type that you or your Rav find extremely questionable. It would be *lifnei iver* to supply food that you believe to be prohibited.

If, however, you do not normally partake of food under this *hechsher* because you have personal stringencies regarding various kashrus issues, you may freely give the food to others who follow more lenient (but acceptable) halachic guidelines (e.g., the particular *hechsher* is considered reliable, but you do not accept this *hechsher* in your home due to personal stringencies such as *pas Yisrael* or *yashan*). In that situation you should certainly gift it to friends and neighbors who regularly buy the product anyway, thereby avoiding the prohibition of *bal tashchis*.

Whether serving food or giving it away, one must always be aware of the halachic issues concerning various levels of kashrus observance among Jews. One must balance such halachic issues as *lifnei iver*, *bal tashchis*, and opportunities for *chessed*. One must especially be cognizant of the sensitivities and feelings of others in dealing with these complex *she'eilos*.

Food Stored Under a Bed

*My son resides in a yeshivah dormitory,
and I send him back to yeshivah after
his off-Shabbos with a few weeks'
worth of nosh. I recently discovered
that he is storing the food under his
bed because there is limited space in
his room. I have always understood
that it is prohibited to place food under
a bed, and I have told him to find a
different place to hide his treasures.
The question I have is concerning all
the cookies, cake, and bags of potato
chips that were placed under the bed
but have not yet been eaten. Is there a
problem with eating it? Must it all be
thrown out? What about bal tashchis?*

*On the same topic, I often store my
baby's bottle and other snacks on the
rack beneath the carriage, and I now
realize that my baby sleeps in the*

carriage above the food and drink. Is this a problem?

The *Gemara* in *Pesachim* (112a) states that one should not place food or drink under a bed because of the *ruach ra'ah* (impure/evil spirit) that resides there. The *Gemara* states that this prohibition exists even if the food is covered.[1]

Some *poskim* are lenient if the food was sealed or tied so that it is completely closed. They maintain that the *Gemara's* ruling that a covering is not sufficient applies to a food item that was covered but not sealed. Many *poskim* are strict on this matter even if the item was completely closed.[2]

Even if your son's nosh was not completely sealed, another aspect would allow consumption of the food in question. Many *poskim* rule that *bedi'eved* (ex post facto), the food or drink does not become prohibited.[3] Although there are notable *Acharonim* who rule stringently on this matter,[4] this would be another possible reason to be lenient on the issue of *ruach ra'ah* in order to be strict concerning the prohibition of *bal tashchis* on food.

Some *poskim* suggest that one can wash the food with water (or the food in its container, if the food would be ruined by contact with water) three times (similar to *netilas yadayim* in the morning).[5]

In conclusion, in light of the question of *bal tashchis*,[6] I would advise you to rely on the many *poskim* referenced above who, for the combination of reasons cited, would be lenient concerning the *ruach ra'ah* issue.[7]

As for your second question concerning the baby bottle and other food that is stored in the basket under the baby carriage:

There are a number of reasons cited by the *poskim* that would lead

---

1. *Shulchan Aaruch Yoreh Deah* 116:5; *Shach*, ibid. 4.
2. See *Yabia Omer Orach Chaim* 4:5 for various opinions.
3. *Pischei Teshuvah* and *Chidushei Rabbi Akiva Eiger* on *Shulchan Aruch* ibid.
4. *Birkei Yosef Yoreh Deah* 116:10; *Gra* as quoted by *Binas Adam* brought in *Pischei Teshuvah* ibid. 5; see, however, *Darkei Teshuvah* 116:35 quoting *Sefer Shaarei Rachamim*, who states that the *Gra* was *machmir bedi'eved* only for himself.
5. *Sdei Chemed, Maareches Lamed* 141:31; *Pischei Teshuvah Yoreh Deah.* 91:4; *Yabia Omer Yoreh Deah.* 1:9.
6. *Gemara Berachos* 50b, *Gemara Shabbos* 140b, *Rambam Hilchos Melachim* 6:10 and *Hilchos Berachos* 7:9, *Shulchan Aruch Orach Chaim* 171:1-2 for sources on the prohibition of *bal tashchis*.
7. *Yabia Omer* ibid.; see *Mishnah Berurah Orach Chaim* 4:14, who is lenient concerning food that was touched before *netilas yadayim*.

us to be even more lenient regarding this issue.[8] Some contend that the *ruach ra'ah* only descends on food that is on the ground. Others say that the issue of food under a bed applies only to a bed in which adults normally sleep.

A third possibility is that there might not be such a severe issue of *ruach ra'ah* pertaining to children younger than the age of *chinuch*. See *Shulchan Aruch HaRav,*[9] who is lenient concerning small children who do not wash their hands properly [halachically] upon waking up in the morning. These children often touch food that is then eaten by other family members. He explains that the *ruach ra'ah* attaches itself only to a body that has a *neshamah kedoshah*. When the *neshamah kedoshah* ascends heavenward at night, the *ruach tumah* comes and fills the void.

For this reason, we do not concern ourselves with non-Jews who touch food without prior washing. This is applicable, to a certain extent, to Jewish children as well, who do not have a full *neshamah kedoshah* until they become adults.

Although the *Shulchan Aruch HaRav* encourages the washing of even an infant's hands, he does use the above reasoning to justify the widespread custom of not being overly concerned when a child who has not washed touches food. See *Mishnah Berurah Orach Chaim* 4:10, who rules that one must be diligent in ensuring that even children wash their hands in the morning, since they will be touching food. It is unclear whether the *Mishnah Berurah* refers to children who are of *chinuch* age or even toddlers.

To summarize: There is much room to be lenient to allow the storage of food and drink in the basket of a baby carriage. (The same leniency would apply to placing food under an airplane seat.) However, if you have a bag that hangs from the carriage with sufficient room for these supplies, it is better to avoid the question and place the food and drink into such a bag.

---

8. *She'arim Hametzuyanim Behalachah* 33:5 in *kuntres acharon*; *Minchas Yitzchak* 4:117; *Az Nidberu* 7:72; see, however, sefer *Shemiras Haguf VeHanefesh* Ch. 14, footnote 15, quoting from HaRav Chaim Shmulevitz, who said that his father was strict concerning this issue.
9. *Mahadura Tinyana* 4:2.

Common Hafrashas Challah Issues

When I bake challos, I make sure to use five pounds [2.26 kilograms] of flour, in order to be able to make the berachah on the hafrashah according to all opinions. But since our family is still small we eat very little challah every Shabbos, so I freeze most of the unbaked dough for future weeks.

A friend of mine says she has heard that no berachah is cited for hafrashas challah unless all the challos will be baked right away. If, as in my case, the dough is frozen and defrosted piecemeal to bake a few challos each week, no berachah is recited, although hafrashah must still be done on the original five pounds (2.26 kilograms) of dough.

Is my friend's information correct? If so, is there any way for me to make a berachah and still bake just a few challos each week?

The answer to your question is subject to a dispute in the *poskim*.[1] As a matter of practicality, your friend's information is correct. The final ruling given by Rav Shlomo Zalman Auerbach[2] is that in the case you describe, the *challah* should be separated without a *berachah*.

It is important to point out that there is a requirement to separate *challah* with a *berachah* if one will be baking all the *challos* at one time, even if most of the baked *challos* are then frozen for use in subsequent weeks. The dispute mentioned above concerns only dough that is frozen for future use, but not *challos* that are frozen after they were baked.

Another scenario: In nurseries and kindergartens, the teacher will on occasion have a baking project with the children. The *kinderlach* bake small *challah* rolls to take home and enjoy. In this scenario, even if the original dough that the teacher prepared for use is more than five pounds (2.26 kilograms) of flour, there is no obligation at all to separate *challah*.

This is because the small *challos* that are being baked belong to different people. Each child is particular about bringing home the fruits of her own labor, and therefore wants the *challah* roll that she herself worked on. Therefore, although all the rolls are made from one dough, no *challah* is separated.

---

1. See *Shulchan Aruch Yoreh Deah* 326;2 with *Pischei Teshuvah* 2 and *Beur HaGra* 7, *Shemiras Shabbos Kehilchasah* 2;42;11 with footnote 45.
2. Quoted in *Shemiras* Shabbos *Kehilchasah*, ibid.

HONORING PARENTS

Missing Work to Honor Parents

My elderly father frequently requests that I run various errands for him. On occasion the list of errands is quite lengthy, and as a result I am unable to get to my office on time. On occasion I even have had to use vacation days to settle all the affairs that I have been asked to take care of. Am I required to do this for kibbud av va'eim, or can I postpone the performance of these errands until Motza'ei Shabbos or Sunday when I have more time? I am afraid that as I run out of vacation days, I will be forced to take any extra days as unpaid leave. Am I obligated to take an unpaid day off to properly fulfill my obligations to my parents?

The *Shulchan Aruch*[1] rules that when feeding a parent (or performing any other service that requires an outlay of money), the child does *not* have to pay for the food — with the exception of the case of an indigent parent and a son with adequate resources, where we insist that the son cover the costs of the basic necessities, since charity begins at home. Yet the *Shulchan Aruch* says that one must personally service a parent *(lechabdo begufo)* even if, as a result, the child will not be able to work during that time.[2] (If the job or career will be in jeopardy, the *halachah* may be different; a Rav should be consulted.)

This applies even to a situation where the child will have to ask for *tzedakah* to raise the funds necessary to cover the shortfall that results from the temporary lack of employment (if the child does not have money to cover the food expenditures for *that day*, working would be permitted even if it would preclude *kibbud av va'eim*).

The *halachah* differentiates between the potential profit that the son is obligated to forgo and the actual loss of money he incurs for providing for the parents' needs.

Assisting parents by performing various errands is usually direct *kibbud* (i.e., shopping for food, medicine, and clothing, as well as taking parents to doctors, exercise programs, and the like). Even running errands that do not seem vital for their basic functioning would fall under the general category of *kibbud*.[3]

It is obvious that one cannot steal time from the boss or the company in order to perform personal *mitzvos*. You would therefore need permission to come late to the office (or to leave early) before you undertake your *kibbud av va'eim* mission. If your employer says that if you come late you are required to stay late, you should do so to fulfill this mitzvah.

If it becomes necessary to take the day off without pay for coming late, you would be required to forgo the money. If you would have to accept a reduction in salary, a Rav should be consulted.

These guidelines apply to one who is self-employed as well. One

---

1. *Yoreh Deah* 240:5.
2. Ibid.
3. See *Rema* ibid. 4, "*Veyeshamshenu beshe'ar devarim shehashamash meshameish rabo* — One should serve a parent as a servant would his master."

would be required to pass up a potential business deal if it requires a meeting at a time when one is asked to take care of the needs of a parent.

If their request is not something time-essential, they may not want you to fulfill it as a time that you will forgo income, and they may be distressed that they caused you loss. In such cases, you may want to ask them if the errand or chore can wait till a time that you are off from work.

However, if there is a vital chore that must be taken care of immediately, it is best that you not cause them aggravation by broaching the question. The mitzvah should be done with alacrity despite the missed opportunity for potential profit.

If you find that performing a service for your parents is affecting your *shalom bayis* or your ability to spend time with your children, a *she'eilah* must be asked. The family dynamics are different in each situation, and the topic should preferably be discussed with a Rav who knows you and your particular circumstances well.

You must be very careful as you deliberate the balance of your obligations, for to err in either direction is potentially dangerous and explosive. The need to preserve and enhance *shalom bayis*, educate your children, and honor your parents is a challenging but necessary juggling act.

Bear in mind that the reward for *kibbud av va'eim* is long life, so any time you spend on this precious mitzvah will be returned to you with dividends. You will therefore have the time to make up for any lost income.[4]

It is especially important that your children see your efforts and *mesirus nefesh* on behalf of your parents so that they will learn the importance of *kibbud av va'eim* and emulate your ways. If you are steadfast in your endeavor to fulfill the mitzvah of *kibbud va'eim* properly, you will *im yirtzeh Hashem* be *zocheh* to have assistance and *nachas* from your own children for many years to come.

---

4. See however, *Kiddushin* 39b.

Honoring Parents
Regarding Taking
Vitamins

My mother has asked me many times to cut out most of the nosh that I eat and to take various vitamin supplements every day. I believe that as a normal, healthy 16-year-old, I will be fine on my regular diet (including potato chips and ice cream) and just as healthy without the vitamins. Am I obligated, due to kibbud av va'eim, to change my diet and take vitamins each day?

There is wide debate among the *Rishonim* and *poskim* concerning the exact parameters of *kibbud av va'eim*. All agree that children are obligated to fulfill parental requests for services that give direct physical benefit to the parent. However, when the parents make a request or a demand for something that does not give them direct physical benefit, there are three opinions in the *halachah* to consider:

One view[1] is that in this case, there is no direct obligation of *kibbud av va'eim*. One must add that even according to this lenient view, it is certainly a wonderful and important *chessed* to make parents happy and comfortable whenever possible, even if you do not have a direct obligation. If your mother is more at ease when you eat properly and take your vitamins, it would be thoughtful and caring of you to do so. It is an opportunity to make her happy without a major investment of time and effort on your part. (Many nutritionists assert that vitamin supplements are important for your health, and so you might actually be fulfilling the mitzvah of guarding your health — *venishmartem me'od lenafshoseichem*. This is certainly true when you resist that extra helping of junk food.) It is especially important to bear in mind that even according to this opinion that there is no *obligation* to obey your parents when their request does not give them any direct benefit, there might still be a *fulfillment* of the mitzvah of *kibbud av va'eim* by giving *nachas* to one's parents in any way. This concept would apply equally to a situation where parents are *mochel* on their *kavod* and waive the honor or service that is due to them. Although the child is not obligated to do it, if he does so nevertheless, he fulfills the mitzvah of *kibbud av va'eim*.

A second view maintains that there is indeed an obligation of *kibbud av va'eim* even when the request is not for the physical benefit of the parent.[2] The Rosh deals with a case where a father demanded that his son not speak to a certain Jew whom the father greatly disliked. The Rosh rules that not only is the son not obligated to obey his father, but he is actually *prohibited* from carrying out his father's wishes. The reason he gives is that a parent has no right to ask a child to transgress the *halachah*, and maintaining a dispute with a fellow Jew violates many *halachos*. The implication is that, in the absence of the halachic objections, the son would have been obligated to honor his father's demand, despite the fact that there would have been no direct service or benefit to his father. Similarly, in discussing the *halachah* that a son does not have to obey his parents concerning his choice of spouse,

---

1. *Ritva, Yevamos* 6a; *Teshuvos Maharik* 166, quoted in *Darchei Moshe* 240:10.
2. See *Teshuvos HaRosh*, quoted in *Shulchan Aruch Yoreh Deah* 240:16.

Teshuvos Noda BiYehudah,[3] explains that this is a unique *halachah* that does not apply to other instances.

There is a third view[4] that although the mitzvah of *kibbud av va'eim* applies only when the parent has direct benefit, there is still a Biblical obligation of *mora av va'eim* — awe for (or fear of) a parent.[5]

I would suggest that in deference to the opinions that hold that your situation would fall either under the category of *kibbud av va'eim* or *mora av va'eim* (or both), you comply with your mother's wishes. This is because refraining from excessive noshing, as well as taking vitamins, will not cause you extreme discomfort or embarrassment.

In the case of a parental request that does *not* involve physical benefit or service to the parent but *will* cause the child much embarrassment or discomfort, consult your Rav. The dynamics of each individual situation can easily affect the determination.

There is an important aside for parents who are reading this *teshuvah.* It seems perfectly reasonable for parents to make demands in areas that can affect the health of their children. All parents and *mechanchim* agree that it is important to train children in the mitzvah of *kibbud av va'eim* and to occasionally insist on following through with what are sometimes unpopular practices. This is crucial for the success and well-being of the child. However, it is incumbent upon parents to refrain from overburdening their children with requests that the children find especially difficult to fulfill. A possible example would be a demand that *all* nosh be avoided at *all* times. *Chazal* were concerned about creating a possible situation of "*lifnei iveir lo sitein michshol* — You shall not place a stumbling block before the blind."[6] It is prohibited to put anyone into a situation in which he or she will do an *aveirah.* Parents, therefore, should be careful not to make a request of a child if it will more than likely be ignored.

Fulfilling *kibbud av va'eim* and *mora av va'eim*, with all their nuances, is a challenging task. One must examine each circumstance with

---

3. *Even Ha'ezer* 45.
4. *Sefer Hamikna* on *Kiddushin*, 31b, *d"h Tanu Rabbanan.*
5. *Vayikra* 19:3.
6. *Kiddushin* 32a and *Shulchan Aruch Yoreh Deah* 240:19. See ibid., 240:20 for the example concerning the prohibition to strike an older child, due to the concern that the child will be tempted to strike back.

a fresh, optimistic outlook in order to properly focus on the maximizing of this crucial mitzvah. Bear in mind that whatever time and effort is spent on helping parents and giving them *nachas* will be richly rewarded in this world and in the World to Come. As the Mishnah says, "These are the things whose fruits one eats in this world, while the principle remains for the World to Come, and they are: *kibbud av va'eim* ...."[7]

<hr />

7. *Peah* 1:1.

Honoring Parents vs. Talmud Torah

I am an 18-year-old yeshivah bachur living in my parents' home. The yeshivah that I attend is only a few blocks away, so I am able to come home for dinner before I begin my night seder. My parents often ask me to help with various chores around the house before and after dinner. This, on occasion, causes me some loss of time from my learning, as I would like to come to night seder early to prepare the next blatt of Gemara. What are my obligations in kibbud av va'eim when it affects my hasmadah in talmud Torah?

As with everything else in the life of the *ben Torah*, one must indeed search for the correct balance between various halachic responsibilities. This is a delicate balance best addressed by a Rav or rebbi who understands the personalities and the circumstances, so I will not address your question directly, but give a brief halachic overview of the issue.

In *Hilchos Kibbud Av Va'eim*, the *Shulchan Aruch* states, "*Talmud Torah gadol mikibbud av va'eim* — Torah learning supersedes the serving of one's parents."[1] The *Pischei Teshuvah*[2] points out that a son is exempt from *kibbud av va'eim* only if he must, for the greater success of his learning, leave his parents' home to attend a yeshivah out of town.[3] The Gemara tells us that although Yaakov Avinu was punished for staying away from his parents for twenty-two years while he resided with Lavan, he was not punished for the fourteen years he spent away from home learning at the yeshivah of Shem and Ever.[4] Although one may move away from home, thus forgoing serving his parents, for the sake of greater Torah learning, if the son remains at home, he must interrupt or delay his learning for the short-term fulfillment of *kibbud av va'eim*.

The rationale for this is based on the rule that governs when *talmud Torah* supersedes other *mitzvos*. The Mishnah tells us, "*Talmud Torah kenegged kulam* — Torah learning is equal to all the other *mitzvos* combined."[5] As a result, the *Shulchan Aruch*[6] rules that if while learning one encounters an opportunity to do another mitzvah, the learning may be interrupted only if that mitzvah will not be performed by someone else. Honoring parents is a mitzvah that cannot be performed by others, as it is a *mitzvah shebegufo*, a mitzvah whose performance is incumbent specifically upon the child. This is similar to the mitzvah of *tefillin* and *tefillah*. Torah study must obviously be interrupted in order to don *tefillin* and to *daven*, even though this will take time from one's Torah learning.

A son is permitted to leave his parents to attend a yeshivah out of town, making it impossible for him to serve them on a daily basis, due to the overriding consideration of long-range success in *talmud Torah*. The *halachah*, however, insists that the son provide service for his par-

---

1. *Yoreh Deah* 240:13.
2. Ibid. 8.
3. *Shulchan Aruch*, ibid., 25.
4. *Megillah* 16b.
5. *Peah* 1:1.
6. *Yoreh Deah* 246:18.

ents when he is in close proximity. (One might consider the possibility of "talking in learning" or listening to an audio *shiur* while doing his chores. If this is feasible, he will accomplish two important *mitzvos* at the same time!)

There are moments during a child's stay at home when Torah is not being learned in any case. At such times of recreation and vacation the parents may (and perhaps should) give their children the *zechus* of aiding them in the various household chores. As their son, you should run for the opportunity to fulfill the mitzvah of *kibbud av va'eim*, and be *mekadesh Shem Shamayim* by displaying the proper care and concern that your parents so richly deserve.

The parents, of course, should be discriminating in their demands, so as not to cause a loss of *talmud Torah* unnecessarily. They must be cognizant of the fact that uninterrupted *talmud Torah* is crucial to the success of their son's growth, and the balance between family needs and *talmud Torah* must be maintained. This is certainly true when it comes to attending *simchos* that do not really require the presence of their *yeshivah bachur*, such as the wedding of a distant family member or casual friend. Parents must carefully weigh their options before insisting that their son cancel or curtail his night *seder* to attend the *chasunah* from beginning to end. (In general, there is some question whether such a request would be within the obligations of *kibbud av va'eim;* see our discussion of the parameters of *kibbud av va'eim* on pages 223-226. As noted above, every situation is different, and requires a *she'eilas chacham.*)

I find it fascinating that people who fully understand and appreciate that someone's job prevents him from participating in a *simchah* cannot comprehend that their relative the *yeshivah bachur* (or *kollel yungerman*) cannot afford to miss night *seder*. Each situation calls for evaluation, but, as a matter of principle, people should recognize that learning people also have a "job," and their "job" is one of the three pillars upon which the world stands.

Sibling Rivalry and Honoring Parents

Q *I am very annoyed with my sister for not wanting to do her share of chores in our home, since I end up pitching in to cover for what she hasn't done. I do this because I know that my mother becomes upset when she notices the job is not finished, and I want to prevent her from getting angry.*

Although I am generally happy to do chessed and kibbud av va'eim, I hold a grudge against my sister for her laziness. Lately, though, it has been bothering me to the extent that, due to my resentment, I find it difficult to pitch in to make the extra effort.

Should I continue to go the extra mile?

There is no obligation for you to cover for your sister, or to complete her unfinished work. This is true even if she is your elder sister, despite the possible obligation for you to honor an elder sister.[1] Each of your siblings has a responsibility to carry out the specific chore your parents asked him or her to do. That said, the reward for the *chessed* you are performing for your mother, as well as the great *sechar* you will receive for *kibbud eim*, cannot be overestimated.

I would assume that you have tried on many occasions to coax your sister to finish her task. It is obvious that you are not succeeding in curing her desire to procrastinate. If the *mussar* you have been giving her has been causing friction between you, you need not continue your prodding.[2]

You may want to focus on the gain you are receiving in terms of your *avodas Hashem*, and the reward you will ultimately receive, to divert your mind from the resentment you feel because of her behavior. If you are unable to do this, you will have to reconsider your willingness to constantly pick up the slack for your sister. Harboring ill will and possible dislike for your sister might just outweigh the advantages of the *chessed* you have been doing until now.

To help you overcome the resentment, I would like to share the following with you. There is a well-known question: If the purpose of *HaKadosh Baruch Hu* having created the physical world is to give reward and pleasure to *neshamos*, why didn't Hashem simply put our *neshamos* straight into *Olam Haba*? The answer given is that our reward would be *nahama dechisufa*, "bread of shame." This means that it is human nature for people to be embarrassed and uncomfortable if they receive something for nothing, and the *neshamah* would not enjoy its eternal reward nearly as much without having worked for it in this challenging world.

One might pose the question: Since Hashem could do anything, why didn't He simply create the human soul in a way that it would en-

---

1. There is some question concerning the obligation to honor an elder sister. See *Pischei Teshuvah, Yoreh Deah* 240:19 quoting the *Shevus Yaakov*, who exempts a sibling from honoring an elder sister. Many other *poskim* seem to assume that a sister is included in the general obligation to honor an elder sibling.

2. See *Arachin* 16b, *Rambam, Hilchos Deios* 6:7, *Rema* O.C. 608:2 and *Mishnah Berurah* (ibid.) 11, for a discussion as to what lengths one must go when fulfilling the mitzvah of *tochachah*, reproof. The question of what degree of friction absolves one of the obligation of *tochachah* is not completely relevant in your case, since the disobedience is primarily an issue between your sister and mother.

joy receiving everything for free? The *neshamah* would then be placed in Gan Eden and receive its eternal reward without being subjected to the risks, temptations, and trials of *Olam Hazeh*.

The answer is that Hashem created man *b'Tzelem Elokim*, in Hashem's image. This does not refer to any physical image, since Hashem has no physical form. *Tzelem Elokim* means (among many things) that we were given the *middos* of *HaKadosh Baruch Hu*. Throughout our lifetime, we are given the task of polishing and perfecting these *middos*. *HaKadosh Baruch Hu*, therefore, would not create us with a personality that enjoys taking, since *HaKadosh Baruch Hu* never takes but only gives, and such a personality could not be said to mirror the *middos* of Hashem.

Hashem created us with this *Tzelem Elokim* to enable us to gain the maximum benefit and enjoyment. That benefit is our ability to come close to Hashem by emulating His ways. (In your case, emulating Hashem's ways can mean perfecting the art of giving, and of tolerating.)

This means that every time we choose to give rather than take, we are emulating the *middos* of *HaKadosh Baruch Hu* (although it is true that there must be takers in order to have givers, and everyone needs help in some way at certain times). The more we give, the more we strengthen and identify with our own *Tzelem Elokim*. This is certainly true when we have occasion to give to those who don't necessarily deserve or appreciate it, because *HaKadosh Baruch Hu* continues to give to us, despite the fact that we may not always be deserving of His incredible *shefa* and *berachah*.

Bear in mind that, as we have stated, the *halachah* does not require you to continue to help your sister in this manner. If you find the resentment continuing to build, then inaction might actually be the better policy for now.

If you do choose to continue your extra efforts of *chessed* and *kibbud av va'eim*, you will aid your own spiritual development by polishing your *middah* of giving.

HaKadosh Baruch Hu will see your efforts on behalf of those who don't really deserve your help, and this will, in turn, help you to be granted *berachah* and *hatzlachah*.

Waking a Parent for an Important Business Call

I am a young single man living at home with my parents, and I receive various business-related calls on our home phone. Some of these calls come late at night.

On occasion my father is already sleeping when these calls come, and the ringing of the phone disturbs him. I remember from my early years in yeshivah that one is not allowed to awaken a parent even if it will result in a loss of money. If I turn off the ringer, my father will not be awakened, but I stand to lose potential profit by not taking these late-night calls. What should I do?

Your rebbe in yeshivah was certainly correct in teaching that a child must never disturb the sleep of a parent. However, all rules have their parameters.

You no doubt remember the famous story told in the *Gemara*[1] concerning Dama ben Nesinah. Dama was a non-Jew who was approached by the Sages when they wished to purchase gemstones that were needed for the breastplate worn by the *Kohen Gadol* in the *Beis HaMikdash*. They offered a fortune of money for the stones, but Dama refused the sale because the key to the vault where the gems were stored was under his sleeping father's pillow. Hashem rewarded Dama with a *parah adumah,* a Red Cow, which was born among his cattle. The price that this *parah adumah* could fetch more than made up for the potential profit he waived on account of his selfless act of *kibbud av.*

This story is often misapplied to questions such as yours relating to *kibbud av va'eim.* Many incorrectly infer from Dama's actions that one may not disturb the sleep of a parent even if the parent will be upset when he or she learns of the opportunity for profit that was lost. The *Sefer Chasidim* (#337) states clearly that one is obligated to disturb the parent's sleep if the parent will be upset upon learning that an opportunity for potential profit was lost because he was not awakened. It would follow that a child would be allowed (and probably obligated) to wake a parent *even if* the potential profit at stake will go to the *child.* This is based on the assumption that parents would suffer anguish if they knew that the child gave up a large sum of money for their sake.[2] This would depend on the amount of profit involved, as well as on the health and financial situation of the parents.

I would venture to say that most parents would gladly give up some sleep to help their child close a $50,000 deal. If the amount of money in question is relatively small (whether a sum is considered small or large would depend on the assets and income of both the child and the parent), or if the parent has a particular problem with insomnia (e.g., if awakened he will not fall back asleep for the rest of the night), the leniency of the *Sefer Chasidim* would not apply.

---

1. *Kiddushin* 31a.
2. See *Dibros Moshe, Kiddushin* 50:17.

One possible reason Dama might have assumed that his father was not to be awakened despite the potential profit might be that he was extremely wealthy, and therefore his sleep was more important to him than money. (He might have suffered from insomnia as well.)

HaRav Moshe Feinstein[3] suggests that Dama's father was not mentally stable and therefore left instructions that he was not to be disturbed for any reason whatsoever. Dama understood that despite the irrational request (rational people would prefer to make a handsome profit rather than to sleep a bit more), he was bound to honor his father's desire.

According to this explanation, a crucial lesson in *kibbud av va'eim* can be learned from the story of Dama ben Nesinah. If a parent has a wish or desire that is unusual, eccentric, or even irrational, the child must obey and strive to fulfill that desire, despite the fact that most normal people would not make such a request. (This holds true only if fulfilling the parent's desire brings no physical or spiritual danger to the parent or monetary loss to the child.)

Fulfilling *kibbud av va'eim* involves performing actions that enhance the enjoyment and happiness of the parent, and the fact that most other people would not express such a wish or directive is irrelevant. Dama correctly understood that if his father's desire was to sleep undisturbed, it became his responsibility to ensure that this wish was fulfilled, despite the absurdity of the request when balanced objectively against the loss of a handsome profit. All children have the challenging task of attuning themselves to the wish of their parents even when they don't understand the reason or basis for the request.

I do not know your financial situation, but I would venture to say that if you have the opportunity to turn a sizable profit, your father would be agreeable to allow the temporary disturbance caused by a phone call or two. It would be wise to ask your father for an honest directive on how to proceed in the future. If he insists on not being disturbed, you must honor his desire and seek a less intrusive way to communicate with your clients late at night. (Try forwarding all calls to your cell phone and set the phone on vibrate.)

There might also be room for leniency if you will actually *lose* mon-

---

3. *Dibros Moshe*, ibid.

ey (not just forgo a profit) by not allowing the parent to be awakened.[4] This is because the child is not obligated to lose money to fulfill the mitzvah of *kibbud av va'eim* (although there might be a mitzvah to do so under certain circumstances).

If you fear that not taking a call will cause you to lose an important client through whom you could have gained significant profit over the long term,[5] or if not taking the call will cause significant loss or damage (not just for this particular order), a *she'eilah* should be asked. It is possible that your father has a right to demand quiet in his own house. You are living under your parents' jurisdiction and with their generosity, and therefore you might be obligated to follow their rules even if those rules are a liability for your business.

It is obvious that people must be extremely careful to make or receive phone calls or perform any other noisy activity only at a time and in a place that will not disturb parents. It is basic protocol *bein adam lachaveiro* to consider the needs of others and not, *chas veshalom*, to risk "stealing" the sleep of others. This is the type of stealing that one cannot repay, because the sleep lost can never be regained. This applies all the more when care and consideration are given to a parent, thus fulfilling the all-encompassing *halachah* of *ve'ahavta lerei'acha kamocha*, as well as the crucial obligation of *kibbud av va'eim*.

---

4. See *Rema, Yoreh Deah* 240:8.
5. See *Shulchan Aruch, Orach Chaim, Hilchos Chol Hamo'ed* 599:5.

Honoring Parents and Baby-Naming

Baruch Hashem, I was recently zocheh to have my first baby boy. In preparation for the bris, I have been discussing with my wife the issue of a name for our soon-to-be "rach hanimol." We are under family pressure to use the name of a zeide who, unfortunately, was not really a complete shomer Torah umitzvos. We understand the importance of kibbud av va'eim but have also learned of the importance of choosing to name a child after an ehrlicher Yid. What are our options?

This is a very delicate issue and must be dealt with carefully. A similar dilemma would be naming after a relative with less than desirable character traits or after someone who was habitually involved in serious *aveiros*.

If your parents will be very upset or insulted if the name is not used, you must carefully weigh the options. Although *kibbud av va'eim* does not outweigh strict adherence to *halachah*, if a compromise can be found that satisfies the *minhagim* of proper baby-naming as well as the desire of your parents, it is incumbent upon us to find that *derech*.

One can offer the following solution: The *Gemara* in *Shabbos* (12a) quotes a prominent *Yid* whose name was Shevna ish Yerushalayim. *Tosafos d"h Shevna*) quote the opinion of Rabbeinu Tam that the *Gemara* should read Shachna, not Shevna. This is because one is not allowed to name after wicked people, as the *pasuk* says, "*Shem resha'im yirkav* — the name of the wicked shall rot." Shevna was a well-known *rasha* in *Tanach*, and no Jewish mother would have named her child after such a person. *Tosafos* then quote a second opinion, that of the Ri, that confirms our text of Shevna by explaining that there is a Shevna quoted in the *Navi Yeshayah*, and he was a *tzaddik*. Why, ask *Tosafos*, should we assume that the child was named after the *wicked* Shevna when we could safely assume that the child was named after the *tzaddik* Shevna? As a further proof, *Tosafos* explain that just because a certain *Yid* by the name of Avraham was a *rasha* does not prohibit us from using the name Avraham. This is because when Avraham is used for the name of a newborn child, we are certainly referring to the original source, Avraham Avinu.

In your situation, if the *zeide's* name was Yitzchak, for example, you can have in mind that your child is being named after Yitzchak Avinu.

Understandably, this is not a simple matter. What will your response be when you are asked for whom the child is named? To solve that dilemma you will need some guidance on how and when to be *me-shaneh mipnei hashalom*, to bend the truth for the sake of peace. This would require verbal guidance and is not within the scope of a written article.

May you be *zocheh lehachniso lebris be'ito, bizmano … ubeshalom.*

CELEBRATING PROPERLY

Selected Bar Mitzvah Halachos

The actual day of my son's bar mitzvah comes out on Erev Shabbos. We will be hosting many family members and friends for the Shabbos simchah, and the preparations on Erev Shabbos will be quite hectic. How important is it to make a seudah on the actual day that he becomes bar mitzvah, as preparing a seudah on Thursday night or Friday morning will add pressure to the atmosphere in the household? Is there an obligation to mark the occasion of the true birthday with a seudah, or can the seudas mitzvah be fulfilled within days of his thirteenth birthday?

There is a mitzvah for the father to make a festive meal on the day that his son becomes a bar mitzvah. This *seudah* marks the occasion of the bar mitzvah *bachur's* new obligation to keep Torah and *mitzvos*.

It is proper that the *bachur* deliver *Divrei Torah* during the *seudah*.[1]

The Torah tells us וַיִּגְדַּל הַיֶּלֶד וַיִּגָּמַל וַיַּעַשׂ אַבְרָהָם מִשְׁתֶּה גָדוֹל בְּיוֹם הִגָּמֵל אֶת יִצְחָק, *The child grew and was weaned. Avraham made a great feast on the day Yitzchak was weaned.*[2] The Midrash[3] quotes Rabbi Hoshaya Rabbah as explaining that *"the day Yitzchak was weaned"* refers to the day he was weaned from the *yetzer hara*. This is a reference to the fact that when a boy becomes a *gadol* — an adult — he receives his *yetzer tov* and is no longer beholden to the *yetzer hara*. This is a cause for *simchah* and celebration.

When possible, it would be proper to have the *seudah* the very night that he becomes bar mitzvah in order not to delay the celebration of such an auspicious occasion. If it is not feasible to do it that night, it can be done the next day.[4]

Even if there will be a *seudah* on Shabbos (or during the following week for family and friends who could not attend on Shabbos), there is still a mitzvah to make at least a small meal to mark the occasion on the actual day he turns 13. Therefore, despite the time constraints and the pressures of the day, one should try to arrange a small meal for the immediate family on Thursday night or the morning of Erev Shabbos.

Even when the *seudah* in honor of the bar mitzvah is not made on the halachic birthday, it can still be considered a *seudas mitzvah* if the young man gives meaningful *divrei Torah* at the gathering.[5]

I have heard that there are those who do not say Tachanun in shul on the actual day of the bar mitzvah (bo bayom) when the bar mitzvah bachur is in attendance at the minyan. Is this the correct practice?

---

1. *Magen Avraham* 225:4; *Yam Shel Shlomo, Bava Kamma* 7:37, based on *Gemara Kiddushin* 31a; *Mishnah Berurah* 225:6; *Kaf HaChayim* 225:11.
2. *Bereishis* 21:8.
3. *Midrash Rabbah Bereishis* 53:10.
4. See *Divrei Malkiel Orach Chaim* 1:3.
5. *Yam Shel Shlomo*, ibid.

The *minhag* among *most* Ashkenazim is to recite *Tachanun* on the actual day of the bar mitzvah.[6] However, many Sefardim do not say *Tachanun*.[7]

> ## Upon reaching this once-in-a-lifetime milestone, would it not be proper for my son to recite a Shehecheyanu?

Your question is an excellent one. The commentators offer various reasons for why there is no recital of *Shehecheyanu* upon reaching bar mitzvah.

One possible answer is that the *berachah* of *Shehecheyanu* is only made on a mitzvah whose obligation is not ongoing (*mitzvos habaah mizman lizman*), as opposed to becoming bar mitzvah, where one is obligated in all the *mitzvos* from that point forward.[8]

Others suggest that there is no *new* obligation for the bar mitzvah *bachur* to keep mitzvos because he was already obligated for many years before his bar mitzvah because of the mitzvah of *chinuch*.[9]

Others rule that *Shehecheyanu* is recited the first time any mitzvah is performed,[10] and according to those *poskim* the bar mitzvah *bachur* should recite *Shehecheyanu* when he puts on *tefillin* for the first time as an adult.

Since there is some uncertainty regarding why a boy does not recite *Shehecheyanu* when he becomes bar mitzvah and difference of opinion among the *poskim* concerning the recital of *Shehecheyanu* when

---

6. *Minchas Yitzchok* 8:11; *Tzitz Eliezer* 11:17. *Darkei Chaim V'Shalom* 192 reports that in the *beis midrash* of Munkatch, *Tachanun* was not said on the day of the bar mitzvah if it was also the first day the bar mitzvah *bachur* put on *tefillin*.

7. *Yabiya Omer Orach Chaim* 1:27:8; 4:14.

8. Based on *Tosafos Succah* 46a; *Tur, siman* 22; See *Beis Yosef, d"h Ha'oseh*. The same question can be raised concerning the recital of *Shehecheyanu* the first time one performs the mitzvah of *tefillin* on the day of the bar mitzvah.

9. *Igros Moshe Yoreh Deah* 3:14:4. Although the obligation to keep *mitzvos* is now *mid'Oraisa*, whereas before it was only *mi'd'Rabbanan*, the obligation is still not entirely new, and hence no *Shehecheyanu* is recited.

10. *Tur* ibid.; see *Taz* 22:1.

he dons *tefillin* (or performs any other mitzvah) for the first time, it is best that the boy wear a new suit or hat the morning of the bar mitzvah in order to recite a *Shehecheyanu*. While saying the *berachah*, he should have in mind the occasion of the bar mitzvah, as well as the donning of his *tefillin* for the first time.[11]

As the father of a bachur who will soon have his bar mitzvah, I will be reciting the Baruch Shepetarani, the berachah of exemption, on the Shabbos of the bar mitzvah. I have heard that some say it with Shem Hashem, although I have never seen it in practice. What is the final psak in regard to this berachah?

There are indeed many *poskim* who rule that *Baruch Shepetarani* is recited as a full *berachah*: בָּרוּךְ אַתָּה ה' אֱלֹקֵינוּ מֶלֶךְ הָעוֹלָם, שֶׁפְּטָרַנִי מֵעָנְשׁוֹ שֶׁל זֶה, *Blessed are You, Hashem, our God, King of the universe, Who has freed me from the punishment due this boy* ."[12] However, the Rema rules that the *berachah* should be said without Hashem's Name: בָּרוּךְ שֶׁפְּטָרַנִי מֵעָנְשׁוֹ שֶׁל זֶה, *Blessed is the One Who has freed me from the punishment due this boy*.[13] This is because the source for reciting *Baruch Shepetarani* is a *Midrash*,[14] and *berachos* are recited with *Shem Hashem* only if their source is found in the *Gemara*.[15] The commonly accepted custom follows the Rema's opinion.[16]

---

11. *Beur Halachah siman 22, d"h kanah*; see *Halichos Shlomo, tefillah* 4:14.
12. *Beur HaGra Orach Chaim* 225:2;3; *Kitzur Shulchan Aruch* 61:8; *Aruch HaShulchan*, ibid.:4; see *Mishnah Berurah*, ibid.:8, quoting *Chayei Adam, klal* 65:3.
13. *Orach Chaim* 225:2.
14. *Bereishis Rabbah* 63:10.
15. *Darkei Moshe*, ibid.1.
16. See *Kaf HaChaim*, ibid.:16; *Teshuvos VeHanhagos* 2:142.

Q
When exactly is the Baruch Shepetarani recited?

One should recite the *Baruch Shepetarani* immediately after the bar mitzvah *bachur* finishes his *aliyah*. This is because his *aliyah l'Torah* publicly signifies his reaching halachic adulthood. The common practice is to recite it after his *aliyah* on the Shabbos of the bar mitzvah. Others say it after the first *aliyah* he receives, even if it is on a weekday. It can technically be said on the night that he becomes a *gadol* if the boy serves as a *shliach tzibbur* or leads *bentching*, since these also signify that he is now an adult.[17]

---

17. *Magen Avraham*, ibid.; *Maharam Brisk*, ibid.; *Ben Ish Chai, Shana Rishonah Parashas Re'eh* 17.

Paying Your Shadchan

I became a chassan recently, and a friend asked me if my family had paid the shadchan yet. I remarked that we will eventually give the shadchan something for his trouble. My friend claims that my attitude is halachically incorrect for a number of reasons. First, he tells me, there is a strict timetable for when the shadchan must be paid, as well as local customs regarding the amount of the fee. One cannot simply "get around to it" when it is convenient, nor can one arbitrarily give the shadchan "something" for his trouble.

Is it true that paying a shadchan is a strict halachah and not just a nice custom? Is there indeed a set amount that should be paid, as well as an

*established time frame for paying this
obligation?*

*If the fee does depend on local
community custom, what would I pay my
shadchan if he arranged the shidduch
from his hometown (I am from New York
and the shadchan lives in Detroit)?*

*Another complicating matter in this
shidduch is that there are really two
shadchanim. The Detroit shadchan made
the initial introduction, while a second
shadchan in New York carried out the
shidduch to its successful conclusion.
Which shadchan do I have to pay? Do I
pay both? Do they split the fee?*

It is a good idea to associate with friends who are aware of halachic
issues. Even if they are not capable of *paskening she'eilos*, they will at
least advise that a question must be asked.

It is clear that according to *halachah* a *shadchan* must be paid, as
one would pay any broker.[1] Payment is due if the *shadchan* made the
successful match, despite the fact that the *shadchan* approached you
and you did not reach out to him to provide the service. This is based
on the requirement to pay for any services rendered, even when they
were not solicited.[2]

This holds true even if the *shadchan* is not a professional match-
maker but rather a friend, neighbor, or even a family member. (If a
very close friend or family member makes the *shidduch*, and it is *clear*
that he or she did not wish to be paid, there would be no obligation. In
such a case one must make sure that there is absolute reluctance on the
shadchan's part to take money and full *mechilah* before a decision is

---

1. *Rema, Choshen Mishpat* 185:10.
2. *Beur HaGra, Choshen Mishpat* 185:13.

made. Even in such a case, it is customary to give some sort of gift. And even if a friend or family member refuses payment from the side they are close with, they are still entitled to receive the half of the "*sechar shadchanus*" paid by the other party, in this case, the *kallah's* parents).

Although one could argue that, technically, payment is due from the *chassan* and *kallah* themselves, it is common practice today for parents to cover the fee. (This is certainly true when the *shidduch* involves younger singles who are still somewhat financially dependent on their parents. However, in many situations this might apply to older singles as well.)

The *chassan* and *kallah* (or their parents) are each responsible for 50 percent of the fee. If one side was delinquent in its portion of the payment, the other side is not a guarantor to cover the shortfall.

One should definitely pay the *shadchan* "on time," as he would any other worker. Some communities have a custom to pay on or before the wedding day. Many other communities have the custom to pay when the *shidduch* is "clinched."

(The *shadchan* might not be obligated to return the fee if the engagement is broken and the *chasunah* never takes place. This would depend on local or communal custom regarding the time of payment. If the custom dictates that payment is due at the *lechayim* or the *vort*, then the money is technically not refundable if the engagement is broken any time after that. If, however, according to local custom the payment is due only at the time of the *chasunah*, then the parties would not be required to pay the *shadchan* if the engagement is broken; if they did pay in advance, the payment might be refundable.[3] The ruling would also depend on whether or not critical information that contributed to the *shidduch's* dissolution was known to the *shadchan* but was not shared with the parents or the prospective *chassan* or *kallah*.)

The sum that is paid to the *shadchan* in different Jewish communities varies. Let us assume that the fees paid in New York are higher than those paid in Detroit. The fee schedule depends on where the *shadchan* is working, which in your case would be from his telephone

---

3. See *Rema, Choshen Mishpat* 185:10 and *Aruch HaShulchan, Even Haezer* 50:42.

in Detroit.[4] As the starting *shadchan*, he would be paid either one-half or one-third, and the *shadchan* in New York who successfully carried it out receives either one-half or two-thirds. (The division of fees depends on local customs.[5]) The portion, say two-thirds, that the New York *shadchan* receives would be two-thirds of a New York *shadchan's* rate (when most of the work for the *shidduch* was done in New York.[6])

The actual fee structure will depend on the local custom of each community. In a large city such as New York it will vary further, due to different *minhagim* in different *kehillos*. There is no precise sum but rather a general range, so ask the Rav in your community for guidance.

The importance of paying the *shadchan* the correct amount in a timely fashion cannot be overstated. Its importance stems from a direct monetary obligation recorded in *Shulchan Aruch, Choshen Mishpat*.[7] It is also reported to be a *segulah* for a solid foundation in the marriage; and conversely, withholding money that is due the *shadchan* can, *chas v'shalom*, be detrimental to establishing a *bayis ne'eman b'Yisrael*.

The *shadchan* should have no qualms or discomfort regarding accepting money for services rendered. Although bringing two people together in marriage is a *chessed* of the highest order, the *halachah* declares that receiving money for one's involvement in this mitzvah does not detract from the holiness of the mitzvah or from its reward. It is told that the Chasam Sofer used the money he received for *shadchanus* to buy his *lulav* and *esrog* for Succos. (The four *minim* must be unquestionably owned by the user on the first days of Succos. To assure full ownership, it must be paid for with money to which he is certainly entitled, from an unimpeachable source.) He was of the opinion that "*shadchanus gelt*" was the most kosher money he had (not that the Chasam Sofer had any funds from questionable sources).

One can surmise that it is very beneficial for the community to have a monetary incentive for those who are capable of suggesting *shidduchim*. Baltimore's Star-K *shidduch* program, which started in 2005 and ended in early 2011, is a case in point. It is amazing to see how an

---

4. *Igros Moshe, Choshen Mishpat* 2:57.
5. See *Pischei Teshuvah, Choshen Mishpat*, 185:3 and *Aruch HaShulchan, Even Haezer* 50:42.
6. See also *Levushei Mordechai, Choshen Mishpat, siman* 14.
7. Ibid.

additional $2,000 can inspire people to get involved. In fact, the program's incentives were paid for over 130 *shidduchim*. For those unfamiliar with this Baltimore-based program, which has been duplicated in other communities, I will quote an excerpt from *Kashrus Kurrents*:

> Attempting to do its part to alleviate the universal singles "crisis" the American Orthodox community is experiencing, Star-K is offering a $2,000 cash "gift" for the successful *shidduchim* of women in Baltimore's Orthodox community — Star-K's hometown. [The single woman must be a Baltimorean at least twenty-two years and two months old at the time the engagement is announced. There is no upper age limit.] This is an additional incentive, on top of the customary *shadchanus* from the parents of the *chassan* and *kallah*.

Although we all try to do our *mitzvos leshem Shamayim*, for the sake of Heaven, paying *shadchanim* their due will help motivate people to focus more time and energy on this important *chessed*.

Zecher L'Churban at a Wedding

I recently married off my first child, and my son's mesader kiddushin asked me if our family has the minhag of putting ashes on the head of the chassan before he walks down to the chuppah. I could not recall any particular family minhag and do not remember if I did it at my own wedding. With no opposition from me or my mechutan, the Rav proceeded to place a small amount of ashes on my son's head.

I am interested to learn the sources for this minhag.

"Im eshkacheich Yerushalayim tishkach yemini. Tidbak leshoni l'chiki im lo ezkereichi, im lo aaleh es Yerushalayim al rosh simchasi — If I forget you, Jerusalem, let my right hand forget its skill. Let my tongue adhere to my palate if I fail to recall you, if I fail to elevate Jerusalem above my foremost joy."[1]

---

1. *Tehillim* 137:5-6.

Based on these two *pesukim*, *Chazal* instituted various laws and customs to ensure that the destruction of the *Beis HaMikdash* remains etched in the memory of Jews at all times. Although this remembrance is highlighted mainly during the period of the Three Weeks, culminating with the mourning of Tishah B'av, we are admonished to recall the *Churban HaBayis* and our present state of *galus* at times of extreme joy as well. This contrast is most pronounced at a wedding, where we are cautioned to remember that the *geulah* has not arrived and that we have not yet merited to witness *binyan Beis HaMikdash*. We are to remember the destruction of the *Beis HaMikdash* at the very moment that we begin building our miniature *mikdash* by creating a *bayis ne'eman b'Yisrael*.

Among the commemorations of the *churban* at a wedding, the most prevalent ones are: A plate is broken at the *tena'im*; ashes are placed on the head of the *chassan* immediately before the *chuppah*;[2] and a glass is broken at the conclusion of the *chuppah*.

Of these three, the only one mentioned specifically in the Gemara[3] in relation to *zecher l'churban* at the wedding is the custom of putting the ashes on the head of the chassan. (Some have the custom to brush away most or all of the ashes immediately after they are placed on the chassan's head[4].) This custom is quoted twice in Shulchan Aruch.[5] The basis for this particular custom is the verse in *Yeshayah* which foretells that, at as part of the ultimate Redemption, HASHEM will לָשׂוּם לַאֲבֵלֵי צִיּוֹן לָתֵת לָהֶם פְּאֵר תַּחַת אֵפֶר, *to bring about for the mourners of Zion, to give them splendor instead of ashes.* The term פְּאֵר, *splendor,* is a reference to *tefillin,* implying that, during our mourning over the destruction, we put ashes at the place we wear *tefillin.*

While all communities practice some form of remembrance of the *Churban HaBayis*, it is not unanimous that this be done by placing ashes on the *chassan's* head. Although the *Gemara* mentions that example, some *poskim* assume that any practice that serves as a remem-

---

2. *Tur Even Ezer* 65 records a custom to place the ashes at the time of the *berachos* under the chuppah. See *Aruch HaShulchan* ibid. 5.
3. *Bava Basra* 60b.
4. See *Aruch HaShulchan Even Haezer* 65:5.
5. *Even Haezer* 65:3 and *Orach Chaim* 560:2.

brance is acceptable.[6] The communities that do not have the custom of the ashes rely on the breaking of the glass after the *chuppah,* as well as the breaking of the plate at the *tena'im.*[7]

In the very near future, may we merit to share *simchos* without a need to commemorate the *Churban.*

---

6. *Tur* and *Beis Yosef* ibid.; *Chayei Adam* 137:2.
7. *Cf. Kaf HaChaim* 560:21; for other forms of *zecher l'churban.* See *Tur* and *Beis Yosef* ibid.

Kos Shel Berachah
at the Chuppah

As a professional photographer, I
attend many chasunos, and I always
have a close-up view of all the details
of the chuppah. I have noticed that the
chassan and kallah usually take a very
tiny sip of wine, and the cup is then
refilled (after the first set of berachos,
the Birchos Eirusin) or discarded (after
the second set of berachos, the Birchos
Nesuin). I was always taught that one
must drink a sizable amount of the
kos shel berachah at Kiddush and
Havdalah. Are the rules for berachos
on the wine at the chuppah different,
or are they drinking more than my
video camera would lead me to believe?

You are definitely an *observant* Jew, as well as an inquisitive one. Your question is one that is debated by the *poskim*, as we shall explain.

To clarify the following discussion, it would be helpful to list the *berachos* recited under the *chuppah*.

The marriage ceremony has two distinct halachic components: *erusin* and *nisuin*. In the times of the Mishnah, these took place months, or even a year, apart. For centuries, however, the custom has been that they are both performed at the *chuppah*. The *Kesubah* is read in between in order to separate them.

A separate *Borei Pri Hagafen* is recited preceding each of the segments. The *Birchas Erusin* is:

בָּרוּךְ אַתָּה ה׳ אֱלֹקֵינוּ מֶלֶךְ הָעוֹלָם, אֲשֶׁר קִדְּשָׁנוּ בְּמִצְוֹתָיו, וְצִוָּנוּ עַל הָעֲרָיוֹת, וְאָסַר לָנוּ אֶת הָאֲרוּסוֹת, וְהִתִּיר לָנוּ אֶת הַנְּשׂוּאוֹת לָנוּ עַל יְדֵי חֻפָּה וְקִדּוּשִׁין. בָּרוּךְ אַתָּה ה׳, מְקַדֵּשׁ עַמּוֹ יִשְׂרָאֵל עַל יְדֵי חֻפָּה וְקִדּוּשִׁין.

Blessed are You, HASHEM, our God, King of the universe, Who has sanctified us with His commandments, and has commanded us regarding forbidden unions;* Who forbade betrothed women to us, and permitted women who are married to us through canopy and consecration. Blessed are You, HASHEM, Who sanctifies His people Israel through canopy and consecration.

The *Birchos Nisu'in* are the blessings recited as part of *Sheva Berachos*.

The amount of wine or grape juice one must drink to fulfill the mitzvah of *Kiddush* and *Havadalah* is a *melo lugmav* — a cheekful. This amount is equivalent to a *rov reviis*, the majority of a *reviis* (halachic opinions range from 1.6 ounces to 2.7 fluid ounces). Many *poskim* rule that this amount must be consumed by one person, but others are more lenient and allow two or more people to drink an amount that would equal the *melo lugmav* when combined.[1]

It would therefore seem that the *chassan* or *kallah* should ideally drink *a melo lugmav*, and if that is too difficult, they should at least share the required amount between them. Another option might be to have one of the guests drink the required *shiur*, as, according to many

---

1. *Shulchan Aruch, Orach Chaim* 271:13-14. See *Beur Halachah*, which is strict on this issue and suggests that one person consume the proper amount when possible.

poskim, the *berachos* are not only for the *chassan* and *kallah* but on behalf of the guests as well. The guest who drinks must have in mind to be *yotzei* with the *Borei Pri Hagafen* of the *mevarech*, and the *mevarech* must have him in mind as well. It is not the accepted *minhag* to use this option.

However, as you have noticed, the prevalent practice seems to be that the *chassan* and *kallah* each take only a small sip, and the amount consumed is not even a combined *shiur* of *melo lugmav*. Some *poskim* explain this practice by pointing out that the cup of wine used for *berachos* under the *chuppah* is not an absolute requirement that would warrant the consumption of a *melo lugmav*, but rather a post-Talmudic custom requiring that the *chassan* and *kallah* merely taste the wine in order to avoid a *berachah l'vatalah*.[2]

Some limit the leniency of not drinking a *melo lugmav* to the *first* cup of wine used for the *Birchas Eirusin*, but insist that a proper *shiur* be consumed (at least by the *chassan* and *kallah* together) for the second cup under the *chuppah* used for the *Birchas Nesuin* (the six *berachos* recited after the *Kiddushin* and the *kriyas hakesubah*). These *poskim* feel that the second *Borei Pri Hagafen* is not a custom but a requirement.

This might explain why some *poskim* rule that one cannot recite the *Birchas Nesuin* without wine or *chamar medinah*, even though one *may* recite the first set of *berachos* (the *Birchas Eirusin*) without a beverage for *kos shel berachah*.[3] It would seem that the *kos* for *Birchas Nesuin* is a stronger obligation than the *kos* for *Birchas Eirusin*.

Those *poskim* who do not require a *melo lugmav* for either *kos* (*eirusin* and *nesuin*) might hold that neither *kos* is an absolute requirement, and therefore, even if no wine or *chamar medinah* is available, one can still recite both the *Birchas Eirusin* and *Birchas Nesuin*.[4]

In conclusion, it seems that the common custom to sip a tiny amount

---

2. See discussions that touch upon this in *Pnei Yehoshua in Kesubos, Kuntres Acharon 22; Sdei Chemed Maareches Berachos 3:5*, quoting *Knesses Hagedolah; Be'er Heitev, Even Haezer 34:6; Aruch HaShulchan, Even Haezer 62:8.*

3. See *Tur, Even Haezer, siman 2.*

4. *Rambam, Hilchos Ishus 10:4* and *Chelkas Mechokek, Even Haezer 62:1.* See, however, *Aruch HaShulchan, Even Haezer,* 62:67, who *paskens* that the *berachah* on wine or *chamar medinah* is an absolute requirement for *Birchas Nesuin*, even though he *paskens* that a small taste of wine is sufficient for both the *Birchas Eirusin* and *Birchos Nesuin.*

of wine from each *kos shel berachah* has a firm basis. However, if the *chassan* and *kallah* drink just a little more (half a cheekful each, or as little as approximately one ounce each, according to many *poskim*) from the second cup (the *kos* of *Birchas Nesuin*) they would fulfill the mitzvah according to all opinions.

Since it is a once-in-a-lifetime opportunity, it might be worth the small effort involved to achieve this *hiddur.*

Sheva Berachos — Panim Chadashos

As we were about to bentch at the sheva berachos seudah for my daughter and son-in-law, we were reminded that the person who was invited to be the panim chadashos had not shown up. My mechutan went to ask one of the waiters to join us so that we could recite the sheva berachos. A vehement debate erupted at that point, with many family members asserting that asking a waiter to participate at the last moment would not meet the halachic requirement of panim chadashos. My mechutan, however, insisted that it was fine, and I reluctantly agreed, not wanting to start a dispute over the matter.

Was he correct?

One must invite at least one individual to serve as *panim chadashos* at each of the festive meals that are made for the *chassan* and *kallah* during the seven days following the wedding (including the day of the wedding itself). This allows for the recital of the seven *berachos* at the conclusion of *bentching*.

(Although it is not the common custom among Ashkenazim, there are opinions that require at least two men to serve as *panim chadashos*).[1]

The *panim chadashos* (literally, "a new face") must be an individual who has not yet attended any of the festive meals or any of the previous *sheva berachos* recitals.

(There is a dispute recorded in *Shulchan Aruch* concerning a guest who came to the *chuppah* but not to the wedding meal. One opinion rules that he is eligible to serve as a *panim chadashos* for *sheva berachos* during the following week. It is best to invite someone who was not present at the *chuppah,* although there is room to be lenient when required.[2])

Optimally, *panim chadashos* should be a person (or people; see above) whose presence enhances the *simchah* for the *chassan,* the *kallah,* or their parents. An important person,[3] a close friend, or a close family member are examples of *panim chadashos* for whom one would normally prepare a fancier meal, for they bring added honor and joy to the festive occasion.[4]

If there is no one in this capacity, one may invite people who are not necessarily close friends, family, or dignitaries.[5]

However, one should make every attempt to avoid summoning a man off the street or a waiter in a last-minute attempt to fulfill the requirement of *panim chadashos*. Besides not fulfilling the definition of a true *panim chadashos* according to some opinions, the person selected will come with an added halachic disadvantage, because he was not really invited to join in the *simchah* of the *chassan* and *kallah*. Although there are opinions that do not absolutely require the *panim*

---

1. See *Chelkas Mechokeik, Even Haezer* 62:9; *Yabia Omer* 3:11.
2. *Even Haezer* 62:7.
3. See *Ohalei Yeshurun* 4:2.
4. *Shulchan Aruch* ibid. 8; see *Chelkas Mechokeik* 13.
5. See *Yabia Omer,* ibid.

chadashos to eat,[6] preferred *panim chadashos* are at least invited for the entire meal if they so desire and are not merely brought in to solve a halachic dilemma.[7]

One cannot say that your *mechutan* was wrong in insisting that the *sheva berachos* be recited with the waiter as *panim chadashos,* as there are *poskim* who are lenient in such a scenario.[8] The waiter should preferably eat bread, cake, or fruit (in descending order of halachic preference), or drink any beverage besides water. If that is not an option, one may rely on the opinion that *sheva berachos* are recited even if the *panim chadashos* has not eaten or drunk anything (see above). However, you would have been safe in omitting the *sheva berachos* if a more halachically preferable *panim chadashos* could not be found. (Even in the absence of *panim chadashos,* the *berachah* of *Asher Bara* should still be recited.[9])

It was wise of you to not start a dispute with your *mechutan* over the matter, especially if he did have an opinion to rely on. When you marry off your next child, *iy"H*, be careful to choose *panim chadashos* who are fitting and reliable and who will attend the *seudah*.

---

6. See *Rema Even Haezer* 62:7; *Yabia Omer* ibid.
7. See *Sove'a Semachos* 1:7.
8. See *Nesuin Kehilchasah* 14:63 quoting *Chinah V'Chisdah*.
9. *Shulchan Aruch* ibid.

Sheva Berachos at Seudah Shelishis and on the Final Day

My chasunah was six weeks ago, on a Sunday evening. The chuppah took place during bein hashemashos (after sundown but before nightfall), and the meal began at night. The question was raised whether we were permitted to hold sheva berachos on the Sunday after the chasunah, which is the eighth day if we count the chasunah from Sunday, but is still within seven days if we count from Monday. Although we opted to cancel the proposed Sunday sheva berachos due to the halachic uncertainty, I am curious to know if that was necessary.

A second question came up regarding

the reciting of sheva berachos after seudah shelishis. We ended seudah shelishis seventy-five minutes after sunset, right before Maariv of Motza'ei Shabbos. Many argued that even if we had decided not to recite sheva berachos on Sunday, we can certainly recite them at the end of Shabbos, for we had extended the kedushas Shabbos with our long seudah shelishis. Was our decision to recite sheva berachos at that time correct?

If a *chuppah* takes place before *shekiah* (sunset), that day is counted as "day one" of the *shivas yemei hamishteh*, the seven days of rejoicing during which *sheva berachos* are recited after a meal attended by the *chassasn* and *kallah* and at least ten men, at least one of whom was not present at the *chasunah* or at any one of the other *sheva berachos* meals. In the opinion of most *poskim*,[1] this applies *even* if the *chuppah* concluded right before sunset and the festive meal took place after dark (night is halachically considered to be the following day).

Your *chuppah* took place during *bein hashemashos*, between sundown and halachic night — the parameters of which are subject to great debate among the *Rishonim* and *poskim* — and, following the rule that we do not recite a *berachah* in cases of halachic doubt (*safek berachos lehakel*), you were correct in not reciting the *sheva berachos* on the Sunday following the *chasunah*. This is due to the fact that *bein hashemashos* has a doubtful status; we are uncertain whether it is still part of the previous day or if it is the beginning of the following day. To be certain, in your case we should consider Sunday as the first of the seven *yemei mishteh*. *Sheva berachos* are therefore recited for six more days, and Shabbos is the seventh and final day.

---

1. See *Pischei Teshuvah* 62:12, *Aruch HaShulchan* 62:3, *Yabia Omer* 5:7.

However, HaRav Moshe Feinstein, *zt"l*, is quoted[2] as having ruled that when the *chuppah* took place *bein hashemashos*, one can treat the *following* day (in your case, that would be Monday) as day one. Rav Moshe notes that this is a case of *sefek sefeka*, a double doubt. First, *bein hashemashos* itself is a gray area, as we are unsure which day it is. Secondly, there is a question regarding when the seven *yemei mishteh* begin. Although most authorities rule that they begin with the reciting of the *sheva berachos* at the *chuppah*, there are those[3] who maintain that the seven days actually begin with the meal at the *chassunah*. When the *chuppah* takes place during *bein hashemashos* (as it was in your case), the meal invariably begins after nightfall.[4]

Many *poskim* rule that one must complete the meal, *bentch,* and recite *sheva berachos* before *shekiah* of the seventh and final day.[5]

In your case, there was certainly room to be lenient and recite *sheva berachos* after *seudah shelishis*, even if you ended 75 minutes after sundown.

First, your *chuppah* took place *bein hashemashos* and your meal began at night, and as we have learned above, there are opinions that claim that when the meal begins at night, the seven *yemei mishteh* begin then as well (see Rav Moshe's double doubt discussed above).

Second, even if you consider your last day to be Shabbos, since you extended your *seudah shelishis*, one could suggest that just as the sanctity of Shabbos is extended until one *davens* Maariv on Motza'ei Shabbos, the seventh day of *yemei mishteh* is extended as well.[6]

Had you concluded *bentching* and *sheva berachos bein hashemashos,* there might have been yet another reason to allow the recital of *sheva berachos*, since your *chuppah* was held during *bein hasheashos* as well. This last point requires a more thorough explanation, but the intricacies of *bein hashemashos* are beyond the scope of this *teshuvah.*

These *sheva berachos* questions arise not only whenever a *chuppah*

---

2. *Ohalei Yeshurun*, page 32.
3. *Knesses Yechezkel*, siman 60.
4. See *Yabia Omer, Even Haezer* 5:7, where he uses a different double doubt to allow the recital of *sheva berachos* during *bein hashemashos* between the seventh day and the eighth day.
5. *Beis Chasanim* 7:13 in the name of *HaRav Yosef Shalom Elyashiv, shlita; Yabia Omer* 5:7.
6. See *Teshuvas Shevet HaLevi* 1:39, where he discusses such a possibility and concludes that this custom has a basis.

takes place *bein hashemashos*. The *sheva berachos* meal of the final day is frequently extended into *bein hashemashos* following the seventh day, raising many more questions concerning the permissibility of reciting *sheva berachos* at that time. Although it is understandable that the *chassan* and *kallah* do not want to see their *sheva berachos* end, one must make sure that no *berachos* are made in vain as they hold on to their final moments of *simchah*. Those planning the final *sheva berachos* meal should make every effort to end the meal early enough to avoid any question of a *berachah levatalah* (blessing in vain). If it is getting late and *shekiah* is approaching, those assembled can *bentch* and recite *sheva berachos* early, and then they may continue celebrating for as long as they wish.

As with all questions of *halachah*, one must ask a qualified *posek* for a final decision in each scenario, while providing him with the exact details concerning the timing of the *chuppah*.

May you be *zocheh* to build a *bayis ne'eman b'Yisrael*.

Torah Learning vs. Chasunah Attendance

I have an ongoing discussion with my wife concerning my attendance at the various simchos of our family, neighbors, and friends. We are fortunate to have a very large circle of relatives and acquaintances, and we have a vort, wedding, bar mitzvah, or sheva berachos to attend once or twice a week!

I participate in a Gemara shiur every night, and missing one-third of the shiurim due to simchos interrupts the flow of the Gemara and detracts from my understanding of the sugyos I'm attempting to learn. Even if I had time to catch up on the material I've missed, I couldn't make up the time lost from my learning. My nightly shiur is the

*only solid learning I have, and it is the
highlight of my day. (I have a short
seder after davening in the morning
to fulfill the mitzvah of "V'hagisa bo
yomam valaylah," but in the mere
fifteen minutes I have, I can't delve
into any topic with full concentration.)*

*My family and friends are important
to me, but my learning is an absolute
obligation, as well as my lifeline. What
should I do?*

The *Gemara* in *Kesubos* 17a states, *"Mevatlin talmud Torah
l'hachnasas kallah* — one must interrupt learning to participate in
a *chasunah.*" The Rema[1] rules accordingly, writing that one should
interrupt Torah study to join the *chuppah.*

Is there a requirement to interrupt learning for a wedding that has
sufficient attendees to honor the *chassan* and *kallah?* Would there still
be an obligation to attend in order to add more *simchah* and *kavod* to
the occasion?

The *poskim* are divided on this issue,[2] but in practical terms it is almost a moot point. This is because most *poskim* agree that in order to
trigger a real obligation to interrupt one's learning to be *mesamei'ach*
the *chassan* and *kallah,* one must actually witness the *chuppah* in for-
mation or in progress.[3] Since this is not often the case, there would be
no official obligation to go to a wedding that one merely knows about
(or has been invited to), since he is not witnessing the actual event.

There is another issue concerning not partaking of a *seudas mitzvah*

---

1. *Even Haezer* 65:1.
2. See *Shittah Mekubetzes Kesubos*, ibid. *d"h v'kama kol tzorchah; Teshuvos Maharam Shick #2;
   Sdei Chemed Maareches Chassan V'kallah* 22.
3. *Chelkas Mechokeik*, ibid.:2, suggests that perhaps one should not interrupt his learning if he
   merely knows that a *chuppah* is taking place in some other part of the city. See *Haamek She'eilah,
   shilta* 14:12 and *Sdei Chemed Maareches Chassan V'kallah* 22, who rule that there is technically
   no obligation to join the wedding if one does not actually see the procession, cf. *Beis Shmuel,*
   ibid.:3.

that one was invited to. For some reason that is not at all apparent, people are careful to avoid inviting others to a *seudas bris milah*[4] but are not careful when it comes to sending wedding invitations. Some suggest that the wedding invitations are sent to all family and friends even though it is understood that many will not or cannot come. It is therefore not an official invitation, but rather a customary friendly gesture.

Your dilemma is therefore a halachic and hashkafic question of a different nature. It is indeed a mitzvah to bring joy to the *chassan, kallah,* bar mitzvah *bachur,* etc. It is also a mitzvah to learn as much Torah as one can find time for. Which one takes precedence? Can we choose based simply on the dictates of our mood?

The answer is clear-cut, although its application requires dedication and honesty. As we have mentioned elsewhere, there is a general rule that one is permitted to interrupt Torah learning only in order to perform *mitzvos* that cannot be performed by others, such as *mitzvos* that are incumbent upon each individual to perform (*mitzvos sheb'gufo* — e.g., *tefillin,* matzah, *succah*) or any acts of *chessed* or community needs that will not be taken care of by others who are not learning at that time.[5]

The fact that the mitzvah of *talmud Torah* is more important than any other mitzvah is not just an important *hashkafah* and a codified *halachah;* it should impact, in a very practical way, many of the decisions we make on a daily basis. Everyone's time is limited, and we are consistantly faced with the challenge of where to place our focus during the precious hours (or minutes!) that we have free.

This is especially relevant in recent times, when we have merited to witness a tremendous population growth (*kein yirbu*) in the community, and modern transportation has made the numerous *simchos* accessible by car or short flight. Although these are certainly positive developments, it does make the decision-making process more complex.

The application of this *halachah* pertaining to your attendance at various *simchos* is as follows. You must honestly assess the importance of your presence (or the disappointment and frustration your absence

---

4. See *Gemara Pesachim* 113b and *Tosafos d"h V'ein; Rema Yoreh Deah* 265:12.
5. *Yerushalmi Pesachim* 3:7; *Rambam Hilchos Talmud Torah* 3:4; *Shulchan Aruch* 241:18.

might cause) at the *simchah* in question. If you are close family or very good friends, your presence will probably be necessary in some capacity.

Even when there is a requirement to attend, there are many opportunities to learn and enable others to learn at various times during the *simchah*. One should always remember to bring a *sefer* or photocopies along in order to utilize the downtime for learning.

Depending on his circumstance, one must decide whether learning in public will be viewed as *yuhara* — arrogance — in which case he shoud learn unobtrusively, or whether his Torah study will inspire others to follow his example, in which case he should not hide the fact that he is learning.

For the hour or more between the *chuppah* and the first dance, one can often find a *beis midrash* next door (or a vacant room in the facility) to learn or organize a *shiur*. The very positive phenomenon of attending a *shiur* during this time slot is gaining popularity and momentum. Many of the men at any given wedding are from the same shul or *beis midrash* and would naturally welcome the opportunity to continue their nightly *shiur* when possible, despite the lively and somewhat challenging atmosphere.[6]

If you are a more distant relative (or not-so-distant but one of thirty first cousins), or simply a casual friend who was really invited so that no one would be insulted, the assumption can be made that your personal *talmud Torah* takes precedence over attendance at the wedding.

If there is little travel time to the location of the *simchah*, it would obviously be proper to schedule a brief appearance to wish *mazel tov* and join the participants for a short dance.

One must factor *shalom bayis* issues into the decision as well. You must inquire about how your spouse or in-laws feel about the issue. If they feel very strongly that you should attend, perhaps you can delicately inquire if they are interested in asking your *posek* whether or not their demands are correct *al pi halachah*.

It is important to stress that no one is suggesting that one avoid doing *chessed* and performing *mitzvos bein adam lachaveiro*. How-

---

6. See *Rambam Hilchos Talmud Torah* 3:13 concerning the special importance and status of Torah learning at night.

ever, it is incumbent upon us to realize that *talmud Torah* is an all-encompassing obligation with strict, detailed parameters. One must be cognizant of the ongoing obligation and privilege of learning Torah, without disregarding the *mitzvos* and *chassadim* that demand attention in their proper time.

Striking the delicate balance between your obligation to learn as much as possible and obligations that are *bein adam lachaveiro* takes formidable strength, focus, and statesmanship. You will merit tremendous *siyatta* di'Shemaya if you act *lishmah,* for the sake of Torah, *chessed,* and *shalom.* May you be *zocheh* to share many *simchos* with others, and at the same time succeed in all your Torah-learning endeavors.

Celebrating a
Chanukas Habayis

**Is there an obligation to celebrate a
chanukas habayis upon moving to a
new house?**

If one builds or purchases a home in *Eretz Yisrael*, there is a *min-hag* to make a *chanukas habayis*.[1] The *chanukas habayis* is a festive meal that is made to celebrate the momentous occasion of purchasing a home in *Eretz Yisrael*. Although this festive *seudah* is not an actual obligation, it is a meritorious custom that is performed to express *hakaros hatov* to *HaKadosh Baruch Hu*.

There are *poskim* who feel that the building or purchase of a home outside of *Eretz Yisrael* is not a cause for celebration, but instead an occasion of mixed feelings because the home is being occupied in *Chutz La'Aretz*.[2] Others rule that a *chanukas habayis* is considered a *seudas mitzvah* even in *Chutz La'Aretz* if the celebration is carried out in the proper way and for the right reasons.

If the *chanukas habayis* is made to thank Hashem for His kindness and the *seudah* is replete with *divrei Torah* and words of *hakaros*

---

1. *Be'er Sheva* 73, quoted in *Be'er Hetev Yoreh Deah* 217:32 and *Pischei Teshuvah*, ibid. 16.
2. *Magen Avraham* 567:5.

hatov, it is considered a *seudas mitzvah* even when it is for a home purchased outside of *Eretz Yisrael.*[3]

A meal that is merely a social event, devoid of Torah and *yiras Shamayim,* is not a *seudas mitzvah.* And if one's intent is to show off his magnificent new home, causing needless jealousy and possibly *ayin hara,* it is certainly detrimental.

The Imrei Emes posits that the primary feature of a *chanukas ha-bayis* is the affixing of the *mezuzos,* citing *Targum Yonasan* on the *pasuk,* "*Mi ha'ish asher banah bayis velo chanacho* — Who is the man who has built a new house and has not inaugurated it."[4] The *Targum Yonasan* interprets "*velo chanacho*" as "*velo kava bei mezuztah le-shachlalusei* — and did not affix on it a *mezuzah* to bring to complete it." We see from this *targum* that the main aspect of inaugurating a new home is the fulfillment of the mitzvah of *mezuzah.*

---

3. *Yam Shel Shlomo, Bava Kamma* 7:37; *Magen Avraham* ibid.; *Yad Ephraim* ibid.; see also *Igros Moshe Yoreh Deah* 3:161.
4. *Devarim* 20:5.

MAASER, MONEY, AND MORE

Maaser From Your Paycheck

I recently began working, and my paycheck indicates that my employer withheld Federal, Social Security, and Medicare taxes. Do I calculate maaser based on my gross or on my net earnings?

Would Social Security tax be different from the other taxes, as I am really putting away money for my own use in the future?

My employer also withheld money to cover a major medical health plan. Is that amount subject to maaser?

Lastly, I requested that money be withheld for a pension plan and life insurance. What would the maaser obligations be concerning these funds?

Maaser is calculated based on the net salary earned, after taxes are withheld. This would be true even if the taxes were not withheld by the employer, but rather paid by the employee.[1]

Social security taxes are no different from other taxes that are due. This is because one is obligated by United States law to pay in to the Social Security system, and one never sees benefit from the money until retirement age. However, any Social Security benefits paid out are also subject to *maaser*, assuming that giving *maaser* would be affordable. (If the Social Security benefits are needed to cover *basic* living expenses and there is no other supplementary income, one would be exempt from giving *maaser*.)

Regarding medical insurance, if one would in any case purchase a similar major medical plan, it is possible that he should take *maaser* from the amount deducted by the employer. If he would not purchase such insurance or would purchase a less-expensive plan, and if the employer is packaging the plan together with the salary whether he requests it or not, then *maaser* money need not be deducted (or would be deducted only on the amount one would have spent had he been self-insured).

In regard to the pension plan, there is a choice. One can either take *maaser* on the amount deposited into the pension account, or separate *maaser* when the funds become available at retirement age.

Since you requested the life insurance, you must separate *maaser* from the amount of the premium. If life insurance is given to all employees whether they request it or not, it would depend on whether you would have purchased such a policy, as outlined above, with regard to health insurance

---

1. *Igros Moshe, Yoreh Deah* 1: 143.

A Gift for Our First Home

Our parents gave us money for a down payment on a starter home. We would like to know if maaser kesafim, separating 10 percent for charity, applies to this sizable gift. They are also buying us living-room and dining-room furniture. Would the halachah of maaser be different in regard to the furniture?

Although there are opinions that take a stricter approach, the common custom dictates that one need not separate *maaser* on a gift that is not cash (or its equivalent). You therefore need not calculate the value of the furniture in order to separate *maaser*.[1]

The *halachah* in regard to the money received for the down payment is a bit more complex. If your parents merely informed you that when you find your starter home they will issue a check for the down payment, there is no obligation to give *maaser*.

If, however, money was given to you to be used in the near future

---

1. *Minchas Tzvi*; 8:4.

as a down payment for the house of your choice, it will depend on the leeway they extend concerning your actual purchase. If you are able to buy the house without using all the money and you believe that your parents will have no problem with your diverting 10 percent of their gift to *maaser*, you will be obligated to give *maaser* from the money.[2] If you discover that your parents object to your separating 10 percent from the money they have given you, you are exempt from separating *maaser* from it. (You have the option of giving *maaser* on the amount at a later date, at such time that you can afford to do so. This option would be commendable, although not mandatory.)

If you are unsure about your parents' feelings in this matter, you should respectfully discuss the matter directly with them.

---

2. *Sefer Derech Emunah*, in the name of the *Chazon Ish*.

Recovering From a Bad Debt

Over a year ago I lent a friend $3,000 and he still has not paid me back. Upon investigation, I discovered that he is in serious debt due to financial reversals in his business. I therefore believe that I will not receive my money any time in the near or distant future. May I inform him that I forgive the loan completely and then recoup the money from my maaser account by separating the amount owed and withholding it to pay back the outstanding loan?

I understand from your question that the borrower is now halachically eligible to receive *tzedakah* (an individual who cannot meet payments for regular living expenses and does not have a job or investments that would ensure those payments within a reasonable time frame). If he is not, you certainly may not simply use *maaser* funds to write off bad loans.

If the borrower is now in a position that he can receive *tzedakah,* the answer to your question will depend on what was known and decided at the time of the loan.

If the borrower was, at the time of the loan, someone eligible to receive *maaser* money, and it was decided then that the lender would take repayment from his *maaser* funds in case of default, the borrower would be allowed to use *maaser* funds to repay outstanding debt.[1]

If the default was not anticipated and no such stipulation was made, one should not use *maaser* money to recover his loss.

The only scenario where it would then be permissible to use *maaser* is if the lender would — even if this man had not owed him the money — have given the borrower this amount of *tzedakah* from his *maaser* money. In such a case, the borrower must also be informed that *tzedakah* is being used for the recovery of money owed, and permission must be granted.[2]

---

1. See *Rema Yoreh Deah* 257; 5 based on *Gemara Gittin* 30a.
2. *Noda BiYehudah, Yoreh Deah* 2: 199.

Settling Disputes
the Kosher Way

Q *I am involved in a dispute with my partner and asked him to come to beis din and settle the matter in a proper way. He insists on submitting the matter to binding arbitration, claiming that there is no prohibition of going to secular court when two parties willingly bring a case before knowledgeable professionals who will arbitrate and render a fair decision out of court.*

Can I allow the case to go before arbitrators, rather than our own dayanim?

A It is apparent that your partner is aware of the serious prohibition concerning adjudicating in a secular court. The *halachah*[1] clearly forbids one to settle a dispute with a fellow Jew in a secular court. This prohibition

1. *Shulchan Aruch, Chosen Mishpat* 26:1, based on *Gittin* 88b.

applies even if the gentile judge uses Jewish law to reach a decision,[2] or when a Jewish judge bases the decision on a non-Jewish legal code.[3] It is prohibited even if both parties are agreeable to such action.

Those who bring their disputes to secular court cause a *chillul Shem Shamayim* because it sends a message that the parties involved give more credence to the laws and courts of the nations than they do to *Toras Moshe*. One who brings a fellow Jew to secular court must return the money awarded (if the same award would not have been received from a *beis din*),[4] as well as pay for damages and expenses incurred.

Although there are instances when *beis din* will give permission to take the dispute to secular court (such as when one of the parties is completely uncooperative during the proceedings in *beis din* or is delinquent in carrying out its rulings),[5] one must not sue in secular court until he has received a clear *psak* and specific parameters on how to proceed.

There are *poskim* who rule that one may bring his case in front of non-Jews for a judgment that is based solely on either common sense or industry-specific custom (arbitration at the Diamond Club for members of its industry is a case in point). It is permissible because one is not submitting to the authority of a recognized gentile court, nor is one following a decision based on a non-Jewish code of law.[6]

There are those who feel that this leniency should apply to modern-day arbitration. They claim that submitting to the decision of arbitrators who are not functioning as official judges and are not part of the governing legal system should not be a violation of adjudicating in a secular court. Many disputants prefer to litigate before an arbitration panel in order to save both time and money. The impartial individuals render a decision after hearing the arguments and examining the evidence, as would any official court of law. Their distinct advantage is that they are not bound by all the technicalities and red tape that make the legal system cumbersome, time consuming, and extremely expensive.

This matter, however, is far from simple. Most arbitration panels

---

2. *Shulchan Aruch*, ibid.
3. See *Chazon Ish, Sanhedrin* 15:4.
4. See *Chidushei* Rabbi Akiva Eiger ibid.
5. See *Shulchan Aruch*, ibid. 2.
6. *Aruch HaShulchan, Chosen Mishpat* 22:8, Rabbi Akiva Eiger, *Choshen Mishpat* 3, quoting Rav Shach; cf. Shach 22:15 and *Nesivos Hamishpat* 22:14; *Teshuvos Ba'ei Chayei Choshen Mishpat* 1:158 brought in *Tzitz Eliezer* 11:93.

follow guidelines that dictate how the arbitrators should formulate their binding decisions. Organizations such as the American Arbitration Association have protocols that suggest that the arbitrators follow the general dictates of the law of the land and legal precedent to reach their decision. In addition, there are federal guidelines for the procedure of arbitration.

Although the award of an arbitration panel is not often overturned by the court, the possibility of an appeal does exist if it can be proven that the arbitrators overstepped their bounds by handing down a decision that went contrary to common law and legal precedent. It is for good reason that many arbitrators are retired judges and attorneys; they are most qualified to decide how to apply the law to the particulars of each case.

Arbitrators are not strictly bound by case precedent or statutory law. Rather, they are guided in their analysis by the underlying policies of the law and are given wide latitude in their interpretation of legal concepts. On the other hand, if an arbitrator manifestly disregards the law, an award may be vacated.[7] In *Wilko v. Swan*, the U.S. Supreme Court suggested that an award may be set aside if it is in manifest disregard of the law. The Federal Standard for Arbitration states that manifest disregard of the law is a basis to vacate an arbitration award.

Although state law (especially in New York) may differ from federal law in the ability to vacate an award due to an arbitrator's disregard of the law, it seems that the initial expectation is that the arbitrators will use common law and precedent (as well as common sense) to formulate their decisions.

As mentioned, there are cases where arbitration would be permitted according to *halachah*. One may submit a dispute to an arbitrator whose decision is based on industry-specific custom and standards. However, many, if not most, arbitration panels follow the legal code of the country in which they reside. They will be very attentive to legal precedent in formulating their decisions. Submitting to the process of arbitration is extremely similar (in substance if not in form) to bringing one's case for a decision based on a non-Jewish code of law (*arka'os shel akum*) and is therefore often prohibited.

---

7. The Arbitrators' Manual- SICA, 2001.

Aside from the possible prohibition against arbitration, your partner will be losing the opportunity to hear the bona fide Torah view concerning your case. There are honest, professional, *batei din* that can settle your dispute. As is the case in any other field, one must consult knowledgeable people to receive guidance in finding the proper *beis din* for your case. Your Rav should be able to give you direction in this sensitive and crucial matter. Heeding the proper advice will help you and your partner reach the appropriate halachic conclusion and be *mekadesh Shem Shamayim*. It is an opportunity that no *frum* Jew can afford to lose.

The author would like to thank Judge E. Prus, H. Rothenberg, Esq., and S. Rubin, Esq., for the legal information they provided.

Timely Payment for Babysitters

Upon coming home very late from a chasunah due to traffic caused by a major car accident, I found a very tired and agitated babysitter waiting anxiously by the door. I was not surprised, for we were supposed to have been home no later than 11:30 and it was already 1 a.m. I apologized for our late arrival and frantically searched for the $42 that I owed her. When all I found was a $50 bill, she mumbled that it was okay and I could pay her the next day. Thoroughly exhausted myself, I accepted her gracious offer and walked her down the block. The next day, my husband dutifully took the money to our neighbor.

Two weeks after the incident, my

husband learned in a shiur about the importance of paying workers on time. He mentioned to me that what we had done was halachically incorrect. I was surprised, for the babysitter was clearly mochel the payment at the time.

Is my husband correct that we mishandled the situation? What are our options if this scenario repeats itself?

There is a Torah obligation to pay a worker on time. One who does so fulfills a positive commandment (*mitzvas asei*)[1] and one who fails to do so violates several prohibitions (*mitzvos lo saasei*).[2] Halachically, "on time" for a day worker means by the end of the day (before nightfall), and for a night worker, by the end of the night (before daybreak).[3]

This obligation to pay on time applies to minors as well.[4] Even if a child is asked to perform an insignificant job and is promised candy as payment for his/her "work," there is a bona fide obligation to ensure that the payment is made in a timely fashion.[5]

Technically, if the laborer does not demand payment, one would not be in violation of the *mitzvas lo saasei*. As you have suggested, one might assert that since your babysitter had not demanded payment, you have not committed an *aveirah*. However, the argument is debatable, for it is obvious that many children and young adults are too embarrassed to demand money; hence their implied *mechilah* might not be *mechilah* at all.

In your situation, the babysitter might have been *mochel* with a full heart so that she would not have to stay another moment while you searched the house for change. Even if that assumption were correct,

---

1. *Beyomo titen secharo — Devarim* 24:15.
2. There are actually five separate *lavim*; see *Bava Metzia* 111a.
3. *Bava Metzia* ibid., according to *Rabbi Yehudah* and *Rav*.
4. *Rambam, Hilchos Sechirus* 11:6.
5. See *Minchas Tzvi*, Vol. 2, 2:10.

you and your husband still lost the opportunity to fulfill the mitzvah of paying a worker on time. You might have avoided violating the *issur*, but by not having the correct change available, you missed a wonderful opportunity to perform the positive mitzvah. In the event that the babysitter really wanted the money on the spot but was afraid to insist on it, you would have violated the prohibition, as well as an infringing on a *bein adam lachaveiro* issue, by disappointing the young lady who left empty-handed after hours of work.

It would have been wiser to give her the $50 bill and request that she bring you the change the next day, or (if your budget allowed) simply round up the payment, especially considering the inconvenience, and give her the larger bill.

If you did not want to give her the $50 and await change, and she was not *mochel*, you would actually be obligated to seek out a 24-hour gas station or convenience store. In the modern city, and even in the suburbs, proper change can probably be procured within a short time. If this option is available, one would have an obligation to procure the proper change (if the babysitter agrees to wait); the *lo saasei* would be violated if one did not do so.

There is an important ancillary issue that bears mentioning: It is common for young babysitters to be reluctant to take a job for fear of staying up too late. (It is more often the babysitters' parents who voice this concern.) These young people often have school the following day. and must wake up early and rested for a long day of classes. It is extremely unfair to promise the young woman that you will be home by 11 if you know fully well that the first dance at the *chasunah* does not end until after 10 o'clock and the commute from the *chasunah* is at least an hour and a half! It is not thoughtful to come home an hour later than you promised with the unsatisfactory explanation that you were hungry and decided to stay until after the main course.

It is wonderful for the *chassan* and *kallah* when their guests stay for the main course — and for dessert as well — but not at the expense of the exhausted babysitter. (Incidentally, it is halachically problematic and morally unfair to lead those making the *simchah* into believing that you will be partaking of the main course when you are certain you will not!

Such practices frequently lead to aggravation over the enormous sums expended for food that went uneaten due to the lack of sensitivity on the part of unthinking guests. If you do not intend to eat, it is advisable to fill out the reply card of a wedding invitation in a way that indicates that you will be attending the *simchah* but do not want a meal to be reserved. On the other hand, those making a *simchah* would do well to remember how they feel when they are guests, and not needlessly prolong the waiting time. This will ensure that the friends and family can enjoy the *seudas mitzvah* and dancing with the *baalei simchah*.)

I understand that *you* were up-front with your babysitter and gave an accurate estimated time of arrival, and you simply got stuck in an unavoidable traffic jam. The problem is with those who habitually understate the length of time that they will be away from home. It is both proper and obligatory to give an accurate estimate of when you realistically expect to be able to relieve the babysitter and to hold yourself to the time promised.

Lending Money Without Proof

Q *I am a yeshivah bachur currently
learning masechta Bava Metzia.
I recently learned the sugya that
seems to say quite clearly that one is
not allowed to lend money without
proper evidence. It is quite common in
yeshivah for bachurim to borrow small
amounts of money for the purchase
of food, soda, and the like, without
writing any document of proof (shtar)
and without any witnesses. Is there any
justification for such a practice?*

Your question is an excellent one, for it seems to be fairly common
for people to extend small loans without proof they would be able to
use to collect the debt if the borrower denies owing it. This typical
scenario comes up among neighbors, at work, and, as you have mentioned, in yeshivah as well.

As you have learned, the *Gemara* rules that it is prohibited to lend money without witnesses or other legally valid proof of the loan, such as a document signed by the borrower or by two witnesses.[1]

One who lends money without evidence that would enable him to legally demand payment violates the prohibition of *"lifnei iveir lo sitein michshol,"* for he may possibly cause the borrower to sin by not repaying the loan. (Rashi explains that there is an immediate "stumbling block" placed in front the borrower, who might, from the very start, never intend to repay the loan, secure in the knowledge that the lender has no proof.[2])

The *Gemara* adds that the lender also runs the risk of bringing a curse upon himself, for when he attempts to collect the funds and the buyer denies the loan, bystanders might assume that the "lender" is actually a thief and a charlatan who is not really entitled to the money at all.

As the *Gemara* further explains, one should not even lend money to a *talmid chacham* without proof of the transaction. Although there is no reason to doubt the integrity of the *talmid chacham*, we are concerned that due to his constant, total involvement in learning, he might simply forget that he borrowed the money and come to innocently but incorrectly deny the existence of the loan.

Based on the above *Gemara*, the *Shulchan Aruch* rules that it is prohibited to lend money without some form of proof: a document, witnesses, or collateral.[3]

Why, then, is there a prevalent custom to lend small amounts without sufficient proof of the loan?

Rav Yitzchak Blazer is bothered by this apparent contradiction between the custom and the *halachah*.[4]

He notes that, by Torah law, *beis din* does not compel a borrower who completely denies having taken a loan to swear. However, the Sages instituted that such a borrower must swear to verify his claim (a *shevuas hesses*) or else pay.

---

1. *Bava Metzia* 75b.
2. Ibid., *d"h "over mishum lifnei iveir."*
3. *Choshen Mishpat* 70:1.
4. *Pri Yitzchak* 1:48.

He suggests that once *Chazal* instituted that the borrower must swear, there is no longer a real risk that he will deny the lender's claim; since people generally avoid at all costs swearing before *beis din*, the lender's claim will likely result in repayment of the loan.

Although Rav Blazer suggests this as a possible reason to defend the current practice, he concludes that one should *not* rely on any leniency. Rather, one should follow the opinion of the *Shulchan Aruch* and lend money only with proof that can ensure proper repayment.

The Ritva[5] is of the opinion that there is no actual prohibition against lending without proof; the *Gemara* is merely advising that one lend money only with proper proof. It is therefore only a stringency (*middas chassidus*) not to lend money without documentation or witnesses.

As an aside, Ritva's understanding is buttressed by an incident cited in the *Gemara*.[6] Rav Ashi was told that Ravina (his student-colleague) followed everything said by the Sages. Rav Ashi tested him by trying to borrow money from him without proof.

If it was Rabbinically *forbidden* to lend money this way, we would certainly expect Ravina to follow the law. If, however, it was rather Rabbinic *advice* and *middas chassidus,* Ravi Ashi's "test" is understandable.

In reality, however, most opinions maintain that this is an acutal *din* and not simply a *chumrah* or *middas chassidus*. They explain Rav Ashi's test was not whether Ravina obeyed the *takanas Chazal*, but whether he would apply it even to a proposed loan to his *rebbi*. Ravina's response indicated his absolute allegiance to the directives of *Chazal*!

Sdei Chemed[7] quotes the Ritva as a possible basis for the custom of those who are lenient, but also concludes that as a matter of *halachah* the leniency should *not* be relied upon.[8]

I would suggest that if someone wants to borrow a very small amount of money, there is a simple way to avoid the prohibition against lending money without proof. One can simply say that he would like to be paid back, but in the event that the borrower forgets, he hereby forgives the loan with a full heart. This up-front *mechilah* removes any issue

---

5. *Megillah* 28b.
6. *Bava Metzia,* loc. cit.
7. *Klalim Maareches Hei:* 88.
8. See *Aruch HaShulchan Choshen Mishpat,* ibid., for another possible defense of the lenient custom.

of "*lifnei iveir lo sitein michshol.*" It will never result in any criticism that the lender improperly demanded repayment of a loan, because the lender has agreed that no repayment will be demanded at any time.

This is a practical idea when your friends in yeshivah (or co-workers in the office) request a dollar or two for a soda. After making the above-mentioned declaration, you have avoided all problems. Either the loan will be remembered and repaid or, if the borrower forgets, then you have done the *mitzvah d'Oraisa* of *gemilas chassadim*.

When dealing with a loan you would collect if not voluntarily repaid, it seems that the vast majority of *poskim* rule that one must lend it only with proper documentation, witnesses, or collateral.

There is no obligation to document proof when lending an object (e.g., a lawn mower or a car). The Rabbinic enactment applies only when lending money.

Stealing Time at Work

I am a 26-year-old secretary working in a heimishe office environment. My boss tends to get very annoyed whenever he sees me speaking on the phone or spending time on personal e-mails, despite the fact that I manage to finish my work by the end of each day.

I recently discovered that he had the nerve to access my e-mail account to check on my volume of personal e-mails. I've even heard that he monitors the amount of time I spend on the phone (and tracks the numbers I call) via the office phone system.

I would like to confront him and let him know that what he did was completely prohibited. However, I must verify that I am 100 percent correct before doing so. Is there any halachic justification for my employer's actions?

It is clear that the *halachah* forbids an employee to waste time on the job. This includes excessive idle conversation between employees, prolonged personal phone calls, and use of e-mail for personal correspondence. When the boss does not allow these activities if they are not work related, it is a form of theft to use a company phone or computer for personal use. Worse yet, the employee is "stealing" by wasting precious time for which he or she is paid. *Chazal* in many places take a very strict stance on the employer's halachic right to demand sixty minutes of work for every hour of pay.[1]

Although it is clear that in today's work environment managers generally do make allowances for coffee breaks and some light conversation, one should not take advantage of their generosity. This is especially true in a situation where the employee senses that the boss does indeed mind that the time is being wasted, and all the more so in your office, where the employer has made that message crystal clear.

The excuse that you "manage to get the job done at the end of the day" does not have any bearing on the subject at hand. Without the extended breaks and distractions, your productivity would increase and your employer would be able to give you additional work. One cannot continue to steal time from his employer because he perceives that the boss is too strict. If you feel that the work schedule is too demanding and pressured, speak to your boss about it, or else seek employment elsewhere.

Let us now address your question concerning the right of management to spy on their employees. It is certainly preferable that employers notify employees of company policies concerning the monitoring of e-mail and phone use. The employer will thereby instill a sense of responsibility by motivating employees to put in a full day's work or face the consequences, and the employees will thus stay clear of any issue of dishonesty, due to the built-in deterrent. (The monitoring of employees' computer use will also ensure that the staff does not access inappropriate sites.)

There may be halachic grounds to permit the monitoring of employees even if the boss did *not* notify them of his "spy system." Although Rabbeinu Gershom issued a *cherem* (ban) on the reading of another's

---

1. See *Berachos* 16a for examples.

mail without permission (this might apply to e-mail as well), there are two reasons the *cherem* would not apply to your situation: First, the computer and the e-mail system are company property, and management has the right to ensure that no one is misusing its system. The second reason is that Rabbeinu Gershom issued his decrees to protect the laws of the Torah, not to enable people to violate them. One cannot invoke the *cherem* that protects the secrecy of correspondence in order to allow the office staff to waste time and misuse the company's property for personal use.[2] It is obvious, though, that managers should not read personal letters addressed to employees, as neither of the above reasons apply.

An honest work ethic is crucial for your *ruchnius* and *ehrlichkeit*. It is also an important opportunity for you to be *mekadesh Shem Shamayim* in the office and help others to do so as well.

---

2. See *Mishpitei HaTorah* page 337-338.

"Busy Work" for Idle Employees

THE RAMIFICATIONS OF ASSIGNING UNPRODUCTIVE TASKS AT THE OFFICE

Unfortunately, business is slow, and quite often my employees are left with no constructive work to do. This can happen several days a week for a few hours a day. These employees are actually enjoying the time off and fill these hours with extended coffee breaks, conversation, and computer games.

Although it is extremely annoying to see my hard-earned money being wasted on salaries for workers who are not earning their keep, I cannot blame them for not working if I cannot consistently supply them with work.

However, I have noticed lately that the

work ethic in the office has suffered to the extent that the employees do not want to apply themselves even when I do assign various projects that must be done with alacrity. It seems that being idle breeds laziness, and now that they are used to taking it easy, they find it difficult to perform even when there is serious work to do.

To combat and correct this problem, I have instructed my managers to ensure that all employees are given work to do throughout the entire day. My new policy is that if there are no "real" assignments to take care of, they should be given "busy work" — any task that keeps them occupied even though the work is of no value to the company. The advantage of busy work is that the employee does not become lazy or self-indulgent, and certainly does not become used to or come to expect an office environment consisting of coffee breaks, good conversation, and fun.

Although the employees are not told that they are given busy work, one of the frum workers figured out that a recent assignment was not a serious one. He refused to do it and even accused me of violating an issur by demanding that he engage in such nonsensical activities.

This employee could not quote any sources for such a prohibition, but he left me wondering whether my new office policy is really in violation of halachah. Could you please advise me as to whether it is permissible on both halachic and hashkafic grounds to maintain such a policy?

In regard to a possible prohibition concerning the assignment of duties that are not really productive in nature, there would seem to be an obvious source in *Chumash*.[1] The *pasuk* describes a poverty-stricken Jew who must sell himself as a servant (an *eved Ivri*) in order to survive. The *pasuk* warns the master *"U've'acheichem bnei Yisrael ish be'achiv lo sirdeh bo befarech — and with your brethren, the Children of Israel, you shall not subjugate him through hard labor."* Rashi explains that this prohibits the master from asking the servant to do "busy work" that is not necessary. Examples given are assignments such as heating up water that will not be used, or hoeing in the vineyard until the master returns. (The latter example causes psychological anguish. It is extremely difficult to work with an undefined or indefinite goal.)

The Rambam[2] describes *avodas perech* as Rashi does, but adds that the prohibition is violated when the servant is given unproductive and undefined work for the sole purpose of keeping him busy. (Rashi seems to indicate that the *issur* applies when the work is given to him in order to torment him. Rashi and Rambam may differ with regard to "busy work" given to an servant without intent to annoy, but rather so that he not become lazy by remaining idle for long periods of time.)

It would seem clear from the Rambam that there would be no actual halachic objection to giving an employee *avodas perech*, because the

---

1. *Vayikra* 25:39-43.
2. *Hilchos Avadim* 1:6, based on *Sifri*, להעבידו בלבד שלא יבטל.

prohibition is mentioned only in regard to an *eved Ivri*. The logical distinction between the two is that an employee is a free man and has the choice to leave his job at any time.

The *Sefer HaChinuch* (*mitzvah* 346) clearly states that the actual prohibition applies only to an *eved Ivri*. However, the *Chinuch* adds that hashkafically, one should be careful not to mistreat the poor and the downtrodden. The *Chinuch* specifically mentions the poor who are part of one's extended household, possibly referring to adopted orphans or domestic help. One might argue that members of the household are more similar to an *eved Ivri* than employees are, because they have nowhere to go to escape their misery, as opposed to employees who have the option to leave at anytime to find a job elsewhere. However, the reality of the job market (especially in times of economic downturn) dictates that most employees are too apprehensive to leave their job unless the likelihood of finding a better job presents itself.

The *Chinuch* further cautions that those with wealth and power must always bear in mind that wealth and poverty are symbolized by *Chazal* as a wheel that revolves around the world, affecting different people at different points in time (*galgal hu shechozer ba'olam*).[3] One could lose his money and find himself in need of the kindness and generosity of others, and it therefore behooves those who can help others to do so, focusing on the sensitivities and feelings of those on the receiving end.

It behooves every employer to remember the awesome words of the *Chinuch* at all times.

Unlike the Rambam, the *Shaarei Teshuvah* (3:60) rules that the verse in question applies not only to a master and a servant, but to any man and his fellow Jew. *Shaarei Teshuvah* understands it as prohibiting any Jew to command another to perform any work (difficult or easy) if the worker will not refuse the command only because he fears the boss or because he is embarrassed to deny the request.

According to this *Shaarei Teshuvah*, it would be prohibited to demand that an employee perform useless work if the employee is acceding to the request only out of fear for his job.

---

3. See *Shabbos* 151b.

Whether halachically prohibited or not (this may depend on the dispute mentioned above), your practice of assigning busy work is not hashkafically sound, and it is certainly not beneficial for your *middos*.

It would seem that giving your staff "busy work" could backfire and undermine productivity in the long run. The other employees will eventually catch on, and resentment will build. The ill feeling toward management will probably result in an even more lackadaisical approach to work, as well as a source of divisiveness and strife in the office

Although you are correct that idleness has had a detrimental effect on the overall productivity of your staff, I would encourage you to find some productive work for your employees' time. I would hope that this would be a more positive way to motivate people and make proper use of their time.

A Secretary's Dilemma

I work as a secretary in an all-Jewish accounting firm, with many conveniences that greatly enhance the work environment for the mostly Orthodox staff. There are four partners in this small firm, two of whom are frum and two of whom are not.

Despite the generally religious atmosphere in the office, I find myself repeatedly faced with a halachic issue. Ignoring the objections of the other partners and employees, the most senior partner, who is not observant, insists on ordering food from a nonkosher restaurant for clients who come to the office for meetings. We have tried to convince him to order kosher food, with limited success.

I am this partner's personal secretary,

and I am often told to order the nonkosher food and set up the conference room for lunch. I have already tried refusing to do so and have been told in no uncertain terms that as long as he is the senior managing partner, I am to do as I am told — or else!

Is it permissible for me to continue under these circumstances? Is the problem mitigated by the fact that they will get another employee to order and serve the food if I don't?

It is indeed prohibited to order nonkosher food for the Jewish clients or to take part in setting up or serving the meal. (This would, of course, apply to the ordering or preparation of nonkosher food for your boss or any other Jewish staff member.) As we will explain, to do so would violate either the prohibition of *lifnei iver lo sitein michshol* (placing a stumbling block in front of a blind man; in this context, the blind men are the unfortunate people who are not aware of their obligation to keep *mitzvos* in general and to eat only kosher food in particular), or the *issur d'Rabbanan* (Rabbinic prohibition) of *misayei'a lidvar aveirah*, aiding and abetting another in sinning.[1]

The fact that your firm has only Jewish personnel compounds the problem. This is because many *poskim* say that one cannot claim that the prohibition is mitigated by the mere fact that someone else might do it. Since "the other person" is also a Jew who is bound by the same prohibition of *lifnei iver*, all those involved are similarly proscribed.[2]

Although one is not obligated (and is in fact usually prohibited) to

---

1. See *Tosafos* in *maseches Shabbos* 3a, *d"h bava d'reisha*; *Magen Avraham Orach Chaim* 347:4.
2. See *Mishneh LaMelech, Hilchos Malveh Veloveh* 4:2; *Chochmas Adam, Klal* 130, end of paragraph 2.

spend more than one-fifth of his assets on any *mitzvas asei* (a positive mitzvah, as opposed to a prohibition), he must be willing to spend all his money in order to avoid violating a Biblical prohibition.[3]

Losing a job (that cannot be replaced) is similar to losing one's assets, and one would be required to give up a job that entails violating *issurim* (prohibitions) that are *mi'd'Oraisa* (of Biblical origin). Some *poskim* would assert that a client who comes to your boss' office for a lunch meeting would not necessarily be eating nonkosher had he stayed in his own office. It is quite common for a person's lunch to consist of a simple tuna or peanut butter sandwich, which more often than not is, unintentionally, kosher. It is also common for busy employees or executives to skip lunch entirely. Serving them a nonkosher meal in your office, therefore, might entail the *issur mi'd'Oraisa* of *lifnei iver lo sitein michshol*, even if they could have purchased nonkosher food themselves.[4]

Other *poskim*[5] would argue that although the clients are eating nonkosher food at your company's invitation, they could purchase their own nonkosher food if they so desired. Those *poskim* hold that we are therefore not dealing with the *issur mi'd'Oraisa* of *lifnei iver*, but rather with the *issur d'Rabbanan* of *misayei'a lidvar aveirah*.

Even if one were to argue that the clients could purchase their own nonkosher food if they wanted to, and therefore we are dealing not with the *issur mi'd'Oraisa* of *lifnei iver*, but rather with the *issur d'Rabbanan* of *mesayei'a lidvar aveirah*, it might still be an issue to remain at your job. This is because there are many *poskim* who rule that one must give away all his money to avoid even a Rabbinic prohibition.[6]

A detailed consultation with a Rav familiar with your circumstances and these *halachos* is necessary, expecially if it is not possible for you to find another job immediately and your livelihood or that of your family depends on your current income (in other words, the job is not merely providing for luxuries or the general growth of your equity).

---

3. *Rema Yoreh Deah* 157:1; *Rema Orach Chaim* 556:1.
4. See *Chofetz Chaim, Hilchos Lashon Hara* 9:1 in *Be'er Mayim Chaim*. The *Chofetz Chaim* seems to understand that *lifnei iver* is violated even if the transgressor could have performed the *aveirah* himself, as long as he would not necessarily intend to transgress were it not presented to him.
5. *Taz Yoreh Deah* 148:3; *Chochmas Adam, Klal* 130; see parenthetical comment in middle of paragraph 2.
6. See *Pischei Teshuvah Yoreh Deah*, ibid. 4, for a summary of the dispute on this point.

(A possible avenue of leniency for such dire circumstances could be based on *Shach Yoreh Deah* 151:6; *Dagul Mirevavah*, *d'h* "*Mah she'ein kein.*" Other *poskim* take issue with this leniency; see *Rema*, ibid.; *Magen Avraham Orach Chaim* 345:4.One must bear in mind that any possible leniency would only be based on the assumption that we are dealing with the *issur d'Rabbanan* of *mesayei'a lidvar aveirah*. However, as mentioned above, there is reason to believe that the actual prohibition here is in fact an *issur mi'd'Oraisa*, and therefore relying on the *Shach* and *Dagul Mirevavah* would not even be an option to consider.)

It is important to stress that the *halachos* concerning *lifnei iver* are quite serious and very complex. One must give an honest and accurate assessment of each situation, because even one small detail can change the *psak halachah*.

If you are able to stay employed and still maintain your refusal to order and serve nonkosher food, you need not be concerned that other employees might violate *lifnei iver* in your stead.

You mention that you have attempted on many occasions to convince your boss to order only kosher cuisine and have not met with success. If you are able to remain with your company in a halachically justifiable way, it is worthwhile and even obligatory to continue your attempts in a respectful yet persuasive way (although not at the cost of losing your job.[7] One never knows how much effort might be the catalyst to reach the *pintele Yid* within him).

---

7. *Rema, Yoreh Deah*, 334:48; *Rema*, ibid. 157:1; *Pischei Teshuvah*, ibid. :5 quoting *Levush*.

Stealing Clients and Customers

I am an attorney at a law firm in New York City. Throughout my six-year tenure as an associate in the litigation department, I have been given many prestigious corporate clients whom I have represented rather successfully. Although my initial connections to these clients were a result of the hard work and vast experience of the partners I worked for, the ongoing relationships for the past few years have been primarily with me. I am the main contact for most aspects of the litigation, while my superior is still technically responsible for my entire caseload.

Having received a lucrative offer from a competing law firm, I am seriously contemplating leaving my present position. It is obvious that the current offer to me is because I service such extremely profitable clients, and I will be expected to exert every effort to bring them along to the new firm. Am I allowed to lure away these clients from my present firm?

Although this question is quite common, it is rarely posed as a halachic *she'eilah*. I therefore commend you for your realization that your expected cooperation in this matter might possibly be prohibited. **Please bear in mind that this topic is complex and that the answer depends on many specific details and the exact circumstances. A rav must be consulted in each case.**

Presented here is some of the background:

The Rashba[1] deals with a case of a Jewish tailor who had a long-standing relationship with a client. A second Jewish tailor came to town and lured away the client at a heavily discounted rate. The first tailor sued for damages of lost income at the local Rabbinical court. The case was sent to the Rashba, who ruled that it was highly improper for the second tailor to infringe on the first tailor's livelihood by "stealing" his client.

The Rema[2] quotes the ruling of the Rashba, as well as an opposing ruling, stating that the final decision in each individual case should rest with the local *beis din*. However, most later *poskim*[3] accept the ruling of the Rashba as binding, and therefore deem the practice of stealing clients and customers to be unethical. It is certainly prohibited to lure a customer out of a competitor's store or office once he/she is actually making a purchase or actively doing business there. That would be comparable to the case in *Bava Basra* (21b) stating that fishermen are

---

1. *Teshuvos HaRashba* 6:259,
2. *Choshen Mishpat* 156:5
3. See *Pischei Choshen* Vol. 4, Ch. 9, footnote 20.

prohibited from setting up nets near the nets laid by others who were set up there first. Since the fish are accustomed to coming to the bait in the first net, a new competitor may not intercept them.[4]

One would have to examine the particular nature of each industry before applying the ruling of the Rashba. In a business filled with intense competition, where customers are bombarded with solicitations from potential suppliers or where clients constantly seek to change the companies that service them, the Rashba might agree that one need not refrain from luring clients from the competitors. This is because if one will not attempt to lure the customer, someone else inevitably will.

However, when discussing higher-end law or accounting firms, it is common for clients to stay with a firm as long as they are happy with the service. It is unusual for a client to leave a law or accounting firm for the insignificant savings they would gain through a slightly lower hourly billing rate.

It is crucial at this point to differentiate between three possible scenarios.

Scenario number one (which is similar to your situation) is when an associate in a law firm is handed clients on a silver platter. The associate did nothing to cultivate the business. With regard to such cases originated by the firm and merely assigned to the employee, the firm would generally insist on contacting such clients to inform them of the associate's planned departure and would seek to prohibit the attorney from making any contact (either by phone or by letter) with such clients prior to or after leaving the firm. Instead, the firm would handle the client contact either through a face-to-face meeting or through a letter to each client.

It would certainly be prohibited for the associate to attempt to persuade the client to join him, as illustrated by the following true story: A young accountant with no experience was hired by a certain firm, and he was assigned several established clients for ongoing work and service. As you will see from the letter below, the accountant now wishes to leave the employ of his boss to open his own independent practice. There is certainly no halachic problem with doing that, nor is there any

---

4. See *Teshuvos Chasam Sofer, Choshen Mishpat* siman 79.

dina demalchusa (civil law issue), as we live in a free country with laws to protect free enterprise (assuming there is no noncompete agreement in place). *What is prohibited is the writing of the letter and the subtle attempt to convince the client that it is in his best interest to follow the accountant to his new firm.*

(The names have been altered to protect the privacy of the principals involved.)

> Dear Mr. Schwartz,
>
> It has been a pleasure working for you to achieve your annual pension objectives and administrative tax requirements. Please be advised that for over five years I have been responsible for designing and administering the pension plans for Mr. Goldstein's clients. I have made it my responsibility to provide you with exemplary services and hope you have been personally satisfied with my annual work product.
>
> I am writing you at this time to inform you that I will be leaving Mr. Goldstein's employ to establish my own practice, with a continued emphasis on qualified pension-plan design and related tax issues. I have been instrumental in the calculation of your annual pension contribution. I believe that I have a unique and thorough knowledge of your pension-plan design and needs, and would be pleased to continue to provide annual compliance and administrative services to you.
>
> Please indicate by your signature below whether you would like to retain my services or whether you would like to be represented by Mr. Goldstein. It has been a privilege to work with you, and I look forward to a continued relationship.
>
> If you have any questions, please do not hesitate to call.

In *scenario number two*, a partner (or associate) originates business based solely on contacts, such as family, close friends, or clients from a previous venture. It would be halachically permitted for him to *solicit* his clients to join him if these clients came to the firm initially with him or because of him. (The solicitation should not be done during his current firm's time or with use of their resources.)

Scenario number three involves a partner who is servicing sizeable, prestigious clients.

In this case, one would expect the corporate client not only to have developed a close relationship with the departing partner (or senior associate) in charge of such work, but also to demand up-to-date information as to who is performing such work and to approve any changes in personnel. It is then the client's choice to decide whether or not to follow the departing partner (or associate) to his new firm.

For an example of how notification should be written in such a case, I have included an actual business document written by a lawyer who has many institutional clients. The letter was sent from the *new* firm, thus avoiding any inappropriate use of the former company's time, stationery, or e-mail for any correspondence that would be to its detriment.

The names have been altered to protect the privacy of the principals involved.

> Dear Mr. Mason,
>
> This is to notify you that I have withdrawn as a partner in the law firm of Lasky, Cohen & Schwartz, LLP, effective on May 17, 2005. As we have discussed, I am now with Shaffer & Fein, LLP.
>
> The Rules of Professional Conduct of the legal profession guarantee the right of every client to choose his or her own lawyer and to change lawyers at any time. You therefore have the right to determine who shall represent your interests and handle your transactions in the future.
>
> For your convenience, you may indicate your

decision concerning your continued and future representation and provide me and Lasky, Cohen & Schwartz, LLP with written instructions concerning the disposition of your files by checking the appropriate box below.

☐ We wish to continue to be represented by Lasky, Cohen & Schwartz, which should retain our files.

☐ We wish to be represented by Mr. Karlinsky's new firm, Shaffer & Fein, LLP. Please cease all work on certain pending matters.

☐ We wish to be represented by the firm, _____. Please cease all work on certain pending matters.

Thank you for your attention to this matter.

As you have read for yourself, the letter is a concise document that fulfills the halachic as well as the legal requirements and expectations regarding the contact of this client.

In summary — in the absence of an agreement to the contrary — it would *generally* be halachically permitted for a professional to *solicit* his clients to join him if these clients initially came to the firm with him or because of him. When they are not "his clients," notifying them *without solicitation* from your *new* place of business would be acceptable if it is clearly expected and compatible with the ethical guidelines of your specific business environment. (See *scenario number three*, above.)

In marked contrast, the smaller-firm environment, particularly one that services individuals rather than corporations, presents different rules for departures of attorneys. If the professional was assigned these clients as a paid employee of the firm, they are obviously not "his clients" at all. Do not forget that even if he were able to further cultivate their business, it *generally* involved the firm's sterling reputation, with the help of its expense account, credit cards, and paid business trips. The handling of such a professional's departure must therefore be left to the discretion of the firm's management.

If a professional's departure is handled correctly (both halachically and legally), and a client *insists* on retaining your services, there is no requirement to turn down the offer.

When serious money is at stake, people tend to find much room for lenience. It is imperative that objective halachic opinion be sought for such a monumental decision.

A rav must be consulted in each situation, and the employer may have to be given the opportunity to present his side to the Rav as well.

Bear in mind that your decision has the potential to create a *kiddush Hashem* or, *chas veshalom*, a *chillul Hashem* among your colleagues, Jews and non-Jews alike.

Two-Tiered Hotel Rates

The following three letters were originally written to the editor of the Hamodia newspaper. The first two were printed with a short response from this writer. The third letter appears here, together with an in-depth response and a halachic and hashkafic overview of the entire subject.

To the Editor:

I am writing this letter just to alert your readers so that they aren't cheated, as we were.

I was recently at a hotel in Israel for one night. I called to reserve a room before my arrival and was charged an "American tourist" price of $185 per night. After leaving the hotel, I came *to suspect that Israeli visitors get an "Israeli" price of 600 shekels per night (equivalent to $140). I confirmed my suspicions by calling the hotel and speaking in Hebrew. I was immediately given the 600-shekel price. I then called again and spoke in English and was given the "American" price. Be careful! Check twice before reserving! Have an Israeli friend reserve the room for you!*

Hatzlacha Rabbah.
Y.D.,N.Y.

To the Editor:

You recently published a letter regarding different rates for Israelis and non-Israelis charged by hotels in Israel. The writer suggested that an American should have an Israeli friend reserve the room to get the less-expensive rate.

I believe that such a suggestion has no place in a Torah-guided newspaper. Dina d'malchusa dina (the law of the land) would certainly apply in Israel as well as in America. The policy of charging different rates to Israeli citizens and non-Israeli customers is not an arbitrary policy of hotels in order to get more money out of foreign citizens. Rather, it is a government-imposed law, and to circumvent this policy is, in my opinion, gezel and in this situation, gezel from a Yid, chas veshalom.

I can't imagine that the Chofetz Chaim or any other of our Gedolim would sanction the practice suggested by Y.D., and I strongly protest the publication of the letter.

S.S., N.Y.

To the Editor:

Charging tourists more than locals for hotels or any other service is certainly not Israeli government policy. If anything, the opposite is true, because Israeli citizens are obligated to pay Value Added Tax (VAT) for tourism services, while tourists are not.

What is happening is discriminatory pricing, pure and simple. It is an attempt to exploit the assumed "deep pocket" of the foreign tourist.

After repeated reports in various Israeli newspapers (including, incidentally,

Hamodia) about this practice, the Israeli Tourism Ministry conducted its own investigation and discovered that the newspaper reports were accurate; tourists were being charged anywhere from 3 percent to 50 percent more, depending on the hotel and whether it was a weekend or midweek reservation.

The ministry's response to this was reported last week in the Israeli press. According to Haaretz (July 10):

> *It's all true: The Tourism Ministry has found that tourists really are being ripped off at some hotels. The investigation revealed significant differences between the prices that Israelis and tourists are charged, mainly at 4- and 5-star hotels and at Jerusalem and Dead Sea resorts as well. It is illegal to discriminate in that fashion, the ministry reminds Israel's hoteliers....*

> *Tourism Ministry officials are considering whether clamping down could impair the hotels' freedom to adjust prices based on supply and demand.*

The law also defines tourism as a public service. Thus, it would follow [that] hotels are not allowed to discriminate between tourists and local residents.

Israel's tourism minister, Yitzchak Herzog, was horrified. He was quoted in the article as saying, "The phenomenon of price discrimination in hotels between Israelis and tourists is a hurtful problem that arises again and again."

He also mentioned the negative image this casts on the local tourism industry, which is "striving to increase as much as possible the number of incoming tourists." What's more, the hotels' own industry association [is against] this practice. According to the press reports, Hotel Association CEO Tova Pinto distributed a letter to her members that said that the phenomenon of "charging a different price to a tourist and an Israeli at the reception desk on the same date creates a negative image for Israeli hotels [because it] is interpreted as apparent discrimination" against the tourist.

So it is clear that the inyan of dina d'malchusa dina is totally irrelevant in this instance. This is not to say that Y.D.'s original suggestion of getting an Israeli to book a room for you is valid, but it isn't clear that it would be gezeilah [as S.S. contends]. Unless you are assuming that a foreign tourist eats twice as much as an Israeli or is more likely to steal the towels, of what significance is the guest's nationality to the hotel's bottom line?

It would be worthwhile for Rabbi Viener to address these issues. Perhaps he can make this the subject of a future column.

S.A., Yerushalayim

Tricking hotels into providing their rooms and services for the discounted price not intended for tourists is a serious issue of *geneivah* and *geneivas daas*. The fact that the tourist is not eating more than the average Israeli (which might or might not be the case) and therefore does not cost the hotel more is irrelevant. If the seller of goods or services quotes a price and the buyer does not fully pay the requested fee, it is a form of *geneivah* [except for specific instances where a price is being extorted; the parameters of those *halachos* are beyond the scope of this artcle, but they certainly do not apply in this case].

In addition, asking an Israeli friend or relative to reserve the room, or misrepresenting your nationality, can cause a *chillul Hashem* if and when the plot is discovered. (I am told that many hotels demand a *teudat zehut* from Israeli citizens and a passport from tourists.)

This maneuver has other negative repercussions as well. Devious behavior has a terrible effect on one's *middos*. Use of trickery and "shtick" becomes habitual and addictive.

S. A. of Yerushalayim mentioned that the government does not support the practice of price discrimination, and that seems to be absolutely correct. However, it does not follow that hotel-pricing discrepancies are illegal.

The parameters and halachic viability of *dina d'malchusa dina* in general and in *Eretz Yisrael* in particular are subjects of great debate in the *poskim*, and are beyond the scope of this article. Those halachic disputes will, in any event, not affect the *psak* for this particular situation. Since two-tiered pricing is not in clear violation of Israeli law, the hotel owners would not be in violation of *dina d'malchusa*.

I have researched the Israeli law concerning discrimination vis-à-vis hotels and their customers. Some of the foremost attorneys in Israel were consulted for their opinion concerning the case at hand. All were in agreement that there is no official law prohibiting a hotel from maintaining a dual-pricing policy, and this is quite clear from the *Haaretz* article cited by S.A.

Neither the Ministry of Tourism nor the Hotel Association approves of the policy of price discrimination ("Israel's tourist minister, Yitzchok Herzog, was horrified" *Haaretz*, July 10), and they are embarrassed by the negative public relations generated by such behavior. However, the fact that they are unhappy with hotel policy does not mean that it is illegal. No legal expert or judiciary committee even attempted to file a suit or a motion to condemn or disallow the practice (even after the exposé in the Israeli media!).

To further clarify this issue, I will quote pertinent excerpts (translated from the original Hebrew) from the anti-discrimination law that was passed by the Israeli government six years ago.

Purpose:

This law is intended to promote equality and prohibit discrimination when entering public places and when supplying products and services.

Prohibition of Discrimination

A person whose business is the supply of a product or service to the public or the operation of a public place will not discriminate [either] in the supply of the product or public service, [or in] allowing entry to a public place, or [in] the provision of services in a public place, because of race, religion or religious group, nationality, country of emigration, etc.

Definitions:

"Public Place" Any location intended for public use, including a tourist area, hotel, hostel, guesthouse, etc.

"Public Services" Transportation services, communication services, energy, education, culture, tourism, and financial services.

It is clear from these excerpts that an anti-discriminatory law concerning public services does exist, and that tourism is considered a public service. However, the law itself defines discrimination as not supplying the service or not allowing access into a public place on the basis of race, color, creed, or nationality. No law exists regarding hotel-pricing disparity, even though the dual pricing does depend on the nationality of the customer.

This is because the dual-pricing policy does not exist to discriminate against the tourist; rather, it services the economic necessities of the hotel industry. The reason that the hotels have discounted pricing for Israeli citizens is because the average Israeli cannot afford the standard international hotel rate, while the typical tourist can. The rates charged to tourists are not necessarily above the normal price for similar lodging internationally. It is therefore not price discrimination against tourists, but a price reduction for the local population.

The hotels must offer the local population affordable pricing so that they can remain as full as possible during all seasons. Due to the destructive nature of wars and terrorism, it is difficult for the hotels to remain profitable, and providing financial incentive to people who would otherwise not make a reservation insures the survival of the hotel industry.

I do not expect the tourist to be happy with this double-standard pricing. Nor am I insisting that the policy is morally 100 percent correct. However, unless the policy violates *halachah* or government law, one may not resort to trickery and subterfuge to receive goods and service for even one penny less than the price at which the owner is willing to provide them. To do so would violate *halachah*, not to mention that it is detrimental to one's *middos* and risks causing a *chillul Shem Shamayim*.

One visits *Eretz Yisrael* to absorb the *kedushah* and to benefit from the *aliyah* in *ruchnius*. It would be a great pity to squander these transcendent benefits by becoming involved in dubious monetary transactions.

Repaying Creditors

*After two years of very poor sales,
it seems that my business is headed
toward bankruptcy. Although I have not
filed for bankruptcy and there is a small
possibility that with Hashem's help I
might be able to turn things around,
I would like to clarify my halachic
responsibilities toward my creditors.*

*What is the halachic permissibility
of availing myself of bankruptcy
protection? Does the law of the land
allow me to erase debt that is owed to
Jews? Are we not all bound to follow
Torah law as spelled out in Gemara and
in Shulchan Aruch Choshen Mishpat?*

The parameters of *dina d'malchusa dina* (the obligation to follow
the law of the land[1]) is a widely discussed subject in the *Rishonim* and

---

1. See *Gemara Nedarim* 28a.

Acharonim. Some limit its application strictly to matters that directly affect the government, such as the right to tax. Others apply *dina d'malchusa dina* more broadly and include any law that benefits the people of the land.[2] This second opinion would seem to favor the halachic application of bankruptcy protection. However, the concept of *dina d'malchusa dina* as applied between two *Yidden* is the subject of an extensive discussion in the *poskim*.[3]

Regarding the practical *halachah* concerning bankruptcy protection in a business setting, many *poskim* rule that one is absolved from any further payment to any creditor after the bankruptcy court allocates the remaining assets of the company.[4] The logic is ultimately based on the assumption that anyone doing business in a country with modern bankruptcy statutes is extending or receiving credit based on the *minhag hamakom,* the rules and regulations that are prevalent in that particular place.[5]

It is well known that not all companies survive in the very competitive environment in which they operate, and many are ultimately forced into bankruptcy. The investor or supplier extends credit assuming that risk. Therefore, even if both the creditor and debtor are Torah-observant Jews, there will be no requirement to repay the debt above and beyond what is required by the court.

This logic might not apply to relief from creditors via personal bankruptcy. One cannot assume that the loan given or credit extended by a friend or neighbor was with the assumption that the obligation of payment would be based on corporate bankruptcy laws.

(It is important to point out that whether the company is officially incorporated might not be relevant to this halachic application. The issue concerns the intention and assumption of the person extending the credit. Would most creditors in this situation assume that their loan is covered by common business law, or is it a loan of a personal nature that is not bound by the practices of the marketplace?)

Note that although relying on bankruptcy protection is permissible

---

2. *Rema* 369:11.
3. See *Rema Choshen Mishpat* 73:14; *Shach* ibid. :39; *Chazon Ish* CM 16:1.
4. See *Igros Moshe Choshen Mishpat* 2:62, *Teshuvos Vehanhagos Choshen Mishpat* 2:701.
5. See *Igros Moshe Chosen Mishpat* 1:72.

according to many *poskim*, it is not the preferred course of action and should be avoided if at all possible. There are two reasons why the option of bankruptcy should be discouraged.

First, there are *poskim* who do not allow cancellation of debt through bankruptcy protection.[6]

Second, it is not uncommon for the officers and principals of a bankrupt company to leave their creditors empty-handed as they, legally, retain significant personal assets. This might create a *chillul Hashem* and it may create a moral obligation to repay the loan. This would depend on the financial circumstances of the creditor as well as the debtor. One can imagine the consternation in the Heavenly Tribunal when a debtor retires with $15 million in personal assets without repaying a poor supplier who extended credit and then lost all his money due to the bankruptcy protection of the debtor.

This is especially relevant when the debtor saw the warning signs that his business was headed for bankruptcy, yet continued to borrow money or accept merchandise on credit. Even if the debtor has technically violated nothing in a legal or halachic sense, one must seriously question the morality of this business practice. It is therefore imperative that a person contemplating bankruptcy seek halachic guidance before taking such action.

May Hashem grant you much success in your business endeavors, and *iy"H* you will be able to avoid the uncomfortable scenario of causing loss to others. Your scrupulous business ethic as well as your *yiras Shamayim* will no doubt be a *zechus* for your *hatzlachah* in *parnassah* and an impetus for future projects of *tzedakah* and *chesed.*

---

6. See *Chelkas Yaakov* 3:160.

Found Money

*As a contractor who does various
jobs in private homes in the frum
community, I come across some very
interesting halachic scenarios. The
sh'eilos that present themselves need
attention and focus, and when dealing
with money, one always needs a large
dose of yiras Shamayim as well as
bitachon.*

*One of the more fascinating questions
that came my way recently involved
cash that I found inside a homeowner's
dropped ceiling. Pulling an electric line
in the basement required me to remove
the tiles of the dropped ceiling in order
to access the area. As I surveyed the
area with my flashlight, I found (much
to my pleasant surprise) some cash that
looked like it had been there for quite a*

*while. I asked the homeowner if he had
stored any cash there, and he replied
that he had not.*

*Does this money belong to me, since
it is not claimable due to the fact that
money is not usually identifiable (has
no siman)? Does it perhaps belong to
the homeowner because it was found on
his property? Please advise, as I want
this windfall to go to its rightful owner.*

I commend you on your honesty and quest for justice. Unfortunately, your reaction is not as commonplace as it should be. In Schenectady, New York, there was once a similar case where a contractor found money inside the wall of a home in which he was working. The contractor deceitfully took the money without compunction.

The case involved a homeowner, Michael Casadei, who hired Kevin Skoog to do some carpentry work in his house. As Mr. Skoog worked in the basement, he came across some loose bricks. He moved the bricks and found a bag that contained stacks of $100 bills that smelled and looked old. Kevin Skoog "decided" that the money was his to take and promptly went on a spending spree. By the time Mr. Casadei caught his contractor, over $48,000 had been spent.

It is gratifying to receive a request for direction from an *ehrlicher Yid* who has an entirely different approach to such matters.

There is a concept in *halachah* that one's secured property automatically acquires for the owner any object that comes into it, even if the owner does not have knowledge of it. This acquisition applies only when the object in question is *hefker* (has no owner) or became ownerless due to the fact that the previous owner relinquished his rights by giving up hope of ever recovering it.

There are certain circumstances in which a home or property will not automatically acquire an ownerless item found inside. If such objects are rarely found on the premises, the acquisition is not automatically made on behalf of the owner. Property can only acquire for its owner items that the owner might expect to find on his property.[1]

Tosafos[2] rules that property acquires objects on behalf of the owner only in a case where the item would eventually have been found by the owner. If it is probable that the owner would never have accessed the area in question for any reason, the item remains ownerless and unclaimed until found.

According to either explanation, the cash you found while working would not belong to the homeowner. Most owners would not expect to find money in hidden areas of their property, and usually do not access dropped ceilings even if they have been living on the premises for many years. Therefore, the cash you found would probably never have been found by the owner. (Those who are handy and capable of running electric lines and cables themselves do have occasion to look inside their dropped ceilings. However, I will assume that this homeowner hired you because he is either not knowledgeable or not interested in doing such work for himself.)

Although according to both opinions the found money does not belong to the owner, it does not necessarily mean that it belongs to you either, if the previous owners of the house were *Yidden*. This is due to the issue of *ye'ush shelo midaas*. This means that one's lost objects do not become ownerless (*hefker*) unless one gives up hope of recovering them (*ye'ush*). The *Shulchan Aruch* rules[3] that if the owner of the lost object has not yet realized his loss, the finder cannot keep the item. Since the owner can only have *ye'ush* after realizing his loss, the finder can never keep the lost object even after the former owner discovers it missing and then has *ye'ush*, because at the time the finder picked up the object, it came to him in a forbidden way (*isura assi leyadei*).

If the money you found in the dropped ceiling was unintentionally left behind by *Yidden* who previously owned the house, you are faced with a situation of *ye'ush shelo midaas*. This is because the owner

---

1. *Rema Choshen Mishpat* 268:3, quoting the interpretation of the Mordechai to *Gemara Bava Metzia* 25b — 36a; see *Nesivos Hamishpat*, ibid.
2. *Bava Metzia* 26a d"h *Deshasich*.
3. *Choshen Mishpat* 262:3.

obviously forgot it was hidden there, for if he had remembered, an attempt would have been made to retrieve it. Therefore, we cannot assume that the owner realized his loss for *ye'ush* to apply. (This is despite the fact that we are dealing with money, and the general rule concerning lost money is that people realize in a relatively short time that their money is gone because they check their pockets often [*adam memashmesh bekiso bechal shaah*]. We assume that the previous owner despaired of retrieving his money because money does not usually have identifying features on which to base a claim. The finder can therefore assume that the money was found after *ye'ush*, and there is no obligation to return it. In this case, however, it was put aside in a place not frequently checked, and the assumption of *adam memashmesh...* may not apply.)

As explained above, if the previous owner is a Jew and did not yet have *ye'ush*, the finder cannot keep the item. You will therefore need to seek out the previous owner to clarify the issue. If the previous owner can provide some identifying mark (such as the type of bag the money was in, or the exact amount) you will be obligated to return it.

If you cannot find the original owner but have information confirming that he is a *Yid*, you must hold the money (or better yet, put it in a federally insured interest-bearing bank account for the owner's benefit) until Eliyahu HaNavi comes to clarify the issue. If the previous owners are not *Yidden*, you, the contractor, may keep the money.

Monetary Losses Due to the War in Eretz Yisrael

I am writing this not only as a concerned parent but also to "right a wrong." Many people come to visit Israel during the summer. Israeli families rent out their apartments to these summer visitors. This year, because of the "war," many tourists decided not to come to Israel after all and canceled their trips at the last minute, leaving the Israeli families without renters for their apartments, with the result that they lost the rent they were counting on to pay future bills.

Our children had a long list of people who wanted very much to rent their apartment during the summer. They chose one family and had a verbal agreement that the family was coming.

They agreed on a rental price, and the deal was made over the phone. Lo and behold, the family called up and said, "Due to the political situation, we're not coming, and we were told by our Rav that we don't have to pay you anything."

I am not coming to argue with a halachic ruling; could you please explain the halachic parameters.

To begin, it is important to point out that one should not approach a Rav with a question involving *Choshen Mishpat* (any monetary dispute) except in the presence of the other party, as a *posek* needs to hear both sides of the dispute in the presence (or possibly via conference call) of — or at least with the consent of — the plaintiff and the defendant. It is contrary to *halachah* to render a *psak halachah* without fulfilling this condition. It is therefore not proper to simply call up and say, "We were told by our Rav that we do not have to pay you anything."

Similarly, essays like the one you are now reading may not be relied upon to provide halachic guidance; they merely serve to explore the issues.

The halachic question of whether one can cancel the deal begins with whether any sort of *kinyan* was made to finalize the rental of the apartment prior to the family's arrival in *Eretz Yisrael*. That *kinyan* might be in the form of a down payment, a contract, or the transfer of a key to the apartment (the various types of *kinyanim* and their practical ramifications are beyond the scope of our present discussion).

However, even if no official *kinyan* took place, there are many sources in *halachah* indicating that a Jew should keep his word, even if it is not absolutely halachically mandated:[1] *Rabbi Yochanan amar,*

---

1. *Bava Metzia* 49a.

"*Devarim yesh bahem mishum mechusrei amanah* — One who retracts his word is not considered trustworthy."[2] This would depend, however, on how drastic the change of circumstances is.[3]

One must also examine the specific business customs relating to the sale or rental of real estate. One might argue that reneging on a real-estate sale or rental is less of an issue than it would be in some other business dealings, for it is accepted practice (for better or for worse) that a real-estate transaction is never a deal until the actual closing or occupancy. Such behavior is not necessarily commendable, but might be halachically justifiable.

If the potential renters do have the right to pull out without paying (which, again, is up to the Rav agreed upon by all parties), the renter should consider whether he is dealing with a family in need (meaning that they are halachically eligible to receive *maaser* money). If there is no *obligation* to pay, it would be still be *lifnim mishuras hadin* (above and beyond the letter of the law) to offer money that would wholly or partially offset the loss, and this money could then be taken from a *maaser*-money account.

It is important to raise one final issue. Even at the height of the Intifada, at a time when one could argue that it was more dangerous in Yerushalayim than during the war in Lebanon, *Gedolei Yisrael* in *Eretz Yisrael* were quoted as saying that if one is coming to *Eretz Yisrael l'shem Shamayim* (for *talmud Torah* or *dvar mitzvah*), there is no need for concern. I was told on good authority that this message was recently repeated during the recent war. I am not criticizing this family's decision; I am just pointing out that the decision to cancel a trip to *Eretz Yisrael* has serious ramifications and must be treated as such. One must seek guidance from a Rav on such a weighty matter.

This letter has raised some valid points to ponder. Let us all continue to *daven* that there be peace in *Eretz Yisrael*, and that our brothers and sisters there be provided with *parnassah* and *yishuv hadaas* to learn and spread Torah, and to continue to generate *zechusim* for *acheinu kol Beis Yisrael*.

---

2. *Choshen Mishpat* 204:7.
3. *Rema Choshen Mishpat* ibid. 11; see *Shach* ibid. 5 and *Aruch HaShulchan* ibid.8.

May we be *zocheh* to witness the time where **all** *Yidden* in *Eretz Yisrael* appreciate the beauty of Torah and mitzvos, as well as the tremendous *kedushas haAretz*. Until then, it is a special responsibility and privilege for *frum* Yidden in *Chutz LaAretz* to support those carrying the torch of Torah in *Eretz Yisrael*.

Making a
Kiddush Hashem /
Chillul Hashem

A PRICE AGREED UPON UNDER PRESSURE

My car recently broke down in a remote area, and without access to Chaveirim or AAA membership, I had no choice but to call a local towing company to take me to the nearest service station. The tow-truck operator gave me the price on his arrival, and although I thought it was exorbitant and tried to negotiate a lower fee, he would not budge. Having no other choice, I instructed him to begin working.

Upon arrival at the service station 45 minutes later, I tried again to negotiate a discount on his steep fee. I told him that it was grossly unfair of him to

*take advantage of a stranded customer
and that I believed I was entitled to a
reduction. He angrily replied that the
price was the going rate, and that it
was irrelevant in any case since I had
agreed to pay it before he towed. Not
wanting any trouble from him or his
friends, I reluctantly paid the fee.*

*After contemplating the incident for a
few days, I began wondering whether
I should even have attempted to
renegotiate the fee after I had agreed
to pay it. Although I had only agreed to
the price under pressure, perhaps I was
halachically bound to follow my initial
agreement. I am also concerned that
perhaps my conduct caused a chillul
Shem Shamayim.*

What should I have done?

The *Gemara*[1] tells of an individual who, while running for his life, came to the bank of a river. His pursuers would soon find him, and he therefore had to cross the river immediately. Having no boat of his own, he was forced to offer the ferry conductor a fortune of money to take him across. Although the ferry owner only agreed to take him for the prearranged price, the *Gemara* states that he was only obligated to pay the regular ferry rate upon reaching his destination. This is because the exorbitant fee was promised under duress, and an insincere offer does not halachically bind the customer.[2]

---

1. *Yevamos* 106a.
2. See *Tosafos* ibid. *d"h Ein lo ela secharo*; see also *Gemara Bava Kamma* 116b with *Tosafos d"h L'havi*.

Although we see that an unfair price agreed upon under immense pressure is not necessarily binding,[3] one cannot assume that your scenario is similar. One obvious difference is that it is quite possible that the standard rate for towing in remote areas is actually much higher than it would be on a regulated, well-traveled highway. Although that standard price is based on the desperate need of a stranded customer who has few, if any, choices in such a situation, it is nevertheless the going rate in that location. It would therefore be acceptable, from the halachic standpoint, for the tow-truck operator to charge such a fee (a bottle of water in the desert is always more expensive than the same bottle at a local supermarket).

Even if the price charged for towing was not standard for that area, you would be obligated to pay the agreed-upon price if it prevented him from taking another towing job at the rate to which you had agreed.[4]

[One would also have to examine the parameters of "a price agreed upon under pressure." Although we have shown that the *halachah* exempts one from paying an exorbitant fee that was agreed upon only due to the pressing needs of the situation, not all situations of "pressure" are halachically the same. It is quite common that people buy and sell items due to a specific need, yet we declare the transaction binding despite the aspect of duress. The prohibition of *onaah* (overcharging) usually applies when there was no disclosure at the time of the transaction. If there was disclosure and agreement that the price would be paid, the fact that it was agreed upon only due to necessity would not always relieve the payer of his halachic obligation.]

As you have been contemplating, even if the *halachah* were to support your attempt to renegotiate the price, it may have been unwise due to the *chillul Shem Shamayim* that it could (and perhaps did) cause. The tow-truck operator is probably not familiar with the *Gemaras* in *Yevamos* and *Bava Kamma*, and certainly not with the *Tosafos* on the *sugya* and the *psak* in *Shulchan Aruch*. All he sees is a Jew who promised to pay him and is now attempting to renege on the deal.

The Rambam in *Hilchos Teshuvah* 1:4 states explicitly that creat-

---

3. See *Yoreh Deah* 336:3.
4. See end of *Tosafos Bava Kamma*, ibid.

ing a *chillul Hashem* is an *aveirah* of the highest order, and it is most difficult to gain atonement for such a transgression in one's lifetime. All Jews are ambassadors of Hashem and His Torah in this world. Whoever we are and wherever we may be, others will draw conclusions about Hashem and His Torah through our actions. This tremendous responsibility is not to be taken lightly, because people automatically assume that whatever we do represents true Torah Judaism.

Although most people do not view themselves as role models, the fact remains that the behavior of *frum* men and women is constantly under scrutiny. The business ethics of a Jew must be beyond reproach, whether in the office or on the road. One must view every transaction as an opportunity to display honesty and integrity in order to be *mekadesh Shem Shamayim*.

_____ *AMBASSADORS ON THE NY STATE THRUWAY*

I was once driving on the New York State Thruway when my car began stalling. Fortunately, I had enough momentum to roll into a rest area and coast to a full stop in front of a gas pump. I was hoping I was out of gas, but it turned out that there was a hole in the engine. With no other alternative, I called for a tow truck.

As I was riding to the repair shop with the friendly driver, he mentioned to me that he was really fascinated by "my people." He had been covering that part of the Thruway for many years, and it amazed him that he rarely saw any of us stranded by the roadside with a disabled car. When I expressed my surprise that I was the first religious Jew he had encountered who required the services of a towing company, he explained that whenever he saw one disabled car, there were quickly three more of "your people" on the spot offering help. By the time he was called for service, they were chatting and sharing their food like old friends.

"You are all like one big happy family," he said.

What a wonderful *kiddush Hashem*!

He then continued, "Can I ask you a personal question? What happens on Friday afternoon when the sun starts setting? Whenever I come to service a disabled car at that time of day, they give me their keys and say, 'Do whatever you can — I'm leaving.' What is so urgent that people are willing to trust their car to a total stranger?"

I explained to him that Shabbos is extremely important to us and when it begins, we stop all weekday activity.

"But what happens," he asked, "if it's an expensive car — and I've seen you people drive some very expensive cars."

"If *Shabbos* is coming," I replied, "*Shabbos* is coming. It doesn't matter how expensive the car is."

"That's incredible. You people really stand up for what you believe in!" Another *kiddush Hashem*.

Then came the bad news. He told me that some of his colleagues do not pick up Orthodox Jews.

"Unfortunately," he explained, "there have been occasions where we get there, tell them the price, and they accept the service. We then take the car with the passengers, get to the shop a few towns over — and all of a sudden they starting negotiating. Although they agreed to the price beforehand, they complain afterward that it's highway robbery and they could have found someone cheaper. My friends do not want the headache, so they prefer not to respond in the first place."

"Then why do you pick them up?" I asked.

"I know that in every religion there are good apples and bad apples."

He was smart enough to not condemn the entire Jewish people for the actions of a few. Nevertheless, many of his friends do not take such a job because they feel that it is just not worth the hassle.

We have to remember that as ambassadors of Torah we are constantly faced with the wonderful opportunity to be *mekadesh Shem Shamayim*. We must be ever vigilant to show others that our word is sacred. Our dealings — with both Jews and non-Jews — must leave others in awe of Torah values, with the indelible impression that the ways of the Torah are pleasant — *deracheha darchei no'am*.

I would like to illustrate this imperative with a story concerning the positive impression made by a Jewish family over 120 years ago. It is possible that their friendly relationship had historic repercussions, and the story helped me uncover a piece of personal family history that had been unexplained for over 60 years.

I received in the mail an article from someone who thought I might be interested in reading a fascinating story about someone who had the same last name as mine. To the best of my knowledge, I am not related to the family discussed in the following account. The article is entitled "The *Shabbos Goy*," by Zev Roth.

In a small Midwest town in the mid-1880s, Jacob Viner and his wife attempted to bring up their children in accordance with Jewish tradition. [They lived in] their Missouri village, located just outside Kansas City. One of the few advantages of living in such a setting was the presence of a large stock of people who could be used as a "Shabbos Goy." When it was required, it was the Viners' young neighbor Harry who was usually called upon. Harry frequently visited the Viner family to help light a fire to warm the house in the frigid midwest winter[5].... Whenever he came, the Viners made sure to reimburse Harry with a small token of their appreciation — a piece of kugel or gefilte fish was always offered. Harry was particularly fond of matzah.

When Harry returned from duty in World War I ... he tried his hand at politics and performed a number of favors for the Jewish community.... The Viner family no doubt took tremendous pride in the friendship they had shown their Missouri neighbor. But in their wildest dreams they could not have imagined how far the dividends of their *kiddush Hashem* would extend.

The Viner family's close contact with young Harry may have influenced the course of Jewish, and indeed, world, history. Harry's political aspirations were only beginning. In 1934, he was elected to the United States Senate, serving for two six-year terms. In 1946, President Franklin Delano Roosevelt inexplicably dropped his vice president, Henry A. Wallace,

---

5. *Amira l'akum* (instructing a non-Jew to perform a prohibited act on behalf of a Jew) is permitted in cases of inclement weather in order to prevent illness. See *Shulchan Aruch Orach Chaim* 276:5.

in favor of a then-unknown Missouri senator, Harry S. Truman. Shortly thereafter, Roosevelt passed away and Truman became president of the United States.

One of the major problems for the Truman administration following the end of World War II was the United States' policy in regard to the proposed State of Israel. There were many pro-Arab officers within Truman's cabinet who were vehemently opposed to supporting the proposed state. As Truman later wrote, "The Department of State's specialists on the Near East were, almost without exception, unfriendly to the idea of a Jewish State. … [They] thought that the Arabs, on account of their numbers and because they controlled such immense oil resources, should be appeased.

"I am sorry to say that there were some of them who were inclined to be anti-Semitic."[6] In spite of all this, Truman immediately supported the State. … [He wrote in] a personal note: "I recognized Israel immediately … in 1948 … against the advice of my own Secretary of State, George Marshall, who was afraid the Arabs wouldn't like it. … But I felt Israel deserved to be recognized and I didn't [care] whether the Arabs liked it or not."

To this day, historians debate exactly what influenced Truman toward the newly founded State of Israel, a policy of support and aid which has been in place more or less for the past fifty [now sixty] years.…

The earliest experiences an individual has are often the ones which form the crux of his views for the rest of his life. Is it inconceivable that this stance was ingrained in a young Harry Truman from the Viner family in turn-of-the-century Independence, Missouri?[7]

---

6. This is a fascinating comment coming from Mr. Truman, especially in light of the negative comments about Jews found in his personal diary. These derogatory remarks were written as late as 1947. Mr. Truman was obviously a very complex person. One sees the concept of "*lev melachim b'yad Hashem*" in Truman's treatment of the Jews after he ascended to the presidency. — Y.V.

7. Unquestionably, [Truman's relationship with longtime friend Eddie Jacobson most probably helped matters as well. — Y.V.]

That a *shomer Shabbos* family in Missouri might have had an impact on the American policy of support for *Eretz Yisrael* highlights the importance of leaving everyone we meet with a warm and positive impression of Jews and Judaism.

However, this is not the end of the story.

My grandfather, who lived in Washington, D.C., was very involved in the Vaad Hatzolah during World War II. The Vaad helped save countless Jewish lives during and after the Holocaust. HaGaon HaRav Aaron Kotler, *zt"l*, toiled on behalf of the Vaad with superhuman effort in an attempt to save Jewish lives. The Rosh Yeshivah came to Washington often and stayed at my grandparents' home for weeks at a time. At one point, Rav Aaron asked my grandfather if he could arrange an appointment with Vice President Truman. As a businessman and not a politician, my grandfather did not have access to the vice president, and, to complicate matters, the vice president was under pressure from President Roosevelt and the State Department not to involve himself too heavily with the "Jewish problem" in Europe.

Despite the uphill battle, my grandfather immediately attempted to set up a meeting with Vice President Truman. I never received a clear answer about how he was able to bring this historic meeting to fruition, until I read "The Shabbos Goy."

It is quite possible that a message reached the vice president's secretary that a certain Mr. Viener wanted to schedule a meeting. It did not matter that my grandfather had absolutely no relation to the Mr. Veiner from Missouri, whom the vice president had not seen for many years. Mr. Truman was eager to see an old friend from his youth — and the rest is history. That meeting helped save many, many lives.

It is remarkable to see the *yad Hashem* that may have enabled someone with a similar last name to reap the benefits of a positive impression made decades earlier. A very "small" *kiddush Hashem* made by treating others with respect helped shaped history.

We all have the responsibility to utilize every opportunity to be *mekadesh Shem Shamayim*. The opportunity is constantly within our reach; let us seize it with enthusiasm.

Parking Like a Mentsch

This morning I went out to my car and saw that I had been completely blocked in by someone who had double-parked in front of me. Even when one has an "important" appointment or a tight schedule, such an act, needless to say, is outrageously inconsiderate. I considered calling the police, but since it was very possible the car belonged to a Yid, I thought it might be mesirah. As it turned out, the person was Jewish, and I gave him a piece of my mind when he returned. I am wondering what, if any, halachic recourse one has in such a case.

Unfortunately, an incident such as the one you describe is not as uncommon as we would like it to be. Guidance on this matter is important in helping others deal with this situation as well.

The *Gemara*[1] discusses a case where one's access to his property is blocked by the barrels of a person who had no permission to place them there. Rav Nachman rules that one may take the law into his own hands (*avad inish dina l'nafshei*) and move the barrels, even in a way that they will inevitably be broken, if there is no other way to clear a passage.

The *Shulchan Aruch*[2] rules according to Rav Nachman. It should therefore be permissible to have the double-parked car towed in order to enable you to use your vehicle. There would be no issue of *mesirah*, as you are allowed access to your property at all times, and you are halachically allowed to protect your interests.

The issue of *dina d'malchusa dina* (following the law of the land) does, however, pose a potential problem. The law (at least in New York) clearly states that it is permissible to tow a car only when the vehicle is illegally parked on private property. This would mean that a vehicle that is double-parked or blocking your driveway but is on a public street is not subject to arbitrary towing.[3]

However, police officials at the 66th precinct (Brooklyn, New York) have stated that the police will allow the towing of a car that is double-parked or blocking a driveway after it is ticketed by the police. Once the car is ticketed, it may be towed by a private company at the owner's expense.

Although we always try to avoid causing financial loss to others, it is permissible to call the police and have the car ticketed to facilitate its removal when necessary. It would be proper, however, to make an attempt to find the owner of the vehicle before taking such a drastic step. You will probably have plenty of time to locate the wayward owner due to the fact that the police often have more urgent things to attend to, and ticketing a car that is blocking another vehicle is not their top priority.

According to U.S. law, one is never allowed to damage the car in an attempt to move it. Towing is the only legal option available and, again, (at least in New York City) that can come only after the car has been ticketed. It is certainly prohibited (according to *halachah* as well

---

1. *Bava Kamma* 27b.
2. *Choshen Mishpat* 4:1.
3. NEW YORK CITY CHARTER, CODE, AMENDMENTS & RULES, TITLE 19, CHAPTER 1, SUBCHAPTER 2, section 19-169.1: Removal of vehicles improperly parked on private property.

as U.S. law) to slash the tires or otherwise damage or disable the car as an act of revenge and spite.

Anyone who is searching for a suitable place to park must remember that he or she is not the only one who is in a rush. Everyone is busy, and it is extremely inconsiderate to block someone else's car. Doing so shows a lack of appreciation for the basic laws *bein adam lachaveiro*. This applies equally to parallel parking in a way that immobilizes the other cars, a somewhat common occurrence that can cost the owner of the sandwiched vehicle much time and aggravation. If the space you want cannot accommodate your car without leaving some room for the other parked cars to exit, it is obviously not meant to be your parking space.

These *halachos* apply even when one is rushing to *daven*, catch a *shiur*, or just say *mazel tov* at a friend's *chasunah*. Hashem does not want our *mitzvos* at the expense of others!

I once witnessed a car pull up near a well-known *makom tefillah* so its driver could catch a late-night Maariv. I saw the driver jump out after pulling his car into the neighbor's driveway. He did not merely block the driveway; he actually had the audacity to park *in* the driveway! There was a huge sign over the garage warning people not to park there, and I told the young man that the owner of this driveway (whom I know personally) was *makpid* that no one block the driveway. The perpetrator informed me that he certainly had permission and then ran to catch *Barchu*.

When I came out after Maariv, I noticed that the vehicle was still there, with a note on the windshield warning him never to park there again. The driver had convinced himself that he had permission, but the owner was furious and told me that he had never seen that car before and had certainly never given anyone permission to park in his driveway. I cannot imagine the reaction in *Shamayim* to this driver's *davening*.

Most *Yidden* have the common sense and *yiras Shamayim* to avoid parking in an inconsiderate and prohibited way. Those individuals who rationalize that it is not so bad must understand that there is *no circumstance* (aside from *pikuach nefashos*) that allows them to be the vehicles of *chillul Hashem*, *nezek*, and strife. In an instance of dire emergency, a contact number should be left on the dashboard. The car owner should then move the vehicle as soon as he is contacted.

The author would like to thank Judge E. Prus and his assistant, Shragi Eichorn, for providing the pertinent legal information for this article.

Driving Like a Mentsch

I am a resident of Brooklyn, New York, and, like many others in my neighborhood, I make the two-hour commute to and from my bungalow colony each weekend of the summer. Last July, after a very grueling drive through Manhattan one late Sunday night, I performed a maneuver that I believe was sensible and necessary under the circumstances.

As all New Yorkers know, the approach from the FDR Drive to the Brooklyn Bridge is often congested and extremely slow moving, since several lanes of traffic merge onto a single-lane entrance ramp to the bridge. Many less-aggressive drivers will move to the right lane and patiently wait on line as the traffic proceeds at a snail's pace. The *less-patient individuals will remain in the center lane until the last moment and then attempt to squeeze into the right lane, thereby cutting the line.*

As I had been on the road fighting heavy traffic for over two hours, I was in no mood to be Mr. Nice Guy. I therefore attempted to save time using this maneuver. It was my good fortune that the car that I attempted to cut in front of was driven by a neighbor of mine and he (somewhat reluctantly) allowed me to proceed in front of him.

However, this gracious neighbor met me at Maariv later that evening and proceeded to give me mussar for my chutzpah! He claimed that what I had done was against halachah, illegal, and could be the cause of a tremendous chillul Hashem.

I was most surprised to hear his tirade against a most common practice, and I'm wondering whether there is any merit to his argument.

Although this *she'ailah* was asked as the summer months began, the topic of impetuous driving habits is relevant at any time of the year.

You are correct in assuming that many people think and drive as you do, but, unfortunately, that does not make it right.

The *Gemara Sanhedrin* (32b) teaches that traveling ships that reach a narrow passage proceed on a "first-come, first-serve" basis. It would seem that one must wait on line in an orderly fashion, and that one who cuts is "stealing" time from others.

As much as you would like to save time, it is extremely inconsiderate to do so at the expense of others. It is unfair to take advantage of others and portrays a lack of *middos* and *kavod habriyos*.

Your friend was correct in pointing out that aside from the halachic and legal considerations, there is potential for a *chillul Hashem*. The drivers who are cut off will most probably notice that the aggressive operator of the vehicle is a *Yid*, and their reaction and verbal response usually bear this out. Even if an adverse reaction is not noticed, they are certainly not wishing you well, to say the least. One will never hear, "This fellow who cut me off is such a wonderful guy — I am so happy that he is able to get home a little bit sooner."

Chillul Hashem applies whether the other drivers are *Yidden* or not, and if the impression is given that *frum* people are inconsiderate, a *chillul Shem Shamayim* has indeed taken place. As should be well known, the *aveirah* of causing a *chillul Hashem* is among the worst transgressions, for which severe punishment is required before atonement is possible.[1]

It is important to mention that aside from the very problematic issue of a possible *chillul Hashem*, there is an underlying danger in receiving a *klallah* (curse) from anyone (Jew or non-Jew) when that *klallah* is somewhat deserved. The *Gemara* in *Megillah* (28a) warns that a curse of any person, even someone who is not a *talmid chacham* or a *tzaddik*, should not be taken lightly (*Al tehi killelas hedyot kallah be'einecha*). The *Gemara's* example of a curse that was effective involved one from a non-Jew.

These sources are important to bear in mind whenever you get behind the wheel of your car. Proper driving etiquette is not an option or a *chumrah*. The impression you make in public in front of hundreds of drivers and pedestrians on a daily basis leaves an indelible mark on their consciousness. Reckless and aggressive driving (perhaps some-

---

1. See *Rambam, Hilchos Teshuvah* 1:4.

what more common among city dwellers) is a malady that we must try to cure. It is crucial that we not only avoid any action that may create a *chillul Hashem*, but that we go the extra mile, and spend the extra time, to create a *kiddush Hashem* via careful and courteous driving.

A Salary Increase and Torah Study

Q *I am 26 years old and have been working at my present job for about two years. My income covers the expenses of my family, but leaves very little in terms of savings.*

My learning is very important to me, and I try to use the available time before and after work to be kovei'a itim (have a set time for learning). After davening I have only half an hour to learn before catching my train to work, and I learn at night for another hour and a half. My boss recently offered me a raise on condition that I come to the office a half-hour earlier in the morning. This new schedule will not leave me any time to learn after davening. Perhaps I should take the opportunity, for after all is said and done, I only manage to learn for a maximum of 30 minutes anyway.

What halachic and hashkafic issues should I examine in order to come to the proper decision?

You deserve much credit for contemplating the options carefully. Your *talmud Torah* is of paramount importance, and you will continue to grow by treating it as such. Many of us make decisions in life that we do not take seriously, simply because we don't think they will affect anything in the long term. It takes a strong focus to remain cognizant at all times of the fact that winning these "small" battles is what life is really all about.

The first halachic issue that plays a role in your decision is that of *nedarim*. When one designates a time for learning, it may be considered as if he has actually vowed to learn at that time every day. This would obligate you to maintain your *seder* as though you had made a *neder* to do so, and one is not permitted to cancel (or reduce) his set time of learning unless there is genuine urgency. Terminating your morning learning, even when justified, might require *hataras nedarim*.[1]

The second issue is the obligation of "*V'hagisa bo yomam valaylah*" (*Yehoshua* 1:8). This *pasuk* teaches us that one must learn to the best of his ability by day and by night.[2] There is special significance in learning Torah immediately after one *davens* Shacharis.[3]

Despite the halachic imperative mentioned above, if one absolutely must work longer hours in order to cover basic expenses, there would be reason to accept the offer of an increased salary, even if it requires you to expand your morning work hours.

The difficulty is in determining which expenses are really necessary

---

1. *Nedarim* 8a; see *Shulchan Aruch Yoreh Deah* 214:1; *Mishnah Berurah* 238:5.
2. *Shulchan Aruch Yoreh Deah* 246:1.
3. See *Shulchan Aruch Orach Chaim* 155:1, based on *Gemara Berachos* 64a; see also *Orchos Chaim l'HaRosh* 44.

and which are luxury items. It is crucial to bear in mind that the *yetzer hara* must pick and choose its battles. Like any good general, it knows it cannot win every battle, and it therefore focuses on winning the crucial ones. There is nothing that bothers the *yetzer hara* more than a *ben Torah* who is being *moser nefesh* to learn as much as he possibly can.

However, the *yetzer hara* knows it will not succeed simply by telling us not to learn at all. Rather, it tells us that our actions are not so important. "You're not going to accomplish much by learning for half an hour," it says. "Don't bother with the small stuff; do something bigger."

There was once a *mispallel* in my shul who, I felt, wasn't attending enough *shiurim*, and it was one of my responsibilities as his Rav to make sure he was learning according to his ability. I mentioned that I had not see him at recent *shiurim* and asked if he was feeling well.

"Yes, I'm feeling fine," he replied.

"We missed you. Did something come up?"

"Yes," he told me, "I have a plan. I can't come for the next week — or perhaps the next month or year — because I plan on learning a lot more than I've been learning until now. I am now planning to set up a much longer learning *seder*."

He explained that he would be pursuing a business opportunity that might take a year, working sixteen hours a day. He would have no time to learn and little time to *daven*, but in the end it would afford him the ability to retire early and learn much more.

This is the advice of the *yetzer hara* wrapped up in a seemingly logical business model. Hashem has a reason for wanting us to have set times for learning Torah every single morning and evening. We do not have a contract on life and we do not know what tomorrow will bring. It is therefore imperative to have set times to learn every day, even if the time seems insignificant.

The *yetzer hara* is expert at deflecting this imperative. I knew another young man who agreed to set up a time to learn, yet every time I presented an idea for a *chavrusa*, he would say something like, "No, that fellow can only learn an hour each day, and I need someone serious who will learn for at least an hour and a half." He shot down every idea I suggested because it was "too small."

Putting off decision-making ensures that we will not accomplish anything substantial in the window of opportunity we call "life." If we realized that even small accomplishments add up, we would not miss a chance to do all within our reach *at the present time*.

If you really need the extra money now and this is your only opportunity to earn it, you may have no choice but to accept the offer. However, you would be obligated to make a strong attempt to make up the lost learning time at night.[4] If this is not possible, you should make an effort to compensate with additional learning on Shabbos and Sunday.[5]

You state that your expenses are covered at the present time. It therefore might not be halachically or hashkafically wise to tamper with your *sedarim*.

May Hashem grant you *yishuv hadaas*, strength, and continued *siyata di'Shemaya* in your learning and *avodas Hashem*.

---

4. *Shulchan Aruch Orach Chaim* 238:2 with *Mishnah Berurah* 4; *Talmidei Rabbeinu Yonah* on *Berachos* page 6a of the *Rif, d"h v'amar*.
5. See *Pischei Teshuvah Yoreh Deah* 241:1.

SECTION TWELVE

PRACTICAL *HASHKAFAH* MATTERS

The Vanishing Nisayon

The topic of *nisyonos*, tests and challenges we face in life, is too broad to cover in one sitting. We will focus, therefore, on three aspects of the topic that I believe are very relevant on a practical level to anyone facing a *nisayon*, whether big or small.

The first issue we must address is the purpose of *nisyonos*. We will examine but one approach, with the understanding that there is much more to say on the topic.

The first appearance of the root term of *nisayon* is in *Parashas Vayeira*, where the *pasuk* introduces the portion dealing with the *Akeidah*: "*Vayehi achar hadevarim ha'eileh, veha'Elokim* **nisah** *es Avraham* — And it happened after these things that Hashem **tested** Avraham"[1] A *midrash* in *Bereishis Rabbah* 55:1 explains that the term *nisah* is to be understood in the context of the verse, "*Nasatah liyirei'echa* **neis** *lehisnoses* — To those who feared You, You gave a **banner** to be held high."[2] The *midrash* explains that Hashem tests those who fear Him with *nisayon* after *nisayon*, for their own sake. *Nisyonos* help a great person demonstrate his true level of devotion, so that it is "uplifted" and displayed for all to see, like the *neis* (flag) on the mast of a ship, which proudly proclaims the ownership or nationality of that ship.

Ramban (on this *pasuk*) explains this concept: Every person has a certain capacity for greatness, but in many cases that capacity lies

---

1. *Bereishis* 22:1.
2. *Tehillim* 60:6.

dormant within one's *neshamah*. We live in the *Olam Ha'asiyah* (the world of action), and we are considered great only when we display our capacity for greatness through concrete actions.

The tests Hashem gives us are very different from the tests we took in school. In a school setting, the person administering the test is no more aware of the score that will be achieved than the one taking the test. When Hashem tests us, on the other hand, the test is one-sided. Hashem *knows* that we can pass the test, and He administers the test for the sole purpose of allowing us to bring to the fore the capabilities that lie dormant within us, so we can receive reward not only for having the capability, but for the action that we were able to perform as a result of that capability.

This means, says Ramban, that Hashem will test a person *only* — *only!* — when He knows for certain that the person is capable of passing the test.

When we feel that we are being tested, it is important to step back at some point and identify the situation as a test, and remind ourselves that we are perfectly capable of passing it — because otherwise Hashem would never have placed us in that situation to begin with.

WHEN WILL IT END?

Another issue we deal with when we are in the midst of a *nisayon* is the overwhelming feeling of not knowing how long the test is going to last. Anyone who has had to deal with a difficult medical condition or has suffered through one with a family member can tell you that there are days when he wondered how he could carry on. Someone who is jobless or is having difficulty with a child's *chinuch* has also experienced this feeling. One of the worst aspects of such a *nisayon* is the time factor. People wonder, *When will I [or my loved one] get better? When will I get a job? When will my child want to learn again?*

I would like to examine a *midrash* regarding a *nisayon* that many of the greatest women in our history faced, and that many couples face in our times as well, because it delivers a deeply inspirational message for those who are suffering.

At the very beginning of *sefer Shmuel*, we learn that Chanah, who would eventually become Shmuel HaNavi's mother, was childless. She decided to improve her chances of having children by allowing her husband to marry another wife, just as our matriarch Sarah did. Contrary to popular understanding, the mechanism of bringing a second wife into the home to serve as a merit for the barren woman is helpful not because it causes Hashem to be "more aware" of the situation. Sarah Imeinu did not think to herself, *If I bring another woman into the home and I am miserable because of it, perhaps Hashem will have mercy on me and give me children.*

Rather, the merit comes from helping another person fulfill a mitzvah. These great women realized that their husbands had a mitzvah to bring children into the world, and they were willing to allow their husbands to fulfill that mitzvah even if it came at the expense of having to share him with another wife. It was that merit that eventually resulted in Yitzchak Avinu being born to Avraham and Sarah, and Chanah wanted to tap into that merit.

She allowed her husband Elkanah to marry a woman named Peninah, and sure enough, Peninah began to bear children. Chanah watched as Peninah bore one child, then another, and another ... but she remained barren. Finally, when Peninah had borne her tenth child, Chanah could no longer remain silent. She cried her heart out at the *Mishkan*, and she was granted a child, the great *navi* Shmuel.

In explaining this story, a *midrash*[3] expounds a verse in *Mishlei* and extracts from it an important principle regarding *nisyonos*. The verse states, "*Matzreif lakesef vechur lazahav, ve'ish lefi mahalalo* — A refining pot is for silver, and a crucible for gold, and a man according to his praises."[4]

What is the connection between the two parts of this verse? The *midrash* explains that just as a refiner of precious metals will leave the metals in the crucible only for the exact amount of time necessary to refine them, because leaving them in any longer will ruin them, so too, when Hashem "refines" a person by giving him or her a *nisayon*,

3. *Pesikta Rabbasi* 43.
4. *Mishlei* 27:21.

that test lasts exactly as long as the person can handle it, and then it is removed.

To illustrate this point, the *midrash* cites three examples of people who were all challenged with childlessness: Sarah, Rivkah, and Chanah. Each of them was tested for a specific amount of time: Sarah was barren for 25 years, Rivkah for 20 years, and Chanah for 19 years. Why? Because Hashem tested each one according to her ability to withstand the test. (The mere difference in the number of years each of these three *tzidkaniyos* had to live with her *nisayon* does not necessarily indicate their relative levels of greatness, as there were many factors, besides duration, that contributed to the *nisayon*.)

This *midrash* bears another comforting lesson for us as we go through tough challenges in life: Although it may seem as though the situation is dragging on and on, we may find comfort in the thought that Hashem is calculating *each minute* of the *nisayon*, and He knows exactly how much we can handle. As soon as the *nisayon* enables us to display the level of devotion and faith we were supposed to achieve through it, Hashem will immediately remove it.

_____ *RIGGING EVENTS TO CREATE A NISAYON*

Whereas the first two aspects of *nisyonos* we discussed are lessons drawn from sources in *Tanach* and *midrashim*, the third aspect is one that I myself have learned while trying to help people deal with challenging situations. I have often encountered a phenomenon that I call the "vanishing *nisyonos*."

As we have seen, the purpose of a *nisayon* is to cause us to demonstrate our true colors by passing the *nisayon*. While some *nisyonos* we deal with will be recurring problems or issues in our lives (such as medical or financial difficulties), a "vanishing *nisayon*" is one that shows up suddenly, and then, just when we decide on how to react to the challenge, the circumstances disappear. Often the details of these *nisyonos* are so intricate that it amazes me to see how Hashem will orchestrate such a situation just to enable one *Yid* to demonstrate his dormant strength of character.

I would like to share three stories in which such *nisyonos* — in varying degrees of difficulty — were presented to, and passed by, the protagonists.

_____ *NOT THAT BASEBALL CAP!*

A psychologist I know was to attend a convention in California. A few days before he was scheduled to depart, he came to discuss with me the halachic ramifications of attending the convention. (I highly recommend that people follow his lead. If you travel to such conventions, you know that dozens of *she'eilos* (halachic questions) can arise in the few days during which you are detached from the community. This psychologist had a litany of questions, ranging from *hilchos Shabbos* to *kashrus*, and many areas between.)

One question he asked was whether he should wear a yarmulke at the convention. The general question of whether a man should wear a yarmulke at work is one that needs to be addressed on a case-by-case basis. Rav Moshe Feinstein, *zt"l*, rules[5] that if someone cannot get a job unless he removes his yarmulke, then he may remove it. It is important to bear in mind, however, that this ruling was issued many years ago, and in the interim it has become quite common for people to wear yarmulkes to work. Even prestigious law firms that would never have considered hiring an attorney who wore a yarmulke a few decades ago now have yarmulke-clad attorneys on staff. Certainly in the New York metropolitan area, people are accustomed to dealing with Orthodox Jews who wear their yarmulkes to work. But aside from the halachic considerations, it is important to realize that a yarmulke is a "chaperone" of sorts. Whether or not you have *semichah*, the yarmulke on your head will cause your co-workers to view you as the "company rabbi," and that will be reflected in their interaction with you. They will frequently know to choose their words and their topics of conversation — and especially their jokes — more carefully when you are in the room; this will shield you from the steady flow of profanity and innuendo that has become part and parcel of corporate-office relationships.

---

5. *Igros Moshe, Orach Chaim* 4:2.

Getting back to my convention-bound questioner, he explained that he does wear a yarmulke in his office in New York, but since this convention would draw people from all over the world who are not accustomed to seeing yarmulkes, perhaps he should remove it when attending the symposiums.

I discussed the *she'eilah* with him at length, and although I told him that according to Rav Moshe he is not *required* to wear his yarmulke, I encouraged him to wear it nonetheless.

We reached the conclusion together that since secular and gentile associates from his office would be attending the convention with him, the sudden disappearance of his yarmulke would be impossible to explain. When we parted ways, he seemed to indicate that he considered it a *kiddush Hashem* (sanctification of God's Name) to wear his yarmulke to the convention meetings and that he would, therefore, do so.

His first few hours at the convention center were uneventful. He landed in California in the afternoon, spent a few hours at the hotel, *davened* Maariv, then collapsed into bed in sheer exhaustion.

He awoke early in the morning to *daven* before the first symposium, but to his consternation, his yarmulke was nowhere to be found. He remembered having worn his yarmulke when he said *HaMapil* the previous night, so he knew it couldn't have gone far — but where was it?

Of course, he hadn't thought of packing a second yarmulke to take to the convention, and to his knowledge there was no Judaica store in the vicinity of the convention center. Unfortunately, his wife wasn't with him, so he couldn't rely on her to find it. He began to search his room frantically, figuring it would be only a matter of minutes before he found it. Alas, after a long hunt that left his room in shambles, he was still sans yarmulke.

The clock was ticking, so he decided he had better *daven* in the baseball cap that he had brought with him. He finished *davening* at ten minutes to nine, then sat down on his bed and began to contemplate his next move. He couldn't go down to the convention in a baseball cap — showing up at a convention in such attire would be a worse *chillul Hashem* than going without a yarmulke. He removed the baseball cap and headed toward the door, but as he reached for the doorknob, he changed his mind and sat back down on the bed. *I decided I was going to wear my yarmulke to the convention*, he thought resolutely, *and I gave my word.*

As he was thinking — and morosely watching the second hand on his watch moving ever forward — he suddenly recalled that the night before, he had removed his shirt and tossed it in a heap into the corner of the room.

He ran over to the pile of clothing, peered into the undershirt he had been wearing the previous day, and lo and behold — there was his yarmulke!

Why hadn't he thought of looking in that pile of tangled clothing during the hour that he had spent searching for his yarmulke? Because that was the point of this *nisayon*. Hashem wanted him to have to make a decision on how committed he was to wearing a yarmulke! Once he made a firm decision that he was not going down to the convention hall without a yarmulke, Hashem "returned" his yarmulke to him, because he had already passed the test.

"DON'T JUMP!"

The second story was one that I witnessed myself. Our shul had two sets of doors. The outer doors, facing the street, locked with a combination, and the inner doors' doorknob had a button on the inner side that anyone in the room could push to lock the door, and which could be opened from the outside only with a key. We never bothered locking the inner lock, as the locks on the outer doors were secure enough to prevent theft.

One Shabbos we arrived at the shul for *Daf Yomi* at 8 a.m., and after unlocking the outer doors we were surprised to find that someone had pushed the locking button on the inner door the night before. Thankfully, the shul has two entrances. We went around to the other side of the building, but there, too, someone had pushed in the button to lock the inner door.

Someone said, "Don't worry, Yossie never misses *Daf Yomi*. I'm sure he has the key."

"How can he carry the key?" another person responded. "There's no *eiruv* here!"

"He probably has it on his belt," the first man countered.

Two minutes later Yossie walked in. "Do you have the key to the inner door?" we asked.

"Why should I have the key?" he answered. "We don't lock the door."

Another few minutes passed, and by this time we had about twenty-five people crowded into the small hallway, trying to find a way to get inside. The fact that in an hour we would have another hundred people standing around wasn't much on our minds at that point. The people who were there had made an effort to get to shul early for a *shiur*, and they didn't want to miss the *Daf*.

One of the *baalebatim*, a man in his mid-50s named Dovid, was feeling very impatient. "This is ridiculous," he said. "We want to learn. What are we going to do?"

Dovid was growing more impatient by the minute, and suddenly he said, "I'm going up to the *ezras nashim* to jump down from the balcony into the shul."

"Dovid," I said, "I'm very pro learning, and I also want to start the *shiur*, but you can't jump into the shul. You could break your leg!"

"Don't worry," he said. "I'm young at heart, and I'm in good shape."

Dovid made a start for the door to the *ezras nashim*, and I followed close behind to make sure he didn't do anything rash.

By the time I got up to the *ezras nashim,* Dovid already had one leg over the railing.

"We'll wait for someone to come open the lock. Please don't jump," I pleaded.

"Look!" he pointed. "I'm directly above that *shtender*. It is very wide and sturdy, and I can lower myself down most of the way so that it'll only be a short drop. I'll land on the *shtender*."

"What if you miss the *shtender*?" I asked. "We're not insured for this!"

I was talking myself blue in the face, yet Dovid would not be deterred. By this time he had both legs over the railing and was gingerly lowering himself down, when someone suddenly shouted from down below, "Don't jump! It's open!"

He hoisted himself back up over the railing, and we went down to join the crowd in the shul. The man who had opened the door explained that he had been fiddling with the handle for the full 20 minutes that we had been standing there, and it had finally popped open on its own.

Human curiosity being what it is, as soon as the *shiur* was over, several participants went to check the distance between the *shtender* and the *ezras nashim*, in case this scenario would ever repeat itself. I'm not sure what they found, but shortly after Shabbos we had the locks of the inner doors removed so that we wouldn't be locked out again.

Now, who opened that door? The guy fiddling with the doorknob? I don't think so. The incredible timing leads me to believe that it was Dovid who got that door open. Hashem wanted to see whether anyone in our shul was willing to put himself on the line for the *shiur*. As soon as Dovid demonstrated the will to ensure that we would have a *shiur*, Hashem sent a message: "I don't want you to jump — you can have your *shiur!*"

The *nisayon* had vanished.

THE BUILDINGS THAT DIDN'T CHANGE HANDS

The third story was the most astounding of all. There was a *mispallel* who was involved in commercial real estate. An *ehrliche* young man, he would call frequently to ask whether his deals were halachically sound before signing the contracts.

"Rabbi Viener," he said one day when he called, "I have a deal on the table now that makes anything I spoke to you about in the past look like child's play.

"Rebbi," he added, "if I pull this off, I can retire and sit and learn for the rest of my life!"

"Tell me the *she'eilah* first," I said, "and then we'll discuss what you'll do after the deal is completed."

It took 25 minutes for him to explain the entire background of the deal. When he finished walking me through the details, he said,

"There's one part of it that might be a little bit shady, and I want to know if I can go ahead with it."

He spent quite a while explaining the shady aspect. The reason he thought it was a "little bit" shady is that it was actually *extremely* shady.

"I'm very sorry," I said, "but it's *assur*. Don't get involved in this deal in any way."

He accepted my ruling like a real trouper. He was looking at a very substantial commission. He was the broker of record, but if he wouldn't finalize the deal, someone else who was not as scrupulous would no doubt grab the opportunity. It was a very tough *nisayon*.

He called me back three times that day, each time with a new angle to the situation he had presented. I was happy to hear him out, because I was hoping it would work out for him somehow. Unfortunately, however, each time I had to tell him that it was still not permissible.

I usually don't do this, but on the third round I couldn't resist asking him whether he was going to follow the *psak*. At that point there was no option halachically other than to refuse the deal, but such a large amount of money posed a tough challenge.

After a long pause he said, "I think so." He had until the end of the day to finalize the deal, but he was leaning toward canceling it based on my *psak*.

This story took place on a Tuesday. He came two minutes early to the Tuesday-night *shiur*, just as I was preparing my final thoughts for the *shiur*, and hit me with a bombshell.

"Rebbi," he said, "you're never going to believe this."

"Try me," I countered.

"I made up my mind that I was going to pass the *nisayon*. I would give up the deal, and all the money.

"I went to my client's office to inform him of my decision. By that time all the documents had been prepared. I swallowed hard and told my client that I couldn't go through with it.

"I cannot explain what happened next. *Less than an hour later, the entire deal fell apart.* Even had I told my client that I would go through with the deal, I wouldn't have made any money at all!"

This story is so amazing to me because Hashem concocted such an intricate plot — one that had the potential to cause several large buildings in Manhattan to change hands — simply to test the integrity of one nice Jewish boy. Once that young man made his decision to act as *every* Jew should, there was no longer a reason for those buildings to be sold.

From time to time we merit to be shown that a *nisayon* was no more than a mirage that allowed us to catapult ourselves to ever-greater heights in serving Hashem. This can be seen only after we've made the decision to display the dormant strength that lies deep within us. Those episodes should inspire us for the many other times that we pass the *nisayon* but things don't end up quite as tidily.

Nice Guy or a Shmattah?

A while back, a fellow left a message on my answering machine. "My name is Aron Goldberg,"[1] he said. "I need to speak to the Rav as soon as possible! Please return my call — even after midnight!" And he left his number.

"Thank you very much for calling back," Mr. Goldberg said when I returned the call. "I really, really appreciate that you took the time to call me...."

He thanked me for a few more minutes, and after that peculiar greeting, he said, "I really need to talk to you."

"I'm ready," I said.

"I don't have time right now," he said. "Can you call me back?"

This was getting stranger by the minute.

"I apologize," I said," but I receive a few hundred phone calls each week, and I might forget. Can you call me back?"

"I would greatly prefer if I could trouble you to call *me* back," Mr. Goldberg insisted.

This left me in an awkward position, but after thinking about it for a few moments, I decided to humor him. "When should I call you?" I asked.

He gave me a time he thought would be good.

I called him back at the appointed time. Once again, he spent five full minutes thanking me profusely for calling back. Then he said, "I *really* need to talk to you."

---

1. Not his real name.

"I understood that from our last conversation," I replied, "and I'm listening."

"I can't discuss this matter over the phone," he said, clearly uncomfortable. "I must speak with you in person."

"Can you tell me what you'd like to discuss?" I asked.

"It's too complicated," he said. "I can only explain it properly face-to-face."

"I should be able to free up some time later this week. When do you want to meet?"

"I don't know yet," he said. "Can you call me back?"

At this point, I was in a quandary. On the one hand, I would have been glad to do the *chessed*. On the other hand, a rav can devote only a certain amount of time to returning phone calls, and to call someone for a third time might come at others' expense. Was I obligated to do *chessed* with this fellow at all costs? And if the letter of the law didn't obligate me, was it within the spirit of the law of *chessed* to do it anyway?

This incident — the outcome of which I will soon share with you — leads to a broader question with which many of us grapple. We all understand the importance of *chessed*, and we are eager to help others in need. But there are instances in which we are certain that those asking for favors are eminently capable of doing for themselves what they have asked us to do for them. If we do help them, we will clearly be rewarded for doing *chessed*.

Sometimes, however, we might feel that the person is taking advantage of us. Or, to quote the eloquent words of someone who was in this position: "I have no problem doing favors, but he is not asking for a favor — he is making me into a *shmattah.*"

Is this position valid? Does the Torah advocate helping others no matter what they request, regardless of whether they are physically, mentally, and emotionally capable of helping themselves? Or, if we can determine that the other person is asking for the favor only because he is too lazy to help himself, are we permitted to refuse— especially considering that helping him might just encourage him to continue relying on others and result in his being less successful in life?

NARROWING THE FOCUS

Before we proceed, let us discuss three important factors that limit this question somewhat:

1. We must be careful to differentiate between "big" favors and "little" favors. Regardless of the conclusions we arrive at in our study of *chessed*, I don't want anyone to think that if he comes home from shul one night and his wife asks him to bring her a drink of water when he comes upstairs, it is okay to bang on the table and shout, "You are perfectly capable of coming down to get yourself a drink. I'm not going to allow you to turn me into a *shmattah.*" In addition to the *shalom bayis* considerations of this particular example, it is obvious that when doing a *chessed* requires minimal effort and would require greater effort on the part of the one asking, we should jump at the opportunity to help.

2. Moreover, there are certain relationships in which the guidelines we are discussing certainly do not apply. The obvious example is the *mitzvah* of *kibbud av va'eim*, honoring one's parents, which also has specific parameters, but those are different from the parameters that we are about to discuss.

In marriage as well, there are many situations in which spouses do, and should, go above and beyond the call of duty and perform acts of *chessed* for each other that the recipient does not absolutely need.

3. We are not going to discuss the question of whether it is proper for people to ask others to do things that they are able to do for themselves. If people do not realize that they should not burden others if it is not necessary, it is not our responsibility to teach them that. Our focus is on what *our* response should be when a person asks us to do something for him that he is perfectly capable of doing on his own.

An incident that happened in yeshivah provides a perfect example of when this question would apply.

One fellow — I'll call him Shmaya — turned to his tablemate in the *beis medrash* and said, "Can you please pass me a pen?"

"I don't see any pens around," his tablemate responded.

"There's one," Shmaya said, pointing to a table ten feet away.

When this incident repeated itself several times, Shmaya's tablemate exclaimed in exasperation, "Each of us would have to put in the same amount of effort to get a pen that's a few tables away. Why should I get it for you?"

""Well," Shmaya replied, "I'm two feet farther away from the pen!"

Our discussion will not address the question of whether Shmaya was correct in making this request. Our concern here is whether his tablemate was correct in feeling that Shmaya was lazy and trying to manipulate the friend into doing something he should have done himself — and whether he was therefore justified in his refusal to do the *chessed*.

As a final caveat, I want to make it clear that even if refusing to do a *chessed* is justified under certain circumstances, we must be very careful to determine that our refusal does not stem simply for our *own* laziness at the time the request is made.

A LESSON FROM A MATRIARCH

We find two instances, one in the Torah and one in the Talmud, that seem to indicate that *chessed* has no boundaries, and no matter how outrageous a request for *chessed* may seem, we should not turn it down:

The first instance: In *Parashas Chayei Sarah*, we read that Avraham Avinu charges his servant Eliezer with the task of finding a *shidduch* for Yitzchak, and Eliezer heads to Aram Naharayim to find a relative of Avraham who would be a suitable match for Yitzchak. En route, he devises a plan through which to test the prospective bride's mettle: He will ask a maiden at the town well to draw water for him. If she offers to draw water not only for him but for his ten camels as well, he will know that she is a suitable match for Yitzchak, because she will automatically fit into Avraham Avinu's empire of *chessed*.

When he reaches the well at Aram Naharayim, Eliezer sees Rivkah. Approaching the well, he asks her to draw water for him, and she offers to draw water not only for him but for his camels as well. As we learn in Rashi,[2] Rivkah was very young at the time, but she followed through on her *generous* offer by carrying pail after pail of water to the trough.

Eliezer was traveling with a contingent of strong servants, all of them apparently quite capable of drawing water and transporting it from the well. Eliezer himself was an able-bodied male several decades older than Rivkah. A *midrash* states that Besuel and Lavan wanted to kill Eliezer and take all the valuables he had brought with him from Avraham's home, but when they saw him lift two camels in his two arms, they decided that it would be unwise to attack him.[3] If Eliezer possessed that sort of physical prowess, was Rivkah required to draw all that water for him and his camels? It would seem that an appropriate response to his request for help would have been to say, "Sir, I see that you need help, but I can't draw water for you and all of your camels. I'll be happy to show you and your men how to draw water and pour it into the trough, though."

Yet Rivkah *did* draw all that water, and her behavior toward Eliezer gained her entry into *Klal Yisrael,* and she became one of the three Matriarchs of our nation. At face value, then, it seems that Rivkah's actions were considered reasonable and within the parameters of *chessed.* And if a young girl drawing water for able-bodied men and their camels is within the parameters of *chessed,* then so is every case that we encounter in daily life.

RUNNING FOR A POOR MAN

The second instance of unbridled *chessed* is in the Talmudic discussion of the Torah's commandment that when a poor person comes to us, we should provide him with *"dei machsoro* — his requirement, *asher yechsar lo* — all that is lacking to him."[4] The Talmud explains that the words *"dei machsoro"* mean that we are obligated to give a person only "his requirement" — i.e., the items he needs in order to

---

2. *Bereishis* 25:20.
3. *Yalkut Shimoni, Bereishis* 109.
4. *Kesubos* 67b; *Devarim* 15:8.

survive. On the other hand, the words *"asher yechsar lo"* teach that each individual has things that are lacking "to *him,*" and we are obligated to provide for each person according to his needs.

The Talmud then offers an extreme example of this principle.

There was a person who came from a wealthy family and had grown accustomed to a luxurious lifestyle. Not only did he have a horse to ride on, he even had a servant running ahead of the horse to announce his impending arrival. Today we might consider this the height of hubris, but that was apparently acceptable for extremely wealthy people at that time.

However, this man was now impoverished. Hillel HaZakein was the *Nasi* (leader) of *Klal Yisrael* then, and he engaged a horse and servant for this man so that he would have what was "lacking to *him.*" One day, Hillel HaZakein could not find a servant for hire, so he himself ran before this man for a distance of three *mil* (more than two miles!).

Can there be a more egregious example of someone being treated like a *shmattah* than a *Nasi* running three *mil* before a delusional man who thinks he still needs an honor that brought him no practical benefit?

Yet this passage is cited by *Rambam* and *Shulchan Aruch*[5] as an obligation for each of us: We must provide a person in need with "all that is lacking to him," even a horse to ride on and a servant to run before him.

This is astounding. In modern-day terms, this would mean that if a wealthy man is accustomed to traveling in a chauffeured limousine and having a lackey escort him everywhere, were he to lose his fortune and still feel the need for this service, we would be required to provide him with that service. And if a member of the Moetzes Gedolei HaTorahh was handling the case and was not able to find the requisite underling, he would himself be expected to escort the man.

Generally, the favors that we are asked to do for others fall far short of this level. It would seem, then, that we would be required to fulfill almost any conceivable request for *chessed*.

---

5. *Yoreh Deah* 150:1

LIMITS TO CHESSED

It's not that simple, however. There is compelling evidence that the Torah does place certain limitations on *chessed*.

The Torah states that if someone sees a person's donkey collapsing under the weight of a heavy load, "*Azov ta'azov imo* — you will surely help along with him"[6] — that is, we must help the person unload the weight from his donkey. A *mishnah* deduces that we are required to do so only if the donkey's owner takes part in the effort. If the owner sits down and says, "You have a mitzvah to unload my donkey; do it yourself," we are not required to unload his donkey for him.[7]

In addition, with regard to both this mitzvah and the mitzvah of *hashavas aveidah* (returning a lost object), the Talmud states that a venerable or elderly person is not required to stoop to a level that is beneath his dignity in order to fulfill them.

These passages too are cited by *Rambam* and *Shulchan Aruch*. Clearly, then, *chessed* does have its limits. But what are those limits?

DON'T RUSH TO JUDGMENT

While I haven't found any sources that clearly delineate the conditions under which we are justified in refusing a request for help and those in which we are not, I would like to point out some lessons we can learn from the examples cited above.

While Rivkah's actions were definitely considered *chessed* — and we would certainly be rewarded if we did the same — we cannot extrapolate from her behavior to all cases. Our question, as we explained earlier, was limited to cases in which we know the person asking for the favor and in which we can determine, beyond the shadow of a doubt, that the person is able to help himself. I would suggest that since Rivkah did not know Eliezer, she could not know for certain whether he was capable of drawing water on his own. Perhaps, Rivkah felt, he had some viable excuse for not offering to help. Rather than suspecting

---

6. *Shemos* 23:5.
7. *Bava Metzia* 32a.

him of taking advantage of her, she gave him the benefit of the doubt and jumped at the opportunity to do the *chessed*.

Lesson #1 in *chessed*, then, is to give people the benefit of the doubt. Perhaps they really do need the favor, even if it does not seem that way. Admittedly, giving people the benefit of the doubt may come at the cost of being taken advantage of from time to time. And, yes, when we realize that someone is definitely taking advantage of us, we may indeed be justified in refusing to help him; in fact, we may be doing him an even greater favor by refusing to help him.

In the majority of cases, however, we should follow Rivkah's lead. We should judge people favorably, assume that they have a good reason to ask for the favor, and jump at the opportunity to help. Many *tzaddikim* were, on occasion, induced into doing *chassadim* that they were not required to do, but they are still considered our leaders despite — or perhaps *because of* — their eagerness to do *chessed*, even at the risk of being exploited.

If we are determined to make sure that we are never taken advantage of, we can easily become so suspicious of people's intentions in asking us for favors that we will end up doing no *chessed* whatsoever. We are much better off erring on the side of being taken advantage of than erring on the side of refusing to fulfill legitimate requests for help.

Lesson #2 is based on HaRav Chaim Shmulevitz's discussion of the episode of Hillel HaZakein running before the formerly wealthy man. In *Sichos Mussar* (5732, 29), Rav Shmulevitz, *zt"l*, points out that this story is very difficult to understand, because, as the Torah leader of the time, Hillel HaZakein should not have been permitted to forgo the honor of the Torah in order to provide this man with his needs.

Furthermore, says Rav Shmulevitz, the pauper could not have been entirely insane, because we are not required to fulfill the irrational desires of a deranged person. For instance, if someone would come over to you and say, "I really want you to stand on your head for an hour," fulfilling that desire would not be considered a *chessed*. We must conclude, therefore, that the man in this story was rational in all areas except for one: he had a desperate *need* for honor.

But considering his status as the leader of *Klal Yisrael*, why was

Hillel HaZakein required to fill that need?

Rav Shmulevitz suggests that this man was so desperate for honor that he might have become dangerously ill if he did not have his horse and runner. This was, therefore, a case of *pikuach nefesh* — danger to a life — which overrides the honor of the Torah.

This tells us that our obligation relative to the *mitzvah* of *chessed* can extend to meeting another person's need — no matter how ridiculous that need may seem — as long as the person is rational and sane.

Lesson #3 relates to when a person may refuse to do a *chessed* because he considers it beneath his dignity.

Let's say you are in your pajamas, and you see your neighbor across the street drop a $100 bill out his window and onto the street. He calls out to you, "Can you please get that for me? I can't leave my house now!" Are you required to do that *chessed*, or can you turn down his request because it is beneath your dignity?

The answer is that it depends on what your reaction would be if you were the one who had dropped the $100 bill onto the street. Would you go out in your pajamas to retrieve it? If you would, then you are required to do the same for your friend. But if you can honestly determine that you would be too embarrassed to go into the street in your pajamas if the money was your own, then you are exempt.

But one must be careful when acting in accordance with this exemption. *Chayei Adam* (Introduction) writes that one of the traits of a haughty person is that when he is presented with an opportunity to do a mitzvah, his first reaction is to evaluate whether it is beneath his dignity.

A BITTERSWEET CONCLUSION

Let's return to the story of our friend Mr. Goldberg, who kept asking me to call him back. Based on the lessons in *chessed* that we learn from Rivkah Imeinu and Hillel HaZakein, it would seem that returning Mr. Goldberg's phone call was the correct thing to do, despite my misgivings, because I had no way of determining whether or not this was indeed a *chessed* that he really needed from me.

When I called him back for the third time, at the time we had agreed upon, he said that although it was vital that we meet, he wasn't sure that he would have time that week. He thought that the next week would be better, and said that he would call me (finally!) to confirm.

I didn't hear from him for four weeks.

One day, a fellow walked over to me in shul. "Do you know who I am?" he asked.

I had to admit that I didn't.

"I'm Aron Goldberg."

"So pleased to meet you," I said. To be honest, I was starting to suspect that the whole volley of phone calls had been a prank, and that the prankster had finally had enough. To my relief, not only did he exist, but he seemed to be a normal, upstanding individual.

"I came in person," he explained, "because I realize that if we continue to play phone tag we're never going to meet. Let's set up a meeting right now,"

We arranged an appointment for later in the week. When he finally came to speak to me I could hardly contain myself. I had to hear why he had put me through this peculiar runaround.

"When people call me regarding an important issue and ask for an hour-long meeting, I usually allow them to open the conversation," I said. "But with your permission, I have to get something off my chest. Can you please explain," I asked, "why you asked me to call you back twice, and each time I called you said you didn't have time to talk?

"I try to be *dan l'chaf zechus* [to judge others favorably]," I continued, "and I decided that you must have had a good reason for making this unusual request. But as much as I racked my brain, I simply could not come up with a plausible explanation. Can you share your reason with me?"

Mr. Goldberg smiled sadly and said, "I was actually waiting for you to ask that question."

Fighting back tears, Mr. Goldberg shared his heartbreaking life story.

"I am completely alone in this world," he began. "I am a *baal te-shuvah*. My family is still irreligious, and they hate me for becoming religious. I got married, but it didn't work out, and now I'm divorced. My ex-wife left with my children, who have no contact with me at all.

"Several weeks ago, the thought that no one in the world cares about me began to haunt me. To prove to myself that nobody cares, I decided that I would call a Rav in the neighborhood and ask him to return my call. *Just watch*, I told myself, *even Rabbis don't have time for me, and he's not going to return my call. Then I'll know for certain that no one cares about me.*

"When you called me back the first time," he continued, "I kept thanking you, because I was shocked that you actually returned the call. Your phone call made me feel that perhaps I did belong on Earth. But then I figured that it must have been a fluke. I was sure that if I would have the gall to ask you to call me again, you would tell me that you had no time. When you called back the second time, I was convinced that somebody really did care about me. Life was worth living."

Suddenly, everything fell into place. The entire incident had been a test!

Now, I must say that, had I not returned Mr. Goldberg's calls I might have been justified. I am not suggesting that Rabbanim should make a habit of calling people back repeatedly. His behavior bordered on trying to "make someone into a *shmattah*," and I think I could have made a convincing case for putting my foot down at some point. But by putting suspicion aside and making that phone call, I was fortunate enough to have been able to help renew Mr. Goldberg's faith in humanity.

Maybe Mr. Goldberg *was* taking advantage of me by making me call him so many times. But I'm still glad I made those phone calls!

A Segulah
For Parnassah

*My husband recently lost his job,
and I feel that he has not been
proactive enough in seeking new
employment. This is causing tension
in the home, since he complains that
I am too worried about the situation
and that the pressure I am adding
is counterproductive. I feel that my
complaining about his lack of initiative
is the only way I can push the agenda
since, in my opinion, he is not taking
the situation seriously enough.*

*Doesn't he have a halachic obligation
to provide parnassah? How do I go
about reminding him of this important
role without promoting further strife?*

You are halachically correct concerning your husband's obligation to provide *parnassah* for his family.

The Torah says: "*She'eirah kesusah .... lo yigra* — he may not diminish her sustenance or clothing."[1] The husband has the responsibility to make sure that his wife is taken care of in terms of food and clothing.[2] If proper *hishtadlus* was made and there is still not adequate income to cover the bills, he does not violate any prohibition. However, if the money is accessible and proper effort is not made to acquire it, or if he is not giving his spouse money out of spite or stinginess, he transgresses the *lo saasei.*

(In the inspiring scenario in which the spouse agrees to lower her standard of living in order to enable her husband to learn Torah, the husband is obviously not in violation of this prohibition. She is to be commended and revered for her lofty ideals and willingness to sacrifice her *gashmiyus* for a greater share in *Olam Haba.*)

The husband must take his responsibility seriously for hashkafic and practical reasons as well. Rabbi Yehudah said: One should always be careful [to make sure] that there is food in his house, for strife is prevalent in a house only on account of food, for it is written (*Tehillim* 147:14), "*Hasam gevuleich shalom cheilev chittim yasbi'eich* — He makes peace in your borders, He fills you with the finest of the wheat.*" When will there be peace in your borders? When there is enough food. One should endeavor to ensure that there is enough money in the house to cover the necessities of life.[3]

DON'T ASK TOO MANY QUESTIONS

The *mechaber* of an important *sefer* containing *mussar, hashkafah, hadrachah, and halachah,* the *Shevet Mussar* has very powerful advice pertaining to your scenario.[4]

His first point is that if a woman sees that the money in the house

---

1. *Shemos* 21:10.
2. See *Kesubos* 47b; *Rambam Hilchos Ishus* 12:2; cf. *Ramban to Shemos* 21:9.
3. *Bava Metzia* 59a.
4. *Shevet Mussar,* Chapter 24.

is tight, she should not ask her husband too many questions about the situation; for example, "What's going to happen regarding the bills? How are we going to pay the tuition? Who is going pay the mortgage?"

Trust that your husband is working on it, even if it appears to you that perhaps he could be working harder or faster. There is an obligation to judge even total strangers *l'kaf zechus* (in a favorable way), and so your husband certainly deserves the benefit of the doubt. "*Al tadin es chavercha ad shetagiya limkomo* — do not judge your friend [and certainly not your spouse] until you are in his exact situation and circumstance." You must assume that your husband is trying his best, even if you feel that you would do things differently.

You must bear in mind that it is not at all his fault that there is a recession or that his firm was downsized. Constant inquiries such as "Did you set up any interviews today?" or "Did you send another resume out?" or "Did anyone call back yet?" can be perceived as badgering and only make the atmosphere more tense than it already is. In the best of circumstances, it takes time and effort to find a job. It does not help matters if a husband feels belittled and pressured by his spouse.

(There certainly are situations where the husband does need *hadrachah* and a bit of prodding to ignite his desire to move forward. However, his spouse is not necessarily the one from whom he is willing to accept such *mussar*. It is often better to seek out his Rebbe, Rav, or good friend to convey the message in a delicate and effective fashion.)

PUSHED OVER THE EDGE

It is crucial to realize that if the breadwinner of the family is pressured too much, there is a risk that he may engage in unethical business practices in order to meet the expectations placed on him. Even good people, when embarrassed or coerced, could become involved in shady deals, rationalizing that the end justifies the means. Every good husband wants his wife to be happy, and if she constantly points out what the neighbors have, what her friend's husband is buying for her, and where others are going for vacation, the pressure becomes almost unbearable. (This is not at all to imply that women are prone to act this way, and it should not be taken as an unfair criticism of our *nashim tzidkaniyos*. Men often have a desire for material goods as well and also feel the need to "keep up with the Cohens." I am merely addressing your request for *hadrachah* on the matter, and advise that you attempt to tone down any requests that are not absolutely required at this difficult economic juncture. Extra care must be taken to avoid comparing your *parnassah* situation to that of [seemingly] more affluent friends or neighbors.)

A SEGULAH FOR PARNASSAH

The *Shevat Mussar* has more practical advice on the matter. If the wife sees that *parnassah* is not going well, she should *daven* intensely and ask Hashem to help her husband and the family.

She should also make sure to smile often and remain optimistic. Her constant reassurances are an important step toward rectifying the situation. When a man sees his loyal wife offering encouragement, when she says to him, "I am behind you; I respect you; we will get through this and grow from it," he will worry less — and by staying calm and optimistic, he will merit long life and good *parnassah*.

What does happiness have to do with good *mazal* for *parnassah*? The *Shevat Mussar* is teaching us that having the mindset that one is comfortable and happy is in itself a great *segulah* for *parnassah*. The feeling that you have (or will have) what you need will itself improve your *mazal*.[5] It is, *chas v'shalom*, a *segulah* for poverty if one is too focused on and worried about monetary problems. Although it is true that a penny saved is a penny earned, one has to strike the proper balance without making everyone in the house on edge and agitated about money.

How is it possible to strike that balance when money is really lacking?

Chazal tell us[6] that Rabbi Akiva was a poor, ignorant shepherd when he married his wife, the daughter of one of the wealthiest Jews in the land. Her father disowned her, and the young couple lived in dire

---

5. See *Rashi, Sanhedrin* 20a d"h *dargash arsah d'gada* — *v'dok*.
6. *Nedarim* 50a.

poverty, sleeping in a shed used for straw, and sleeping on the straw. One day, Eliyahu HaNavi appeared at their door in the guise of a poor person asking for a little straw, for his wife had given birth and had nothing comfortable to lie upon.

R' Akiva remarked to his wife, "You see, there is someone even poorer than we are." This enabled her to realize that they still had more than others. The key to a life of contentment is to avoid looking at people who have more and to look instead at those who have less, thus giving one an appreciation for what he has.

The proper attitude, even in the direst times, is a *segulah* for future *parnassah*. Even if that *parnassah* does not manifest itself immediately (or ever) in a large bank account, the peace of mind that comes with the attitude that one is satisfied with one's lot is the greatest wealth. As *Chazal* teach us, "*Eizehu ashir? Hasamei'ach b'chelko.*"

This positive outlook on life will encourage your husband and create a calm, warm atmosphere in the home — conditions that are necessary for the *berachah* of *parnassah* to descend on your family.

Daas Torah, Part 1: A Lesson From Purim

The subject of *daas Torah* is complex and often misunderstood. We will look at an excerpt from the writings of Rav Eliyahu Dessler to gain a deeper understanding of this crucial topic.

Rav Dessler was present at meetings of many *Gedolim* (including Rav Chaim Soloveitchik, Rav Boruch Ber Liebowitz, Rav Chaim Ozer Grodzenski, and the Chofetz Chaim, *zecher tzaddikim livrachah*). "I will tell you with certainty," he writes, "that their genius was self-evident to all. Their depth of understanding was incredible. Before we get to concepts such as *mesorah, ruach hakodesh,* and *siyata* di'Shemaya, we have to understand that we are talking about men of rare genius. They have a greater understanding of any topic than we can ever hope to have. And if they are contemplating an area in which they do not have the information, they know to ask. They would never render a decision without ascertaining the facts."

Their brilliance was only one component in their successful leadership. A lifetime of learning Torah was only the beginning; a person can have that and still never attain *daas Torah*. He must also have total *yiras Shamayim* to do everything *lishmah* for *Klal Yisrael*. He has to realize the great responsibility that lies in making decisions for the *klal*.

Rav Dessler explains that if our understanding seems to contradict *daas Torah,* we should not be surprised, because *daas Torah* is not necessarily our *daas*, the common *daas*, the *daas* of the masses. *Gedolei Yisrael* have a *siyata* di'Shemaya that comes with their genius, *yiras Shamayim*, and sense of responsibility.

Much damage can be caused when one follows one's own opinion, if that opinion is not supported by genuine *daas Torah*. The inside story of Purim is an excellent example of just how dangerous improper decision-making can be.

The story of Purim occurred over a span of nine years. Had we been alive at the time, we would probably not have recognized the connection between events that occurred over such a long span of time. It took Mordechai, one of the *Gedolei Hador*, to understand that the feast at the beginning of the *Megillah* was a cause of Haman's decree of extermination years later.

Rav Dessler explains that Mordechai had declared that it was forbidden to attend the feast, but, unfortunately, people did not listen, although they knew that there might be issues of *tznius* and improper interaction. They felt that their failure to attend would be politically dangerous; they didn't want to be perceived as unpatriotic. They voiced their concerns to Mordechai HaTzaddik, but their apprehensions didn't change his opinion of the situation and the spiritual dangers that it presented.

"Mordechai HaTzaddik knows *halachah* well," they said among themselves, "but he does not know politics."

Many ignored the stern warning of the *tzaddik* and joined the festivities. They did not realize that by going they would be party to the enormous *chillul Hashem* that would take place there. One of the reasons Achashverosh threw the party was to celebrate the downfall of the Jews. He erroneously thought that Yirmiyahu's prophecy that *Klal Yisrael* would be redeemed after seventy years had been proven false. The feast was a celebration that the Jews would remain in *galus* and never return to their land to rebuild the *Beis HaMikdash*.

During the feast, Achashverosh brought out the vessels of the *Beis HaMikdash* and used them for mundane purposes, and he donned the garments of the *Kohen Gadol*. He was also aware that Hashem detests *pritzus*, so he made sure that the marathon festivities were

planned with appropriate immodesty. Although the Jews in attendance certainly felt terrible witnessing all this, they mistakenly thought
that their presence was necessary for political gain. *Chazal* tell us that
18,000 Jews attended the event.

One can be sure that after it was over, many of them remarked, "It
is a good thing we went, because the king is happy we showed up, and
now he is well disposed toward us. Who knows how many evil decrees
we averted by our attendance. Can you imagine if we had not gone?"

Indeed, Hashem didn't punish them immediately. Nothing happened a month later, a year later, or even eight years later.

After nine years passed, Haman gained power and decreed that
everyone must bow down to him. Technically, there might have been
some *heter* to bow down. Mordechai, however, was afraid of *maris
ayin*, the concern that although something is technically permitted, it
should not be done because people might misunderstand and believe
that he was kowtowing to an idol-like figure, and he was therefore intent on not capitulating, thereby making a *Kiddush Hashem*.[1]

Many were upset by Mordechai's decision. "Years ago he gave us bad
advice," they said. "It is a good thing we didn't listen to him then. Now
he is taking on his own personal *chumrah* and putting us all in danger."

Their worst fears seemed to materialize. Haman convinced Achashverosh to issue a decree of extermination against all the Jews. *Daas
Torah was wrong again*, they murmured. *It is all Mordechai's fault.*

Yet Mordechai HaTzaddik insisted that it was necessary to show Haman that the Jews would not compromise on their principles. As for
the harsh decree against the Jews, Mordechai explained that it was not
the result of his decision not to bow down to Haman, but a punishment
for their participation in Achashverosh's party nine years earlier.

Whose side would we have taken had we been there at that time?
Would we have connected the troubles to that party nine years earlier
that Mordechai told us not to attend? Or would we have connected it
to Mordechai's stringent stance not to bow down to Haman?

The common person, with common *daas*, would have concluded
without any doubt that Mordechai was at fault. How could anyone argue

---

1. See *Tosafos Sanhedrin* 61b, *d"h Rava*.

with the facts? Mordechai was the one who had made Haman angry.

However, just the opposite was true.

Mordechai HaTzaddik had an understanding of *darchei Shamayim, Divine* ways, that the *klal*, with their common *daas*, did not have. His way was not the way they saw it … at least at that point in time.

The greatness of *Klal Yisrael* is that they ultimately did *teshuvah*. They came to recognize that Mordechai HaTzaddik had been right all along.

According to a simple reading of the *Megillah*, the turning point that set in motion the salvation of *Klal Yisrael* was Achashverosh's disturbing dream. However, Rav Dessler explains that the real turning point was when *Klal Yisrael* stopped blaming Mordechai and finally accepted responsibility for ignoring his directive nine years earlier. From that point on, Hashem caused the wheels to turn in our favor, beginning with Achashverosh's nightmare.

Rav Dessler warns that there is a great *yetzer hara* to resist authority; to flout *daas Torah*. Many problems in *galus* are rooted in the fact that we have not always followed *daas Torah*. The story of Purim highlights this.

On Purim we rejoice in the recognition that *Klal Yisrael's* success depends on the strength of its leadership and our ability to take counsel from and heed the advice of our *Gedolim*.

Daas Torah, Part 2: Understanding Emunas Chachamim

I read your recent article concerning daas Torah with great interest. It is a topic that pertains to the decision-making of every Jew.

May I be so bold to ask if there is a possibility that daas Torah can err? If it is indeed possible, how does one comfortably follow daas Torah and yet deal emotionally and intellectually with the thought of that possible scenario?

Daas Torah is a term that is misunderstood almost as often as it is used. Daas Torah does not mean that our Gedolei Hador are infallible.

The famous Gemara in Gittin (56b) many read every Tishah B'Av tells how Rabbi Yochanan ben Zakkai, the Gadol Hador, was spirited out of the besieged city of Yerushalayim and granted a private audience with the Roman general Vespasian. Just as Rabbi Yochanan was telling Vespasian that Yerushalayim would be conquered only by a king, a messenger delivered the news that the emperor of Rome had died and that the Senate had appointed Vespasian in his place. He was so impressed with the great rabbi's foresight and wisdom that he granted him any request, whereupon Rabbi Yochanan said, "Give me Yavneh and its sages, spare the life of Rabban Gamliel, and provide doctors for Rabbi Tzadok."

Two generations later, Rabbi Akiva applied to his response the verse, "He turns backward [the wisdom of] the wise ones and makes their wisdom foolishness,"[1] which means that Hashem will on (rare) occasion confound the wisdom of even the greatest chachamim. Either He will cause them to give incorrect answers or He will make them unable to answer at all. According to Rabbi Akiva, Rabbi Yochanan should have asked Vespasian to spare Yerushalayim and instead target his attacks against the Jewish zealots who were responsible for the rebellion. Destroying these ruffians, who in effect had held captive and even murdered the masses, was the only action necessary to restore law and order.

According to this explanation, Hashem caused Rav Yochanan to make a decision that was, objectively, unwise. Hashem put thoughts in Rav Yochanan's mind that took away his impeccable judgment. Hashem's siyata di'Shemaya led the Gadol Hador to make a decision that was ostensibly harmful, because that is what Hashem wanted.

Now, it should be noted that the Gemara also presents the opinion of those who defend Rabbi Yochanan's decision, saying that if he had asked for Yerushalayim, Vespasian would have refused him outright, and the Jewish people would have ended up with nothing. Nevertheless, this Gemara is telling us that it is possible (although extremely uncommon) that there can be crucial situations of great national importance — and certainly in the life of the individual — when Hashem causes Gedolim to make harmful decisions. However, the answer one receives from a Gadol in such unusual and difficult circumstances is still controlled by HaKadosh Baruch Hu, and therefore following his decision remains the will of Hashem in that situation.

The decision-making of Gedolim before the Holocaust is another possible example of Hashem controlling decision-makers at a time of Divine punishment. Although one can never really understand the Heavenly calculations concerning such a tragic and complex era in

---

1. Yeshayah 44:25.

Jewish history, and why it was His will that Klal Yisrael should suffer, it is pertinent to paraphrase a penetrating insight from Rav Aharon Yeshaya Roter, author of *Shaarei Aharon* and a survivor of the Holocaust, regarding the conduct of *Gedolei Torah* before World War II:

There are those who are critical of the way that *Gedolei Torah* acted ... the claim is that had they fled Europe ... many would not have perished.

In my opinion, this claim arises from a failure to understand the nature of the Holocaust and a failure to believe in Divine judgment. Hashem is compared to a shepherd, and if a shepherd decrees death on a part of his flock, is it possible for the sheep to run away? David HaMelech has written, *"Anah eileich meiruchacha v'anah mipanecha evrach* — where can I go to avoid Your spirit [of anger] (Radak)? Where can I go to flee from Your Face?"[2]

All the military strategists agree that during the war in the North African arena, if things had been left to their "natural" course, the Nazi general, Rommel, would have continued east and conquered the Land of Israel too, with all the consequences of a Nazi occupation. He was stopped only by a miracle, for Heaven surely decreed, "Only to here. Not farther."[3] Had Europe's Jews fled to Israel, who says that Rommel would have stopped where he did?

Our *Gedolei Hador* have a special *siyata* di'Shemaya that gives their advice a capacity for success not possible through other channels. When you follow *daas Torah,* you are following what Hashem wants you to do. Of course, it is possible that they can make a "mistake," because, for various reasons, Hashem influences them to make a certain decision.

Although Hashem may sometimes will that someone following the advice of *Gedolei Yisrael* be harmed, our *mesorah* concerning *emunas chachamim* teaches us that we are to assume that their guidance will prove beneficial, even in this world.

We must constantly strive to purify our outlook on life and to seek counsel from those whom Hashem has chosen to lead us through the challenges and vicissitudes of our days.

---

2. *Tehillim* 139:7.
3. It is noteworthy that the Jewish Agency — the official Zionist leadership of the Jewish community — was so certain of Rommel's imminent takeover it had started destroying its documents and almost all its leaders abandoned Yerushalayim.

Reconciliation Before Yom HaDin

I have a neighbor with whom I was on good terms until recently. I asked her to let my child come to play at her house, since I had to go out for about an hour. She replied that she could not have company because it was dinnertime. I am hurt and incensed by her refusal to do this simple favor for me. She should have simply offered to have my daughter join their family for dinner. What angers me is the fact that I have fed her children at our family mealtimes on numerous occasions and would expect a reciprocal relationship.

Due to my pain and frustration I am no longer speaking to my former friend. I am saddened by the turn of events and feel somewhat guilty, especially as we approach Yom Kippur. I am waiting for her to apologize, but she is ignoring the entire issue.

What should I do?

The first step in this process concerns your obligation to judge her favorably (be "*dan lechaf zechus*") and try to understand where she might be coming from.

Family dynamics vary from home to home, and it is quite possible that your neighbor's children are not as manageable at the dinner table when they have their friends eating over. Even if behavior is not the issue, the distractions created by the presence of friends might not be beneficial for children who are poor eaters. It is also possible that they want supper to be an opportunity for special family time together. Or perhaps special circumstances that evening precluded her from having your children over. These are just a few of the many possible reasons for your neighbor's response.

Second, you are assuming that your former friend is aware that you have graciously fed her children on various occasions. If that assumption were *incorrect*, it would explain why your neighbor does not feel indebted to you and would not feel there is any reason to want to reciprocate the favor. In *Beitzah* 16a, the Gemara rules that when one gives a child a gift it is important to let the parents know, thereby engendering *hakaras hatov* and a warm feeling of *achdus* between the parents. Following this sage advice might have prevented much of this dispute.

It is also important to do *chessed* without expecting repayment. Although your reaction is understandable, it is not healthy for a relationship to keep an account of the favors you have done for others. If every *chessed* you do creates in your mind an obligation of reciprocal payment, you will remain frustrated and disappointed at what you perceive to be a lack of *hakaras hatov* when you attempt to call in your credits.

You might want to consider investing some time and effort in forgiving her completely, without confronting her on the issue. That strategy might be beneficial, as it may help you to avoid the argumentative discussion that could ensue if you sit down to discuss the matter. If you do choose to simply forgive her, you will be "giving in," but the benefits of giving in, especially before the *Yom HaDin*, are immeasurable. (See our comment concerning the power of giving in and *tzelem Elokim* found in "Sibling Rivalry and *Kibbud Av Va'Eim*" (page 230)

If you are unsuccessful in eradicating any ill feelings in your heart, you must approach the other party to discuss the matter, as the Torah enjoins us to do.

The Rambam rules[1] that if one feels wronged, he should not remain quiet and harbor ill will but should rather approach the alleged wrong-doer and confront the issues. This is a *mitzvah mi'd'Oraisa*, which we learn from the *pasuk*, "*Lo sisna es achicha bilvavecha* — Do not hate your brother in your heart ...," but rather, "... *hochei'ach tochiach es amisecha* — give reproof to your fellow Jew,"[2] by letting him know of his wrongdoing that has affected your relationship. After the parties have respectfully aired their grievances, striven to understand each other, and asked forgiveness, reconciliation should result.

If this is the case, you should sit down with your neighbor in a calm and quiet atmosphere and lay out your grievances toward her in a pleasant, nonconfrontational way. She will either explain her actions in a satisfactory way or apologize.

It is crucial that you take care of this important business *before* Yom Kippur. The *Shulchan Aruch* rules[3] that *aveiros* between people are not forgiven on Yom Kippur until efforts are made to appease the wronged party. Even if you are 100 percent in the right regarding the issues at hand, it is important for your success in *din* (judgment), as well as for your neighbor's success in *din*, to repair the breakdown of your previously harmonious relationship. It is a *chessed* to afford her the opportunity to apologize if she was wrong; and if you were *chosheid bi'kesheirim* (suspected an innocent person of wrongdoing), it is vital that you are afforded the same opportunity.

In the *zechus* of being a *rodeif shalom* — a pursuer of peace — may you be *zocheh* to abundant *berachos* and *nachas*.

---

1. *Hilchos Dei'os* 6:6.
2. *Vayikra* 19:17.
3. O.C. 608:1, based on the *Gemara* in *Yoma* 85b.

Revenge Is Not Sweet

A relative of mine has been acting in a very obnoxious way and rarely misses an opportunity to insult me.

I have deep feelings of resentment, for I do not know what I have said or done to deserve such treatment. I feel guilty that I am having difficulty forgiving, especially as it is right before the Yemei HaDin.

To compound the problem, I feel a strong desire to take revenge and give back a sampling of what he has been subjecting me to. I understand that the desire for revenge is a very negative trait, yet I am unsure whether under these circumstances it is actually prohibited.

Please help me address this painful

topic so that I can prepare for the
Yamim Nora'im with clear direction.

Although the prohibition of taking *nekamah* (revenge) is clearly stated in *Chumash*,[1] there is ambiguity as to its parameters and practical application.

> *Those who suffer insult but do not insult in response, who hear their disgrace but do not reply, who perform Hashem's will out of love and are happy even when suffering, regarding them the pasuk states, "They who love Hashem will be like the sun going forth in its might."*
>
> Shabbos 88b

There are sources that seem to indicate that although it is not praiseworthy, it is permissible to take revenge for insult or injury that one has suffered. Our text of the *Gemara*[2] apparently limits the prohibition against revenge to monetary issues (*hahu bemamon hu dichsiv*).

Indeed, the example given in the *Gemara*[3] seems to limit the *issur* of revenge to the denial of monetary favor. The *Gemara* describes the hypothetical case of Reuven, who asks Shimon to lend him his sickle, and Shimon's refusal to perform this simple *chessed*. On the following day, Shimon asks to borrow Reuven's hatchet, and Reuven refuses in order to take revenge.

The Raavad[4] explains that the prohibition applies only to the person who is retaliating and not to the one who did not perform the *chessed* in the first place. This is because it is quite possible that the reason the object was withheld had nothing to do with any hatred or negative character traits. Rather, the owner was concerned that the object might not be returned intact, or that it might not be returned at all. One violates the prohibition only when the *chessed* is not extended merely to take revenge.

---

1. *Vayikra* 19:18.
2. *Yoma* 23a; cf. *girsa* of Rav Avraham ben HaRambam in *sefer Maasei Nissim, siman* 1.
3. Ibid.
4. *Peirush HaRaavad* on *Toras Kohanim, Parashas Kedoshim*.

Based on this explanation, one can understand why the *issur* of *nekamah* applies only when a person does not receive the favor he was expecting. The Torah demands that in such a case one judges favorably and assumes that there was a good reason the request was denied.

Based on the *Gemara* mentioned above, there are *Rishonim*[5] who *pasken* that according to the letter of the law, seeking revenge is not prohibited when one is mistreated, either physically or verbally.

However, other commentators seem to take an all-inclusive view of the prohibition of *nekamah*. *Sefer Hachinuch*[6] states clearly that one is proscribed from taking revenge (or even harboring ill will in his heart — the prohibition of *"lo sitor"*) even after physical harm, verbal abuse, or humiliation. (Our discussion relates only to the *issur* of retaliating *after* disengagement, for one can certainly defend himself from physical attack, even from verbal abuse, at the time it is being perpetrated.[7])

The *Chinuch* explains that one must always realize and internalize that all that befalls man, either good or bad, is directly from Hashem. Therefore, if one is pained or harmed by another, he should realize that it has come to him as a decree from *HaKadosh Baruch Hu* as payment for his sins, and therefore he must not take revenge against the messenger but instead contemplate his own actions and thereby be spurred to *teshuvah*. The *Chinuch* cites the famous example of Dovid HaMelech, who refused to avenge himself after the insults of Shimi ben Gera. Dovid HaMelech understood that any suffering he endured was a direct decree from Hashem, and therefore harming the messenger was illogical and counterproductive.

Of course, one may take whatever remedies *halachah* allows to obtain compensation, and, as a person with free choice, the perpetrator will certainly be punished for his actions.

The Chofetz Chaim rules[8] that one is prohibited from taking revenge *in any circumstance*, and you should therefore desist from any attempt at retaliation. It is important to bear in mind that the Torah was not given to angels but to people such as yourself, who have the

---

5. *Shaarei Teshuvah, Shaar Shelishi* 38; *Teshuvas Rashi* 245, *Smag* 12.
6. *Mitzvah* 241.
7. See *Rema Choshen Mishpat* 421:13, *Sefer Chofetz Chaim, Lo Saasei* 8-9 in *Be'er Mayim Chaim*.
8. *Sefer Chofetz Chaim* ibid., based on the above-mentioned *Sefer HaChinuch*, as well as *Rambam Hilchos Dei'os* 7:7-8.

potential for greatness but must struggle to overcome normal human emotions to achieve their potential. If you bear in mind the lesson of the *Chinuch* and internalize the reality that the pain and humiliation you are suffering is actually from *HaKadosh Baruch Hu,* it will be easier to mitigate your desire for vengance.

It might prove beneficial to assume that your relative has problems and deep-rooted emotional difficulties (although they are not readily apparent) that are causing his terrible and senseless abuse of others. In situations such as these, the aggressor is not to be hated but pitied. Perhaps this realization will help you reach out and ultimately help him make *shalom,* not only with you but with himself.

As we explained above (in our discussion of "Reconciliation") the Rambam rules[9] that if one feels wronged, he should not remain quiet and harbor ill will; instead he should approach the alleged wrongdoer and confront the issues. This is a *mitzvah mi'd'Oraisa,* which we learn from the *pasuk "Lo sisna es achicha bilvavecha* — Do not hate your brother in your heart …," but rather "… *hochei'ach tochiach es ami-secha* — give reproof to your fellow Jew"[10] by letting him know of his wrongdoing and how it has affected your relationship. After the parties have respectfully aired their grievances, striven to understand each other, and asked forgiveness, reconciliation should result.

You should therefore sit down in a calm and quiet atmosphere and set out your grievances. Hopefully, he will either explain his actions in a satisfactory way or apologize.

It is crucial that you take care of this important business *before* Yom Kippur. The *Shulchan Aruch* rules[11] that *aveiros* between people are not forgiven on Yom Kippur until efforts are made to appease the wronged party. Even if you are 100 percent in the right regarding the issues at hand, it is important for your success in *din* (judgment) as well as your relative's success in *din,* to repair the breakdown of your previously harmonious relationship. It is a *chessed* to afford him the opportunity to apologize if he was wrong.

If you feel that a face-to-face confrontation would lead to further

---

9. *Hilchos Dei'os* 6:6.
10. *Vayikra* 19:17.
11. *Orach Chaim* 608:1, based on the *Gemara* in *Yoma* 85b.

insult and verbal abuse, you may want to put your thoughts down on paper. The recipient of your letter will have a chance to reflect quietly on the matter. Upon a careful reading of your words of reproof and your request for reconciliation, he might be able to absorb and internalize the ramifications of his errant behavior.[12]

As we noted above, *Chazal* tell us that Hashem promises incredible reward to those who do not perpetuate a feud by retaliation, despite the temptation to do so. If you are able to somehow forgive him for his behavior, it will be a great *zechus* for you.

Hashem is forgiving with those who are forgiving of others, as *Chazal* teach us, "Whoever forgoes his rights, all his sins are forgiven."[13] Life is too short to waste precious time on squabbles. Passing this difficult test will undoubtedly help you obtain the *mechilah* and *kaparah* you need from Hashem to merit a *kesivah vechasimah tovah*.

---

12. Any such letter must be written with great care and sensitivity. The person reading the letter does not have the benefit of the inflection of your voice and your body language, so one must be able to read from your words both the substance of what you are saying as well as your sentiments. Also realize that anything you write may be shown to others.
13. *Yoma* 23a.

Placing the Blame
on Others

As I was waiting in line for dinner in yeshivah, my friend Chaim unexpectedly pushed me from behind so hard that I knocked over the bachur in front of me. Infuriated, the startled bachur turned to me and demanded to know why I had the chutzpah to push him for no apparent reason.

Unfortunately, I reflexively told him that it was not my fault, but rather the fault of my [former] friend Chaim. Was I allowed to blame Chaim for the incident? It was certainly not motzi shem ra because he did cause the problem. However, I am afraid that it might have been lashon hara to point the blame in his direction.

On the other hand, had I not told him the truth, the blame would have been placed on me and I would have been the object of this bachur's anger and contempt. Although I hope this never happens again, I would like to be prepared. What would be the correct reaction in such a situation?

The Chofetz Chaim[1] gives us direction as to how to react in such a situation. He rules that one should simply say, "I did not do it" or "It is not my fault," rather than reveal the identity of the perpetrator. In your case, you could say, "I'm sorry, but I was pushed into you by someone else."

The Chofetz Chaim explains further that this formula works even if there are no other people in line and the blame will then be shifted to the only remaining suspect. This applies, however, only where the deed in question was done willfully. If the original deed (in your case, the pushing that led to this domino effect) was done *by accident,* the Chofetz Chaim is in doubt whether one may say it is not his fault if in doing so he will cast the blame on the remaining person.[2]

Applying these principles to your case, if you are sure that Chaim pushed you on purpose, you would be allowed to say, "It was not my fault," even if there was only one other person in line. Although that person (Chaim) will be implicated by your denial, it is not *lashon hara.* If it is possible that the pushing was an accident and only one other person was there, you might not even be allowed to say, "It was not my fault," as you would be incriminating the only other person involved.[3] In that case, you would want to simply apologize and explain that it was an accident.

---

1. *Hilchos Lashon Hara* 10:17.
2. *Be'er Mayim Chaim* ibid. 43. See there that it might depend on the ruling of the SMA *Choshen Mishpat* 388:10, concerning a person who is pushing a potential damage away from himself and thereby causing the damaging agent to affect someone else. A person who is being blamed for something he did not do is already being "damaged" by the anger and ill will of his accuser. To point a finger at the perpetrator would relieve the person of the discomfort and pressure, but would shift that discomfort onto someone else. Although that other person is indeed the perpetrator, the deed was only done by accident and, therefore, the perpetrator does not warrant becoming the object of hatred and disdain.
3. Based on the *safek* of *Chofetz Chaim* in *Be'er Mayim Chaim* ibid.

This may sound extreme, but wouldn't it be nice if you all had some pocket-size *mussar sefarim* to look into while waiting on line in the dining room? The time on line would become time well spent and will help polish everyone's *middos*. It will also keep everyone occupied, thus avoiding potential *machlokes* as dinner is being served.

Mazal and the Jews

There is an important point that I would like to clarify in regard to my davening during the Yamim Nora'im. Aside from the main focus declaring Hashem as Melech and doing teshuvah, we spend considerable time and energy asking Hashem for long life, health, parnassah, tranquility, etc. Yet I was always under the impression that life's circumstances are determined by a person's mazal. If the mazal is indeed preordained at birth, how can we daven to change it? Is there a part of mazal that is not set in stone?

Please clarify this difficult and confusing topic so that I will be able to relate to my davening with the proper kavanah. (A clarification will also help me understand the berachah I give to others when I wish them mazal tov at their simchos.)

Many misunderstand the role *mazal* plays in a person's life, and as a result, they create unhappiness for themselves. On the other hand, those who understand what *mazal is* will have a much easier time dealing with life's tests. It is therefore vitally important to properly understand the concept of *mazal*. We will explain it according to the approach of HaRav Eliyahu Dessler, *zt"l*.

WHAT IS MAZAL?

To begin, let us correct the first and most common misconception: *Mazal* is not "luck." It has nothing to do with luck.

Rav Dessler, quoting Radak, explains that the root of the word *mazal* is *nozeil*, "something that pours." It is the *hashpaah* — the heavenly influences — that "pour" down from heaven to earth. Aside from their innate abilities and talents, certain circumstances, talents, and abilities are all preordained to "pour down" from heaven, and therefore have nothing to do with luck. The talents we are born with, as well as the circumstances we find ourselves in, are not left to blind chance and coincidence.

Rav Dessler explains that *mazal* comprises the custom-designed tools, talents, attributes, *middos,* and circumstances (this includes one's family, community, financial situation, etc.) that one is provided with in order to accomplish one's purpose in life. The reason that people have different talents, advantages, disadvantages, circumstances, etc. is because they have different purposes in life. Every Jew has a general mission as well as a specific mission that is unique to him, and each person is given the tools that he needs to fulfill his purpose. These sets of tools are your *mazal*. They were not given to you by chance; rather they are perfectly designed for you and your life's mission.

YOUR CUSTOM-DESIGNED MAZAL

The reason *mazal* is also the word for stars and constellations is because their positioning at the time of birth will affect a person's talents and attributes. Someone born under the red planet, Mars, will have a predisposition toward things related to blood. If the person does not refine his *middos* and channel the predisposition in a positive way, there is a strong possibility he will be a murderer. Channeled properly, his talents can be used to save lives as a doctor or to perform *mitzvos* as a *mohel* or *shochet*, etc. The *Gemara* gives many fascinating examples of how people born at a certain time are predisposed to certain circumstances related to their *mazal*.[1] It also notes that depending on what day of the week you are born, you will have certain predispositions, qualities, and *middos*.

The myriad factors that are part and parcel of one's *mazal* are impossibly complex. Moreover, the *sefarim hakedoshim* tell us that most *neshamos* today are not here for the first time. Either it is a *gilgul*, which means the person is here to rectify the *neshamah* of someone who lived previously, or it is a *nitzutz* ("spark"), which is described by the metaphor of one candle lit from another; although the second flame takes on some of the properties of the first, it is not the same candle. Hashem will sometimes take the *neshamah* of a *tzaddik* and use that to "light" other *neshamos*, which will in turn carry out some of the lifework of the precursor *neshamah*, while at the same time facing new challenges as well.

These are extremely lofty concepts, and delving into them at length usually has little positive impact on a person's *avodas Hashem*. It is best to proceed with the simple understanding that wherever one's *neshamah* originated, Hashem caused it to be born at a specific time under specific circumstances to acquire the properties of a specific *mazal*, which are custom designed for its life mission.

MAZAL FOR YISRAEL?

Rav Dessler cites the *Gemara*[2] that discusses whether or not Jews have *mazal*. Rabbi Chanina says that features such as intelligence and wealth are products of *mazal*, and that a Jew is in fact subject to this *mazal*, which Rashi explains to mean that one's *mazal* cannot be

---

1. *Shabbos* 156a.
2. Ibid.

changed. It is fixed, as are the constellations in the heavens. Even *tefillah* will not change it. Similarly, Rava in *Moed Kattan*[3] made a well-known statement: "Children [how many], longevity [how long a person will live], and finances are not dependent upon merit, but on *mazal*." In other words, whatever you are born with — from your innate talents to your environment — is what you have and what you have to work with; there is no changing that.

Rabbi Yochanan and Rav, on the other hand, say that Jews are not subject to *mazal*. This implies that all the talents one possesses and the circumstances one finds oneself in are not fixed. They can be changed.

A simple reading of this *Gemara* would lead one to think there is a difference of opinion. However, as *Tosafos* explain, there really is no difference of opinion; rather, it is a question of degree.

Everyone agrees that great merit (e.g., exceptional accomplishments in *tzedakah, chessed,* and Torah) as well as *tefillah,* can change one's *mazal*.

As with every rule, though, there are exceptions. Some situations are fixed and nothing in the world is going to change them. All the individual's personal merits and *tefillos* are as vitally important as ever and will accrue major returns for the person in *Olam Haba,* and they will help others in need of these *tefillos* as well. However, they will not change the person's *mazal* one iota in this world.

As an example, *Tosafos* cite the case of Rabbi Elazar ben Pedas,[4] one of the Torah giants of his generation. He lived in abject poverty, and implored Hashem to provide him *with sustenance.* He was not asking for a yacht or a Lexus, he was merely asking for basic necessities so that he could better devote his energies to *avodas Hashem.*

As a sign of his greatness, Hashem responded to him, with a question: "Would you prefer that I destroy the entire universe and start things from scratch again so that *maybe* you will be born under a *mazal* that has some chance of *parnassah*?"

In other words, Rabbi Elazar ben Pedas' *mazal* was set in stone and immutable. Hashem would have to begin creation again — and

---

3. *Moed Kattan* 28a.
4. *Taanis* 25a.

then, only "maybe," would Rabbi Elazar's *mazal* change. He was an extremely great person, who *davened* with incredible heart and earned enormous merits through Torah and deeds, but he still could not change his personal situation.

Tosafos use this as an example that some people have a *mazal* that will never change. That might sound very frightening, but as we will discuss, it is just the opposite; it might be the most comforting news.

In summary, there are two types of *mazal*. One type can be changed if the person puts forth superhuman effort over an extended period of time, which was apparently the *mazal* of Chanah, the mother of the prophet Shmuel, who *davened* for a child. The other type of *mazal*, as we will see, is one that is immutable, for the person's own good.

TOOLS

One type of person has a *mazal* to accomplish specific things in life, and his wealth or poverty — or any of the other circumstances he is born into —are his tools to fulfill this purpose.

For instance, imagine a person whose purpose here is to be a *baal tzedakah*: to build *yeshivos*, establish the infrastructure of a community, and help the needy. He is good at what he does and therefore *davens* to Hashem for more money so that he can further expand his *tzedakah* activities. Hashem might decide that since he is using his tools so well, he deserves to be given more.

The same scenario can apply to wisdom. If a person is using his mind for the right things, when he *davens* to Hashem for more wisdom he will be answered in the affirmative.

However, if one does not maximize the use of the talents and tools bestowed upon him, they can be reduced or taken away. Just as Hashem can quickly undo the financial success of the wealthiest person, He can also take away or reduce the wisdom of intelligent people. If one is not properly using the tools given him, Hashem may decide to give them to someone else. The person's *mazal* has changed because he has not made appropriate use of the blessings at his disposal.

The *Gemara* teaches that there is no ultimate reward in this world;

that reward is reserved for *Olam Haba*. How can that be? Do we not read *every* day in the *Shema* that Hashem promises us rain in its season, healthy crops, and natural resources? Is that not reward? Actually, those promises are not rewards but tools to achieve the reward. If we use the tools well the first time, we will merit to receive them again — all in order to help us achieve our goals in life.

Rava used to *daven* to be as smart as Rav Huna, the Rosh Yeshivah of the previous generation, and his *tefillos* were answered. Then he asked to be as wealthy as Rav Chisda, the other great Rosh Yeshivah at the time, and again he was given what he asked for. It is interesting to note that Rava — who maintained that elements such as children, longevity, and wealth do not depend on merit but on *mazal* — davened for these things to change, and they did!

Rava was able to ask for change because the things he was asking for were tools. If one is asking for change in regard to his tools, he can ask for more. The answer might be "no," but there is nothing wrong with trying. Rava was given what he wanted because when he became the leader of the next generation, he needed an expanded set of tools and resources.

TESTS

So far we have discussed the first type of *mazal*. The station one is given in life and the things he has are tools to help him accomplish his soul's mission in life. His *mazal* can change in accordance with merits or demerits related to how he goes about his mission.

Then there is another type of *mazal*. This *mazal* is not a tool to use in life, but a test. The entire purpose of this person's time on earth is to undergo that test. He can *daven* to Hashem all day to extract him from his predicament, but from Heaven's point of view it is not a predicament; it is one of the primary purposes for which he was put on earth. This *mazal* is not changeable, for that would undo the life challenge that was tailor-made for him.

Sometimes it is a person's test to live in poverty or to suffer. All his *davening* will not help. All of his Torah and *mitzvos* and *chessed* will not change the circumstances. His situation is not a tool given to him, but a test: to *daven*, to keep the Torah, to do *chessed*, and to give *tzedakah* despite the adversity he faces.

Such a person wonders, *Why isn't Hashem listening to me?* The truth is that Hashem is listening to him, but the person's *neshamah* can reach its *tikkun* only by living with this challenge. That is the example of Elazar ben Pedas. His *dveikus*, *tefillos*, and deeds might have been at a higher level than anyone else's, extracting him from poverty would have enabled him to achieve even more, yet none of it changed his *mazal*.

To further support his point, Rav Dessler cites the *Gemara* in *Moed Kattan*.[5] Rabbah and Rav Chisda were both Roshei Yeshivah in the generation before that of Rava. They were equal to each other in terms of *tzidkus*, learning, and communal status. Their power of *tefillah* was also equal. However, Rav Chisda lived to the ripe old age of 92, while Rabbah died at 40. Rav Chisda was wealthy and had a large family; he was repeatedly making *simchos*. Rabbah was poor and constantly in *aveilus*. These were two people in the same generation of equal stature, abilities, and merit, yet their material lives could not have been more different.

Rava witnessed this, which is why he came to the conclusion that when it comes to children, wealth, health, and longevity, everything depends on *mazal*, not merit.

Of course, poverty is not the only test. *Chazal* remind us that wealth is just as much a test. A lot of people quip, "Try me." However, the responsibility of those with wealth is much greater. Money comes with its own unique set of stresses, fears, jealousies, and opportunities for sin.

RECOGNIZING THE DIFFERENCE

In either event, the main point Rav Dessler makes is to draw a distinction between *mazal* that is a tool and *mazal* that is a test.

How does one ascertain under which *mazal* he is living: the fixed *mazal* of Rabbi Elazar ben Pedas, or the difficult but changeable *mazal* of Chanah?

---

5. *Moed Kattan* 28a.

There is no magic formula to figure it out. It is a life challenge we all have to face. However, using Rav Dessler's approach. we can at least understand the different types of challenges and learn how to react in ways that turn them into advantages. One has every right to *daven*, to give *tzedakah*, to do *chessed*; to do everything in his power to try to change his *mazal*. However, if after doing so for a long time he does not receive the answer he is seeking, it might be a sign that his particular set of circumstances is his test in life and cannot be changed. His key to *Olam Haba* will be earned by the merit generated through his *avodas Hashem* under trying circumstances.

If we internalize this concept, we can become happier people. Most unhappiness in life is the result of feeling that someone else has something we should have. We fail to understand that the other person has a particular tool to fulfill a purpose in life that we have not been assigned. At other times, the reason we lack something is because we are being tested, and continuing to fulfill the Torah's expectations with a full heart is the very purpose for which we were born. If we could see ourselves in the *Olam HaEmes*, we would thank Hashem for the assignment and understand that exchanging our circumstances would defeat the fundamental purpose of our lives, the personal *tikkun* we are meant to effect.

The bottom line is that *mazal* is not luck. It is a carefully crafted set of circumstances designed in Heaven specifically for each one of us to fulfill his mission in life. Understand that and you have one of the more important keys to a life of meaning and contentment.

Our *mazal* and *hatzlachah* can be altered only with earnest *tefillah*, *mesirus nefesh* for Torah, and a continued push for growth in *avodas Hashem*.

When we wish another person *mazal tov* we are adding our own *tefillah* on their behalf.

It is only possible (but an affirmative answer is not at all guaranteed) to ask Hashem for longer life and health for ourselves if we make full use of the precious time we have now. One can request prosperity only if his present resources are used properly. We must maximize the use of the tools we are given before we ask for more.

INDEX

Index